Lucy and Dando

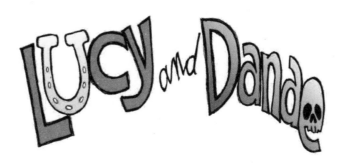

Other *Non Sequitur* Books by Wiley

The Non Sequitur Survival Guide for the Nineties

Non Sequitur's Beastly Things

The Legal Lampoon:
A Biased, Unfair, and Completely Accurate Law Review from Non Sequitur

Why We'll Never Understand Each Other

LUCY and Danae

SOMETHING SILLY THIS WAY COMES

by Wiley Miller

**Andrews McMeel
Publishing**

Kansas City

Non Sequitur is distributed internationally by Universal Press Syndicate.

Lucy and Danae copyright © 2005 by Wiley Miller. All rights reserved. Printed in the United States of America. No part of this book may be used or reproduced in any manner whatsoever without written permission except in the case of reprints in the context of reviews. For information, write Andrews McMeel Publishing, an Andrews McMeel Universal company, 4520 Main Street, Kansas City, Missouri 64111.

05 06 07 08 09 WLS 10 9 8 7 6 5 4 3 2 1

ISBN: 0-7407-5099-2

Library of Congress Control Number: 2004113769

www.uComics.com

───── **ATTENTION: SCHOOLS AND BUSINESSES** ─────

Andrews McMeel books are available at quantity discounts with bulk purchase for educational, business, or sales promotional use. For information, please write to: Special Sales Department, Andrews McMeel Publishing, 4520 Main Street, Kansas City, Missouri 64111.

For every little girl who thought keeping a horse in her bedroom was perfectly rational.

—Wiley

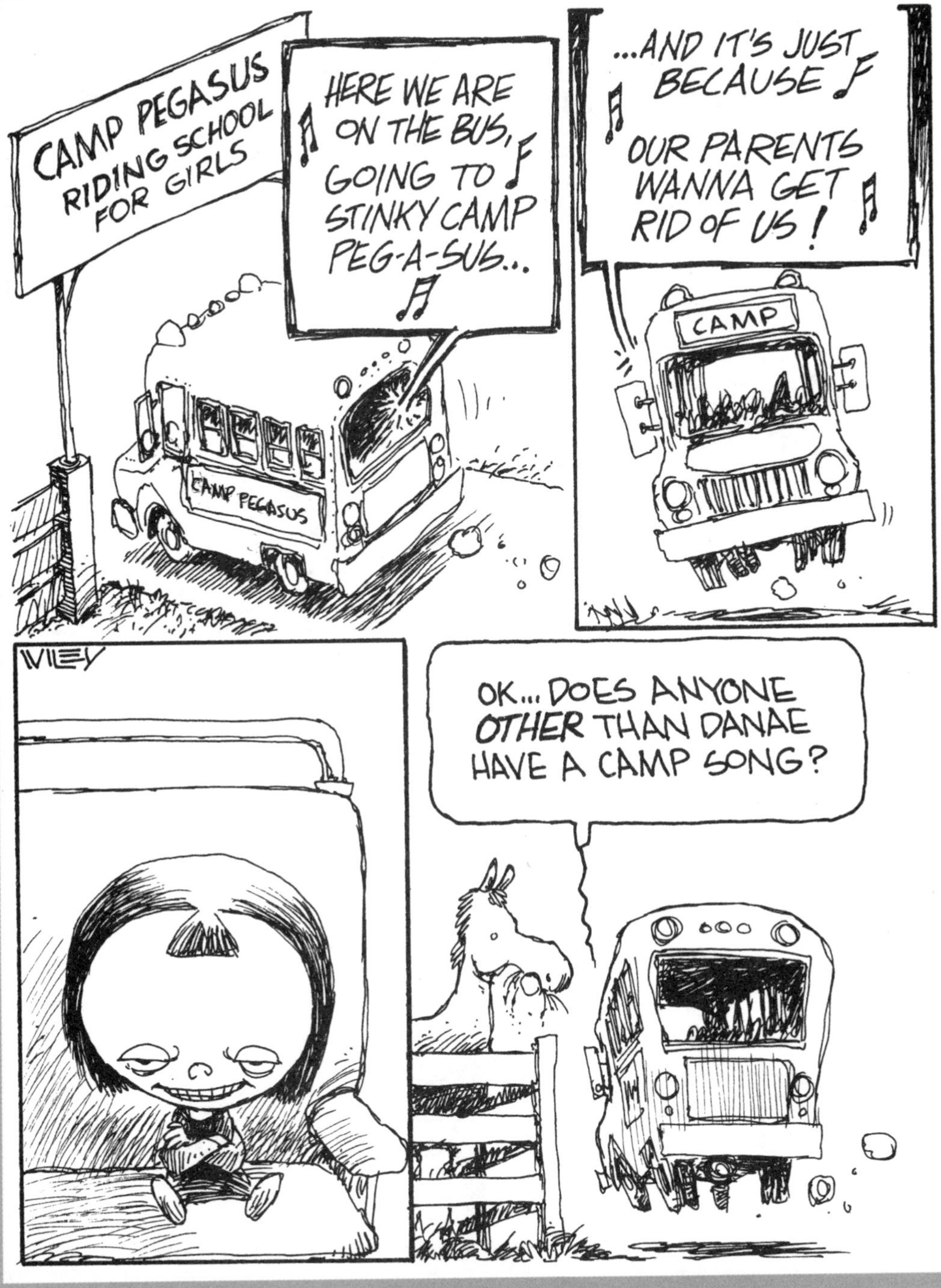
CAMP PEGASUS RIDING SCHOOL FOR GIRLS
HERE WE ARE ON THE BUS, GOING TO STINKY CAMP PEG-A-SUS...
CAMP PEGASUS
...AND IT'S JUST BECAUSE
OUR PARENTS WANNA GET RID OF US!
CAMP
WILEY
OK... DOES ANYONE OTHER THAN DANAE HAVE A CAMP SONG?

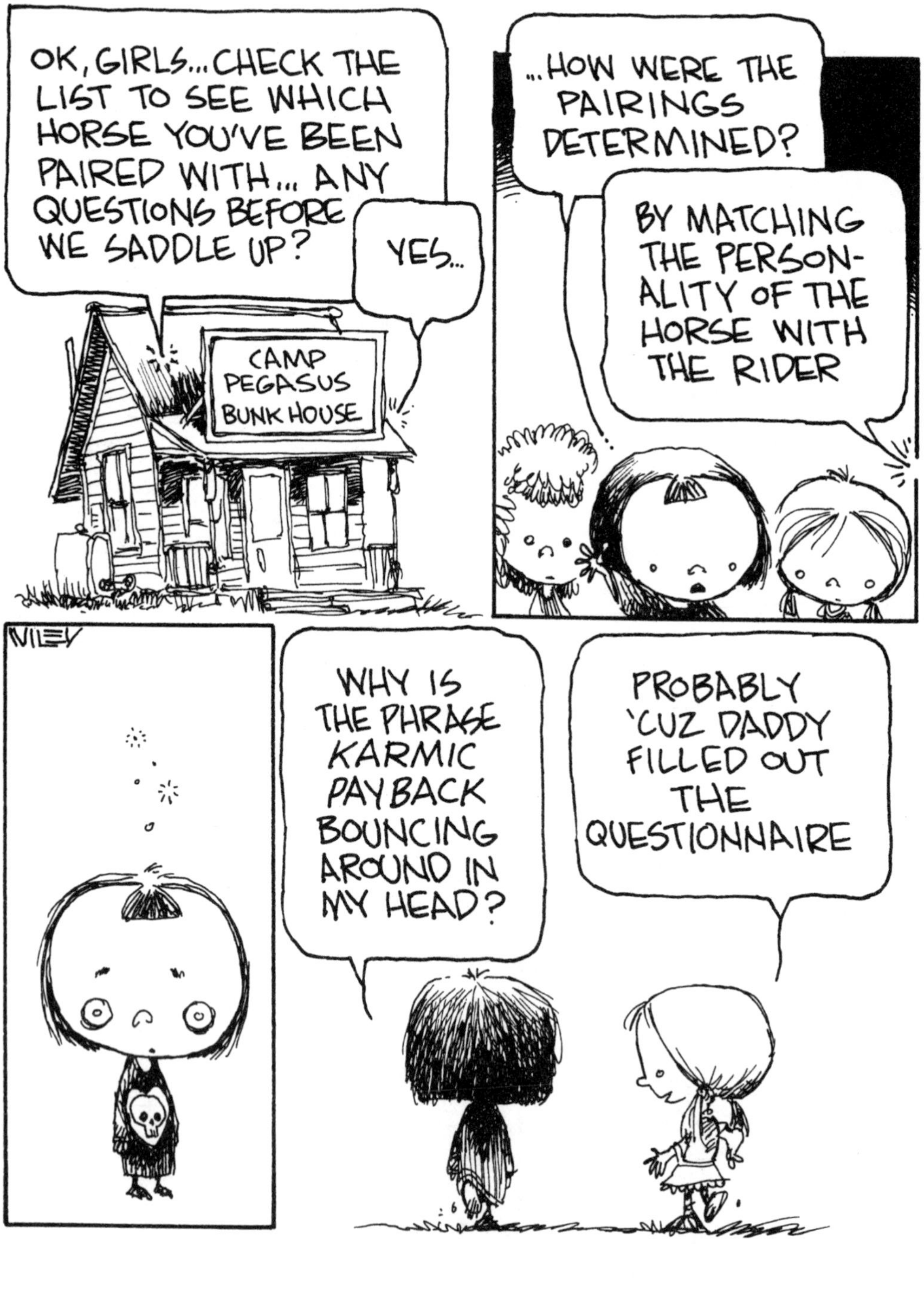
OK, GIRLS...CHECK THE LIST TO SEE WHICH HORSE YOU'VE BEEN PAIRED WITH... ANY QUESTIONS BEFORE WE SADDLE UP?
YES...
CAMP PEGASUS BUNK HOUSE
...HOW WERE THE PAIRINGS DETERMINED?
BY MATCHING THE PERSON-ALITY OF THE HORSE WITH THE RIDER
WILEY
WHY IS THE PHRASE KARMIC PAYBACK BOUNCING AROUND IN MY HEAD?
PROBABLY 'CUZ DADDY FILLED OUT THE QUESTIONNAIRE

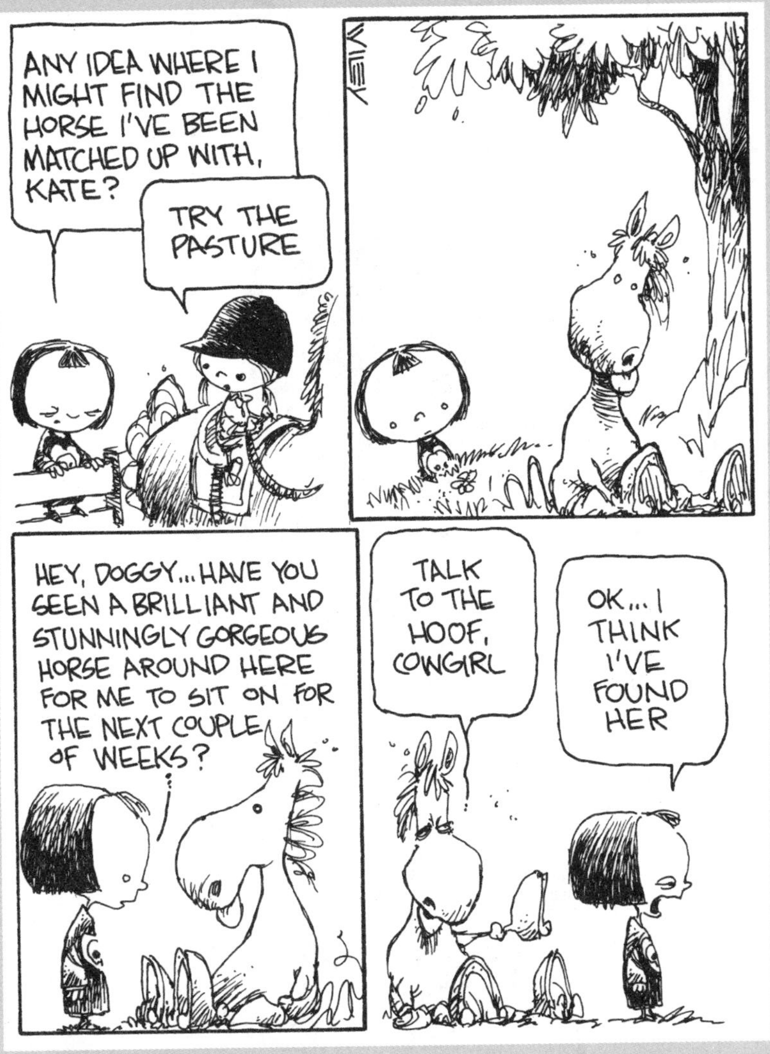
ANY IDEA WHERE I MIGHT FIND THE HORSE I'VE BEEN MATCHED UP WITH, KATE?
TRY THE PASTURE
HEY, DOGGY... HAVE YOU SEEN A BRILLIANT AND STUNNINGLY GORGEOUS HORSE AROUND HERE FOR ME TO SIT ON FOR THE NEXT COUPLE OF WEEKS?
TALK TO THE HOOF, COWGIRL
OK... I THINK I'VE FOUND HER
WILEY

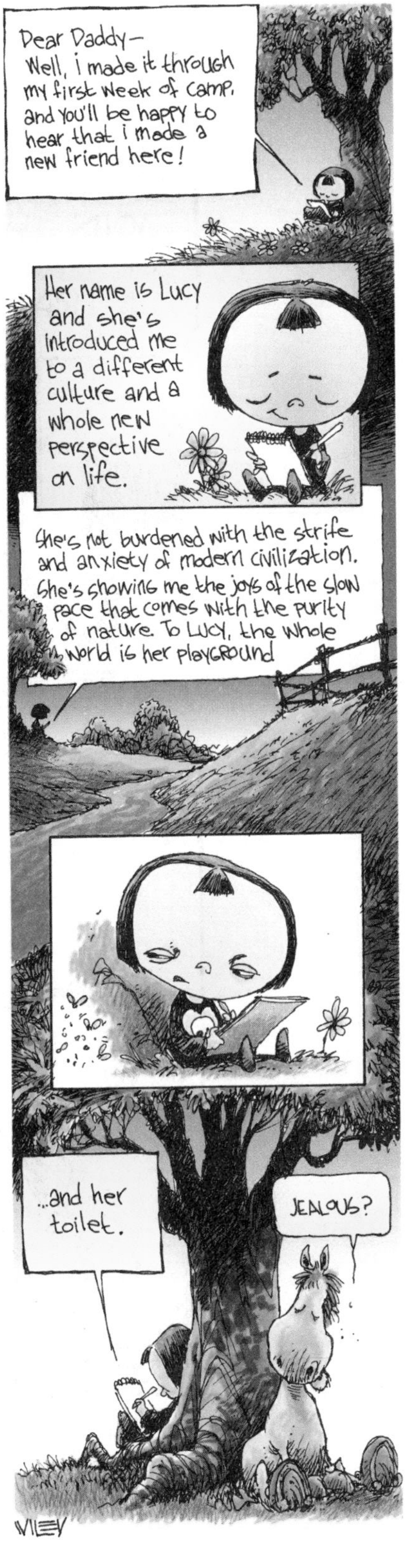
Dear Daddy— Well, i made it through my first week of camp, and you'll be happy to hear that i made a new friend here!
Her name is Lucy and she's introduced me to a different culture and a whole new perspective on life.
She's not burdened with the strife and anxiety of modern civilization. She's showing me the joys of the slow pace that comes with the purity of nature. To Lucy, the whole world is her playground
...and her toilet.
JEALOUS?
WILEY

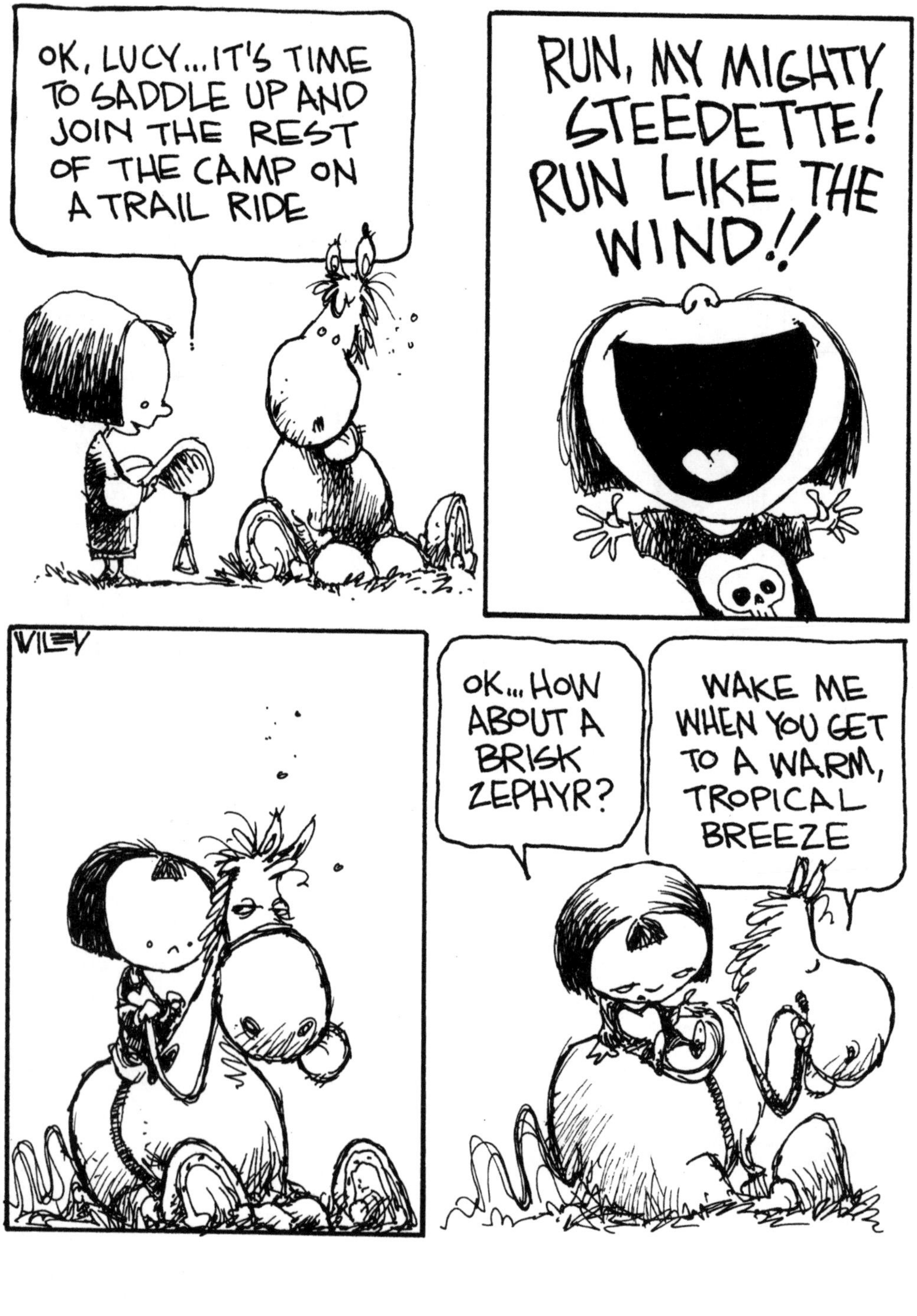
OK, LUCY...IT'S TIME TO SADDLE UP AND JOIN THE REST OF THE CAMP ON A TRAIL RIDE
RUN, MY MIGHTY STEEDETTE! RUN LIKE THE WIND!!
WILEY
OK... HOW ABOUT A BRISK ZEPHYR?
WAKE ME WHEN YOU GET TO A WARM, TROPICAL BREEZE

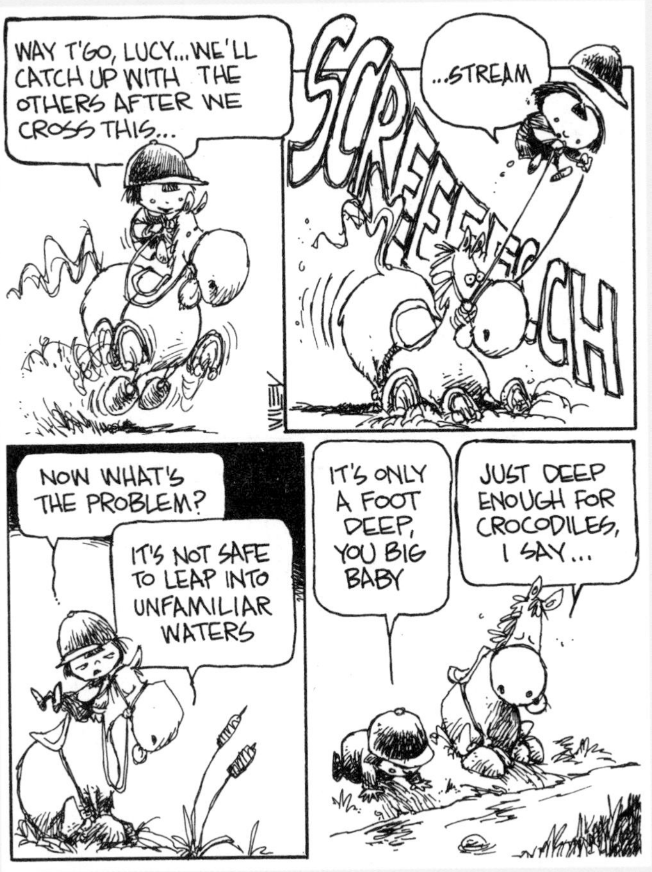
WAY T'GO, LUCY... WE'LL CATCH UP WITH THE OTHERS AFTER WE CROSS THIS...
...STREAM
WILEY
NOW WHAT'S THE PROBLEM?
IT'S NOT SAFE TO LEAP INTO UNFAMILIAR WATERS
IT'S ONLY A FOOT DEEP, YOU BIG BABY
JUST DEEP ENOUGH FOR CROCODILES, I SAY...

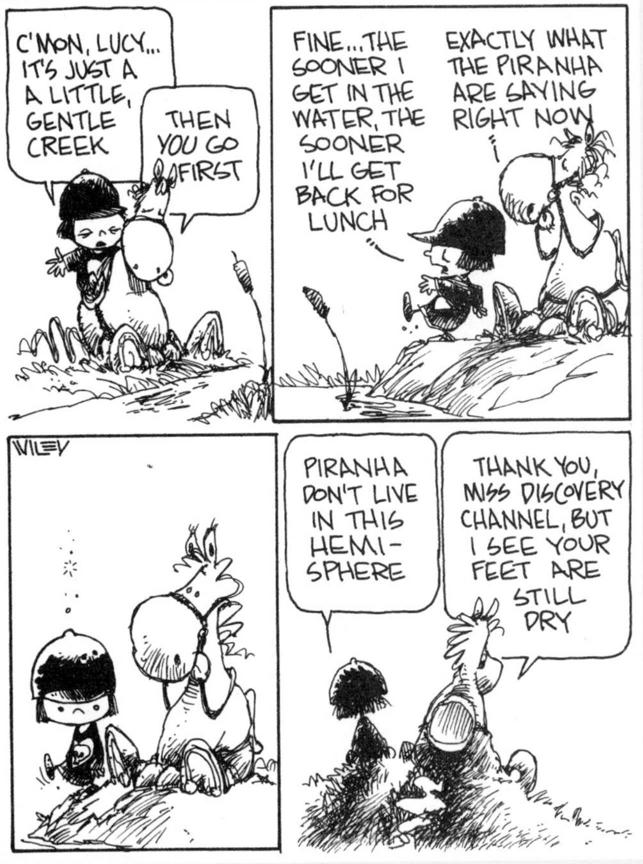
C'MON, LUCY... IT'S JUST A A LITTLE, GENTLE CREEK
THEN YOU GO FIRST
FINE... THE SOONER I GET IN THE WATER, THE SOONER I'LL GET BACK FOR LUNCH
EXACTLY WHAT THE PIRANHA ARE SAYING RIGHT NOW
WILEY
PIRANHA DON'T LIVE IN THIS HEMI-SPHERE
THANK YOU, MISS DISCOVERY CHANNEL, BUT I SEE YOUR FEET ARE STILL DRY

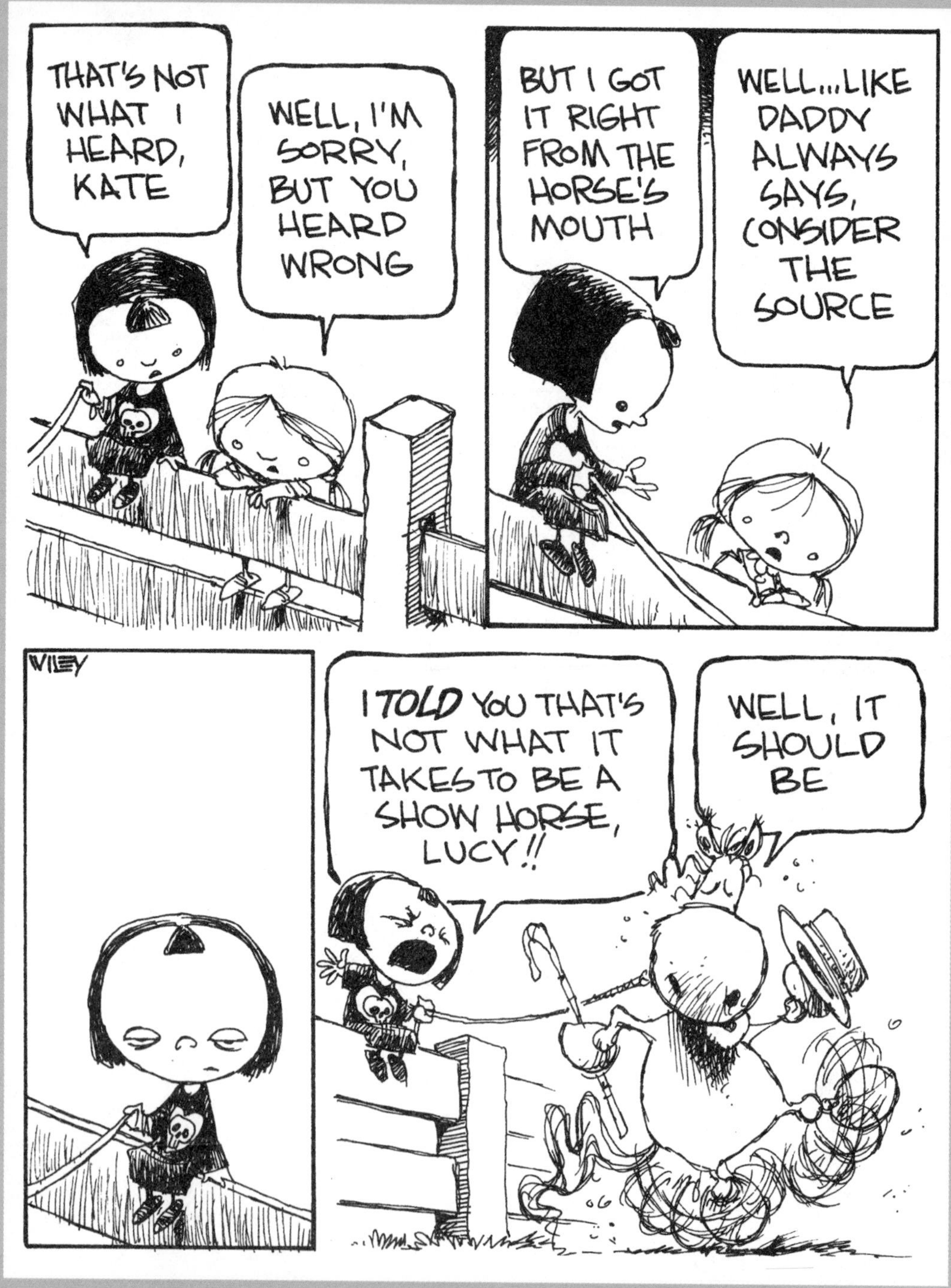
THAT'S NOT WHAT I HEARD, KATE
WELL, I'M SORRY, BUT YOU HEARD WRONG
BUT I GOT IT RIGHT FROM THE HORSE'S MOUTH
WELL...LIKE DADDY ALWAYS SAYS, CONSIDER THE SOURCE
WILEY
I *TOLD* YOU THAT'S NOT WHAT IT TAKES TO BE A SHOW HORSE, LUCY!!
WELL, IT SHOULD BE

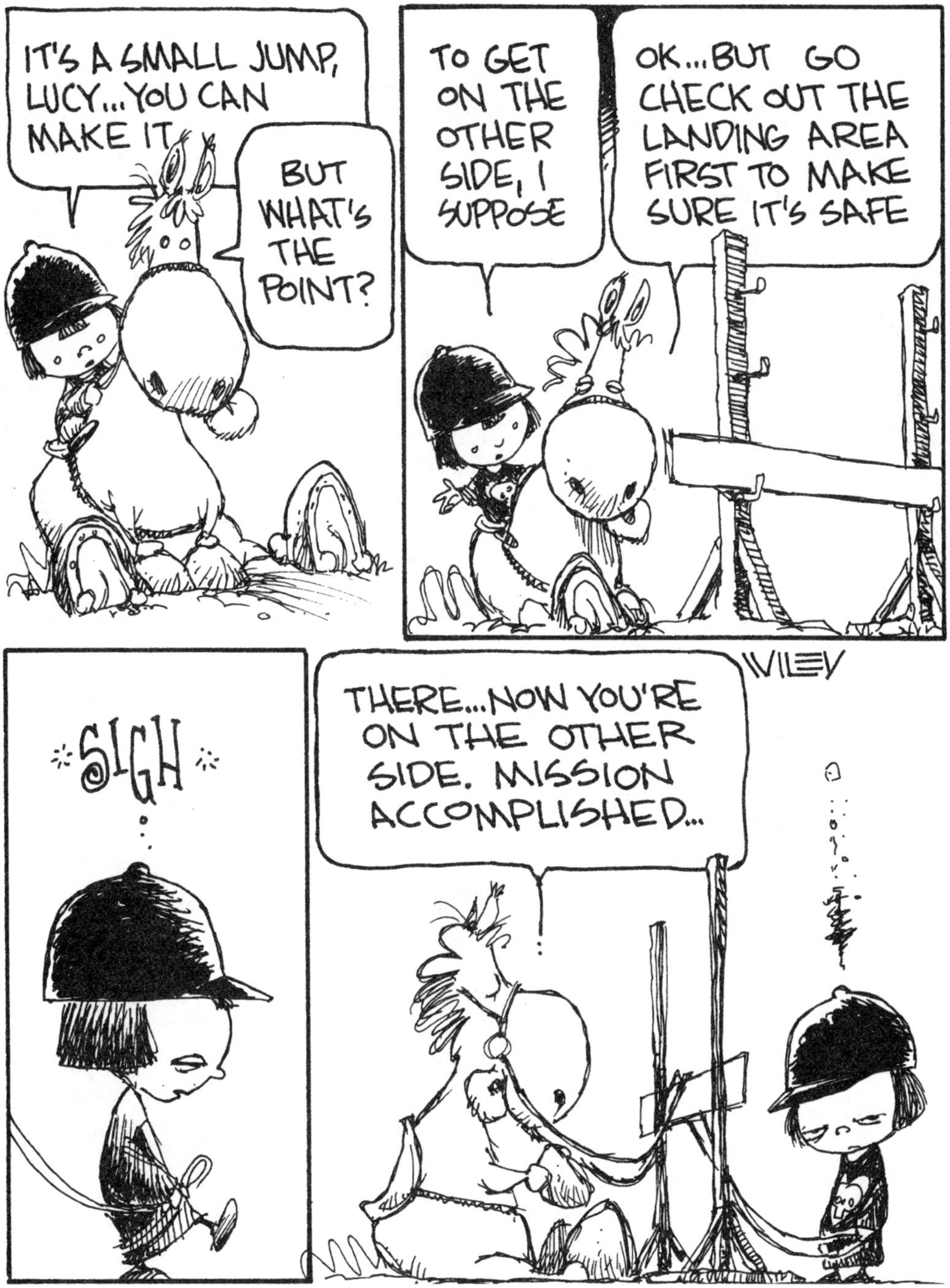
IT'S A SMALL JUMP, LUCY... YOU CAN MAKE IT
BUT WHAT'S THE POINT?
TO GET ON THE OTHER SIDE, I SUPPOSE
OK... BUT GO CHECK OUT THE LANDING AREA FIRST TO MAKE SURE IT'S SAFE
WILEY
SIGH
THERE... NOW YOU'RE ON THE OTHER SIDE. MISSION ACCOMPLISHED...

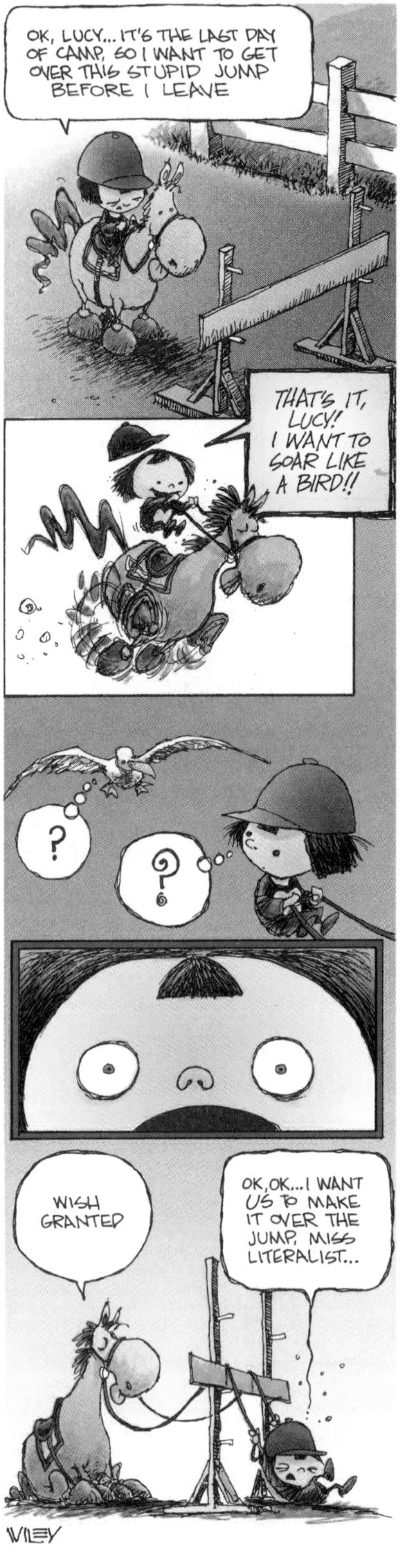
OK, LUCY... IT'S THE LAST DAY OF CAMP, SO I WANT TO GET OVER THIS STUPID JUMP BEFORE I LEAVE
THAT'S IT, LUCY! I WANT TO SOAR LIKE A BIRD!!
?
?
WISH GRANTED
OK, OK... I WANT US TO MAKE IT OVER THE JUMP, MISS LITERALIST...
WILEY

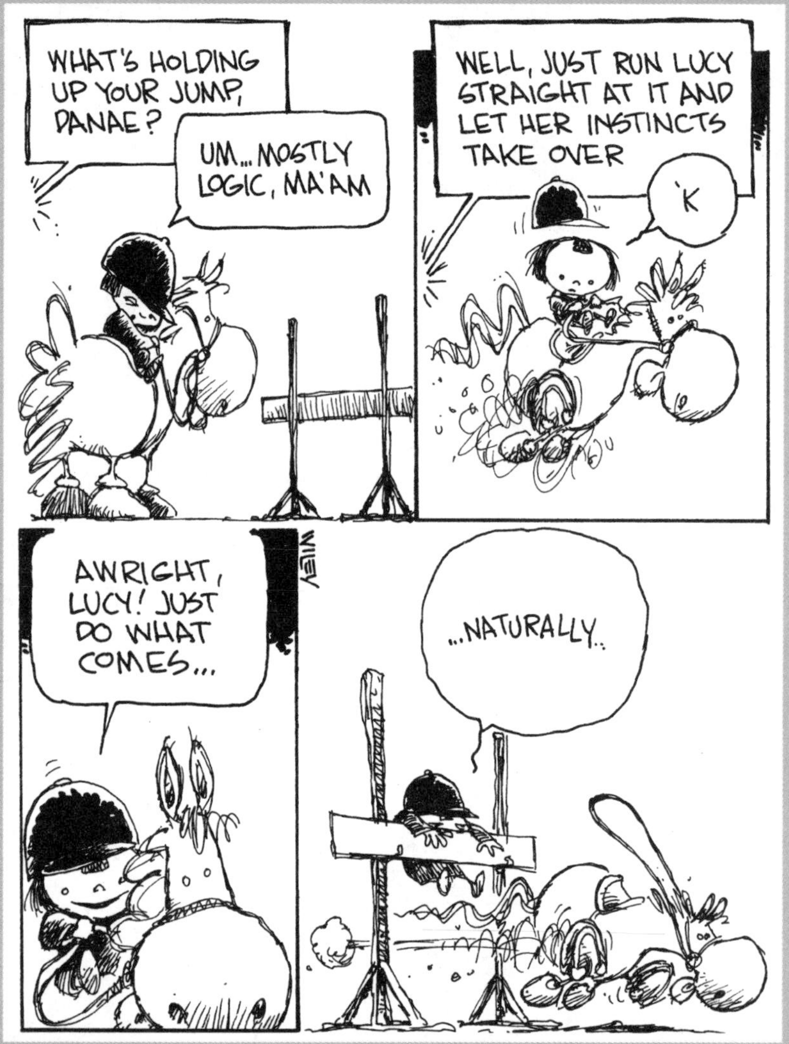
WHAT'S HOLDING UP YOUR JUMP, DANAE?
UM... MOSTLY LOGIC, MA'AM
WELL, JUST RUN LUCY STRAIGHT AT IT AND LET HER INSTINCTS TAKE OVER
'K
AWRIGHT, LUCY! JUST DO WHAT COMES...
...NATURALLY..
WILEY

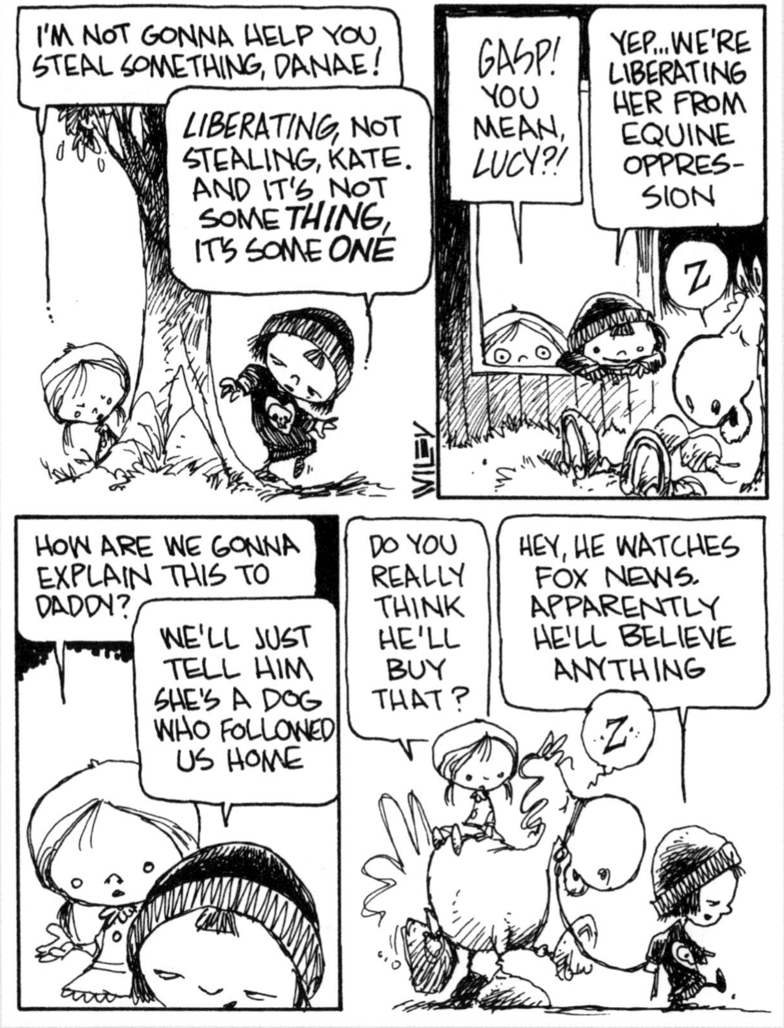
I'M NOT GONNA HELP YOU STEAL SOMETHING, DANAE!
LIBERATING, NOT STEALING, KATE. AND IT'S NOT SOMETHING, IT'S SOMEONE
GASP! YOU MEAN, LUCY?!
YEP... WE'RE LIBERATING HER FROM EQUINE OPPRESSION
Z
HOW ARE WE GONNA EXPLAIN THIS TO DADDY?
WE'LL JUST TELL HIM SHE'S A DOG WHO FOLLOWED US HOME
DO YOU REALLY THINK HE'LL BUY THAT?
HEY, HE WATCHES FOX NEWS. APPARENTLY HE'LL BELIEVE ANYTHING
Z

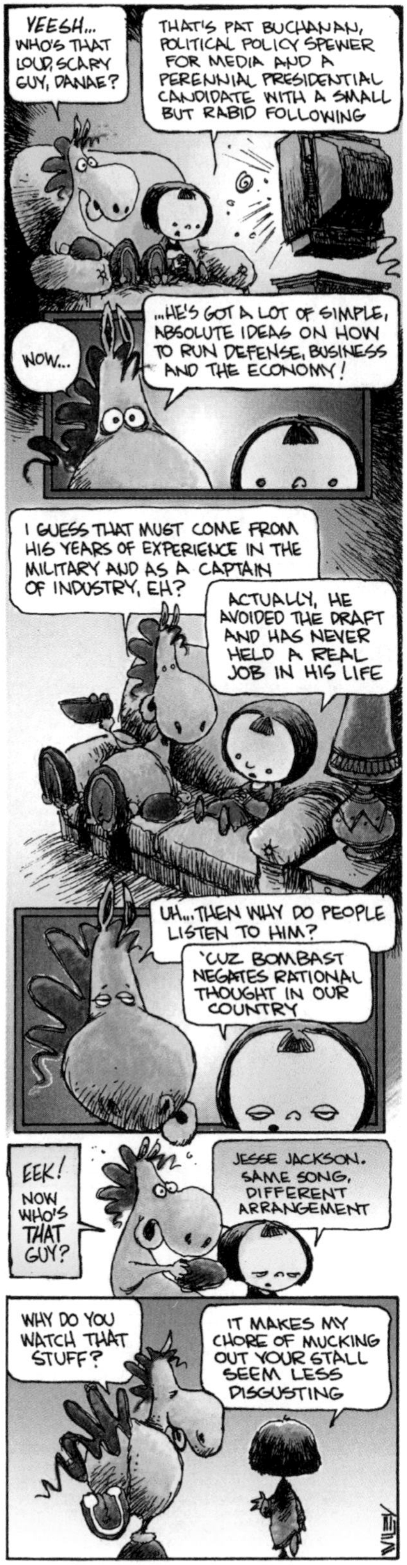
YEESH... WHO'S THAT LOUD, SCARY GUY, DANAE?
THAT'S PAT BUCHANAN, POLITICAL POLICY SPEWER FOR MEDIA AND A PERENNIAL PRESIDENTIAL CANDIDATE WITH A SMALL BUT RABID FOLLOWING
WOW...
...HE'S GOT A LOT OF SIMPLE, ABSOLUTE IDEAS ON HOW TO RUN DEFENSE, BUSINESS AND THE ECONOMY!
I GUESS THAT MUST COME FROM HIS YEARS OF EXPERIENCE IN THE MILITARY AND AS A CAPTAIN OF INDUSTRY, EH?
ACTUALLY, HE AVOIDED THE DRAFT AND HAS NEVER HELD A REAL JOB IN HIS LIFE
UH... THEN WHY DO PEOPLE LISTEN TO HIM?
'CUZ BOMBAST NEGATES RATIONAL THOUGHT IN OUR COUNTRY
EEK! NOW WHO'S THAT GUY?
JESSE JACKSON. SAME SONG, DIFFERENT ARRANGEMENT
WHY DO YOU WATCH THAT STUFF?
IT MAKES MY CHORE OF MUCKING OUT YOUR STALL SEEM LESS DISGUSTING

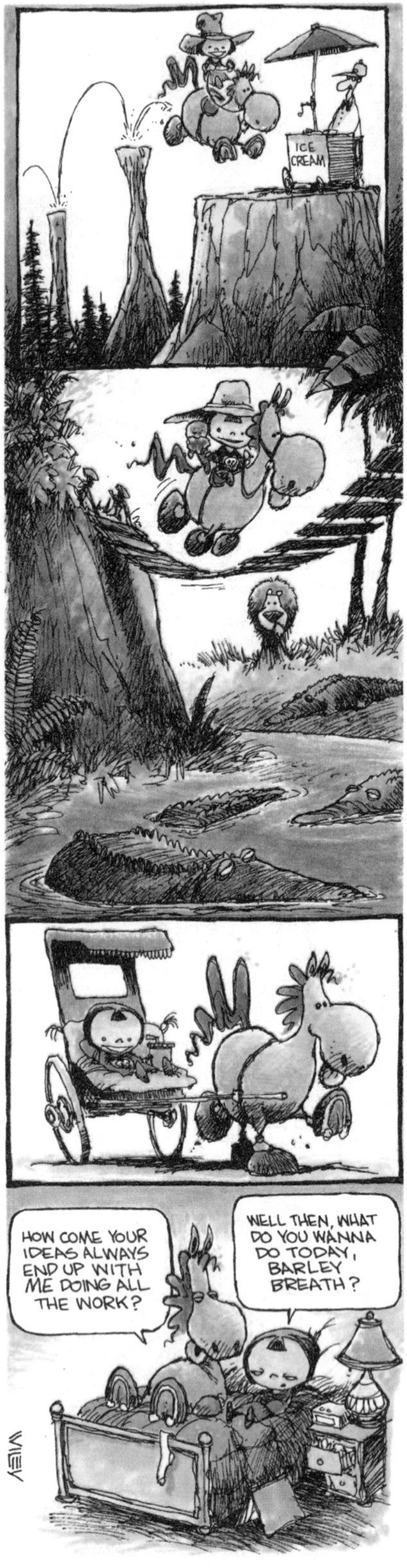
ICE CREAM
HOW COME YOUR IDEAS ALWAYS END UP WITH ME DOING ALL THE WORK?
WELL THEN, WHAT DO YOU WANNA DO TODAY, BARLEY BREATH?
WILEY

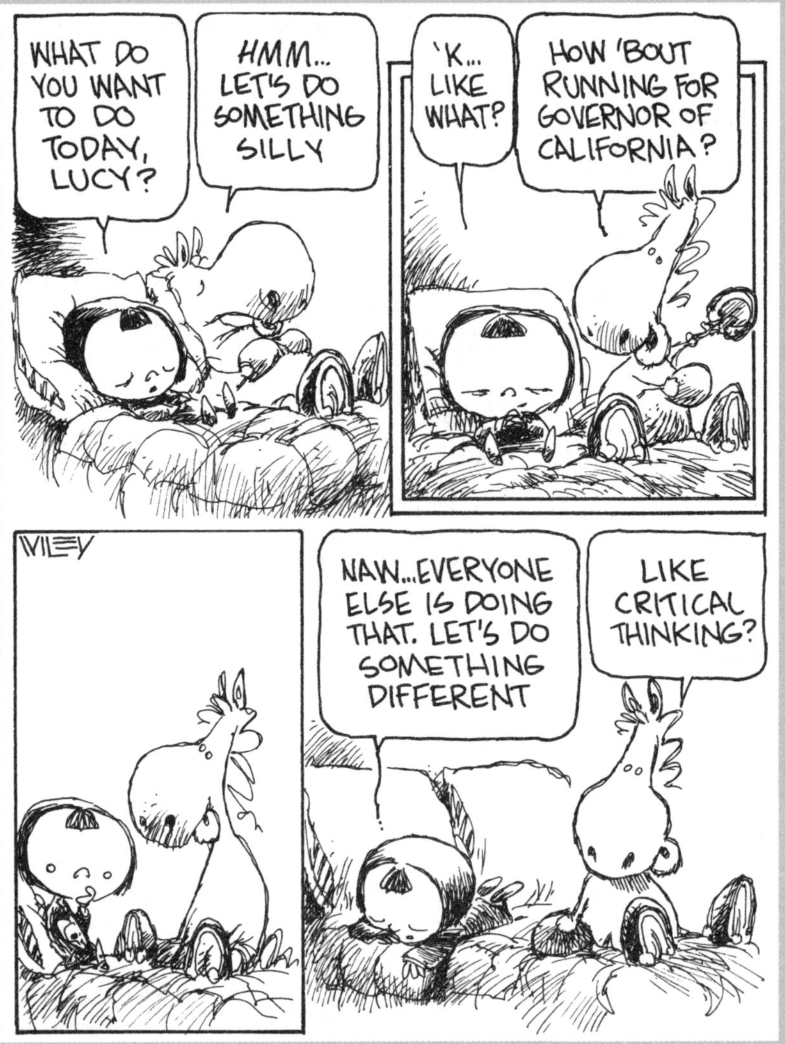
WHAT DO YOU WANT TO DO TODAY, LUCY?
HMM... LET'S DO SOMETHING SILLY
'K... LIKE WHAT?
HOW 'BOUT RUNNING FOR GOVERNOR OF CALIFORNIA?
WILEY
NAW...EVERYONE ELSE IS DOING THAT. LET'S DO SOMETHING DIFFERENT
LIKE CRITICAL THINKING?

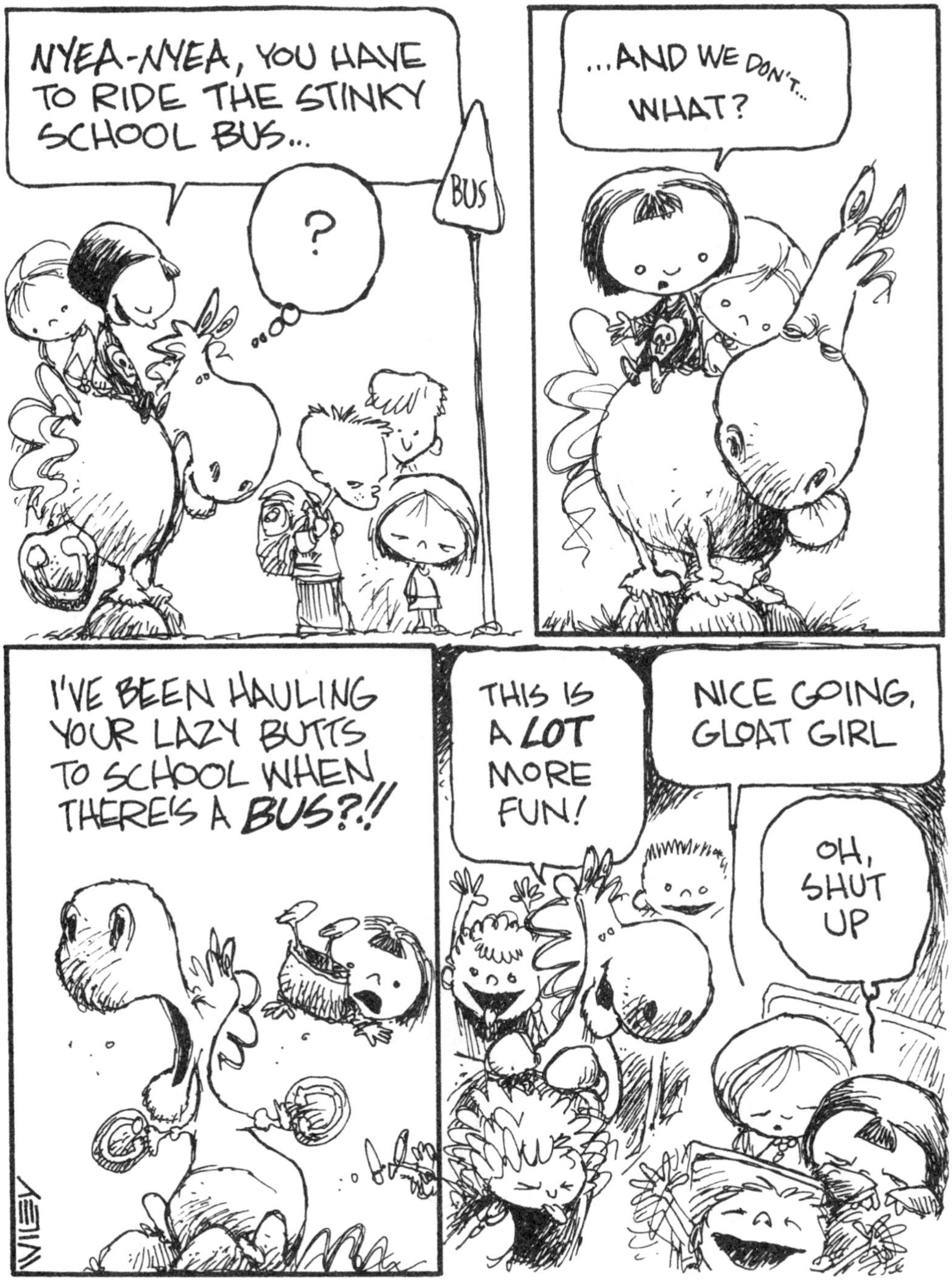
NYEA-NYEA, YOU HAVE TO RIDE THE STINKY SCHOOL BUS...
?
BUS
...AND WE DON'T... WHAT?
I'VE BEEN HAULING YOUR LAZY BUTTS TO SCHOOL WHEN THERE'S A BUS?!!
WILEY
THIS IS A LOT MORE FUN!
NICE GOING, GLOAT GIRL
OH, SHUT UP

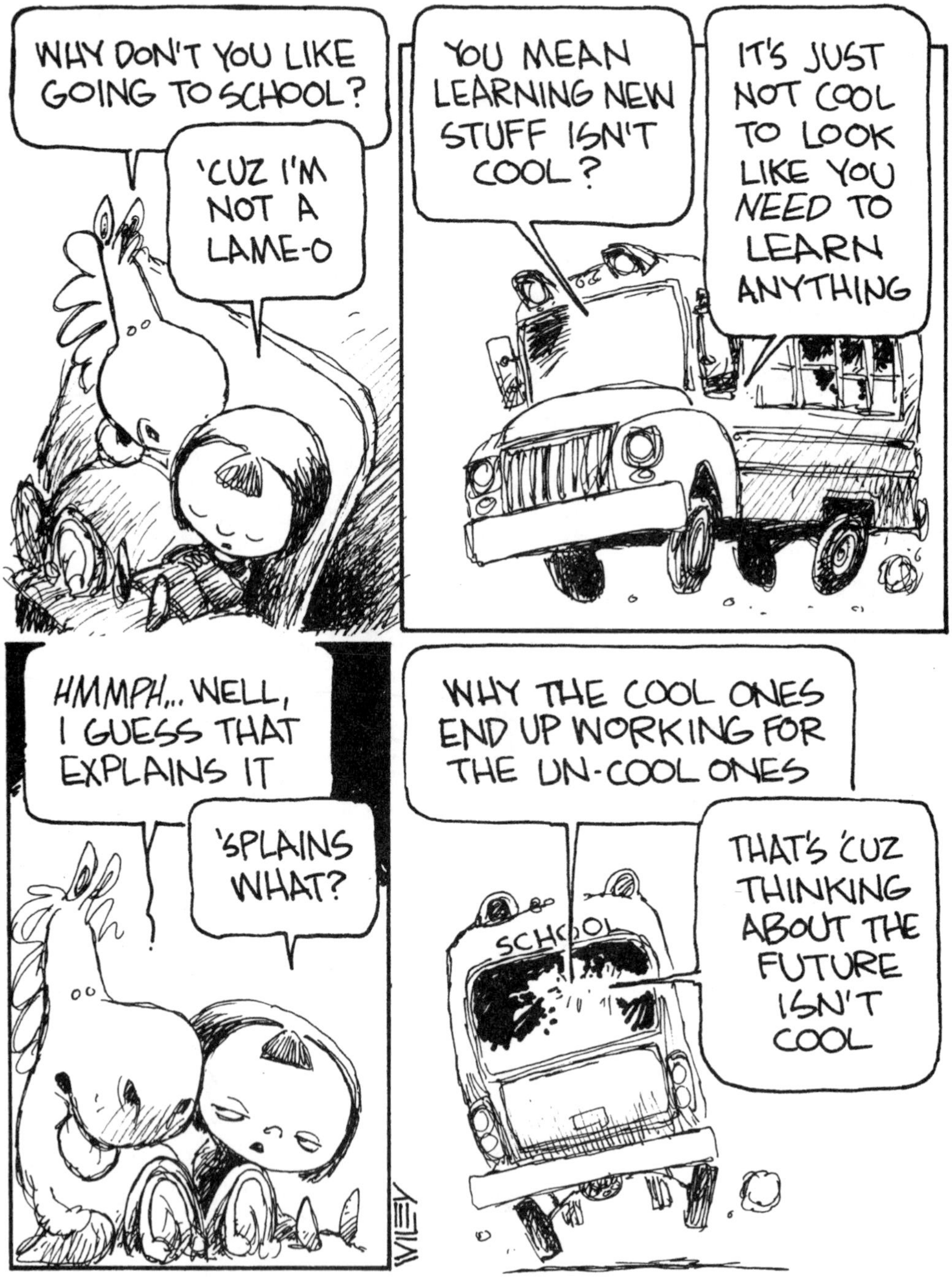
WHY DON'T YOU LIKE GOING TO SCHOOL?
'CUZ I'M NOT A LAME-O
YOU MEAN LEARNING NEW STUFF ISN'T COOL?
IT'S JUST NOT COOL TO LOOK LIKE YOU *NEED* TO LEARN ANYTHING
HMMPH... WELL, I GUESS THAT EXPLAINS IT
'SPLAINS WHAT?
WHY THE COOL ONES END UP WORKING FOR THE UN-COOL ONES
THAT'S 'CUZ THINKING ABOUT THE FUTURE ISN'T COOL
SCHOOL
WILEY

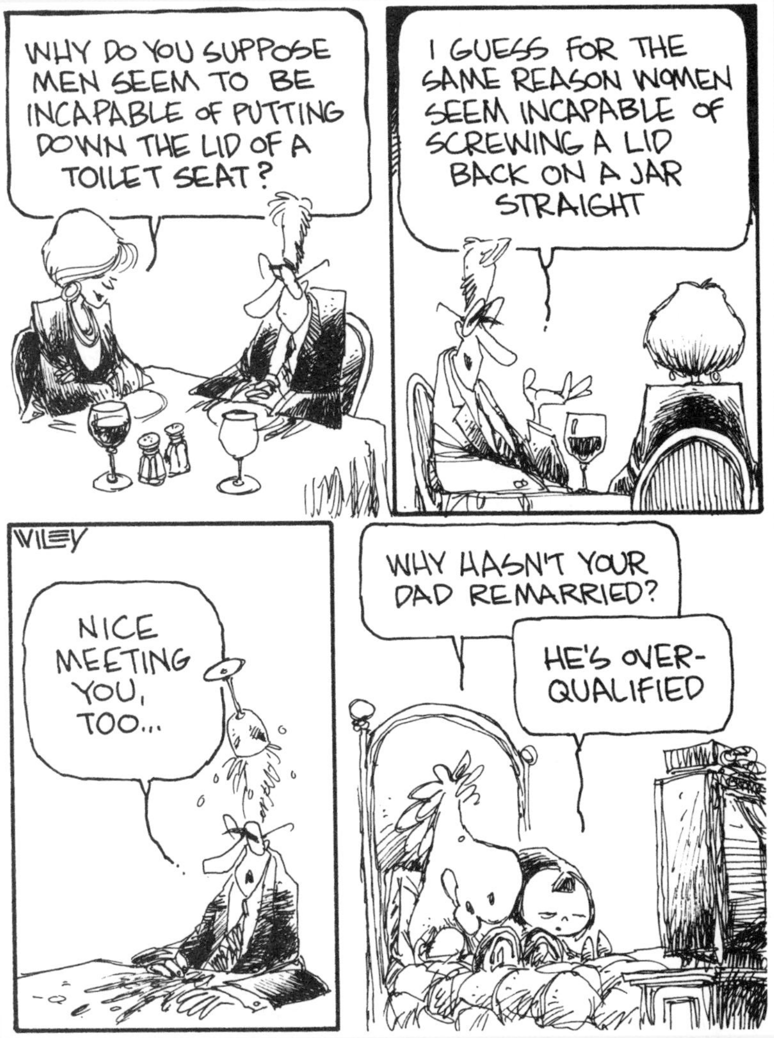
WHY DO YOU SUPPOSE MEN SEEM TO BE INCAPABLE OF PUTTING DOWN THE LID OF A TOILET SEAT?
I GUESS FOR THE SAME REASON WOMEN SEEM INCAPABLE OF SCREWING A LID BACK ON A JAR STRAIGHT
WILEY
NICE MEETING YOU, TOO...
WHY HASN'T YOUR DAD REMARRIED?
HE'S OVER-QUALIFIED

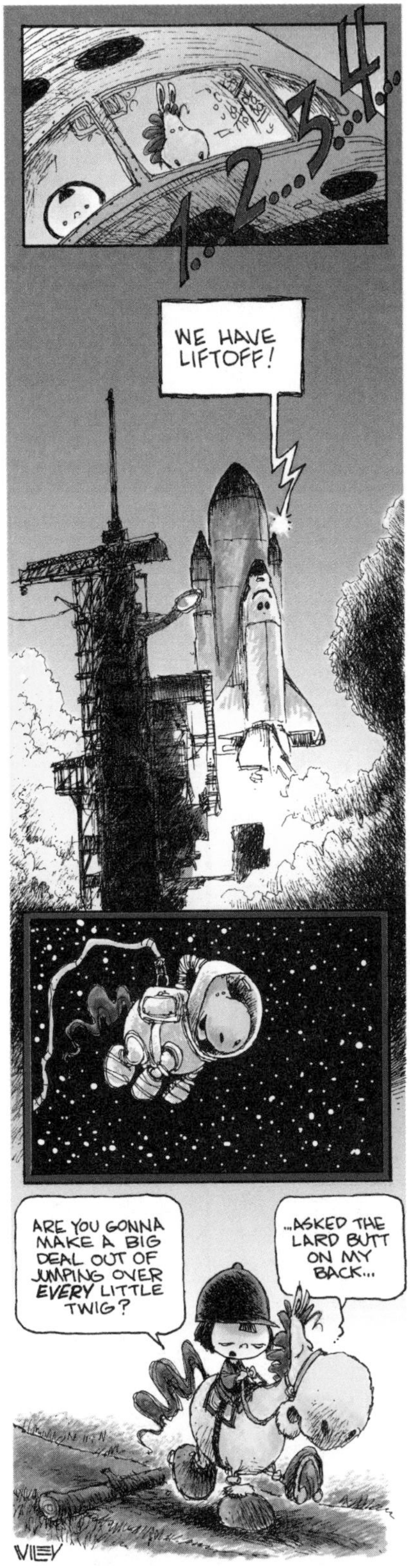
1...2...3...4...
WE HAVE LIFTOFF!
ARE YOU GONNA MAKE A BIG DEAL OUT OF JUMPING OVER EVERY LITTLE TWIG?
...ASKED THE LARD BUTT ON MY BACK...
WILEY

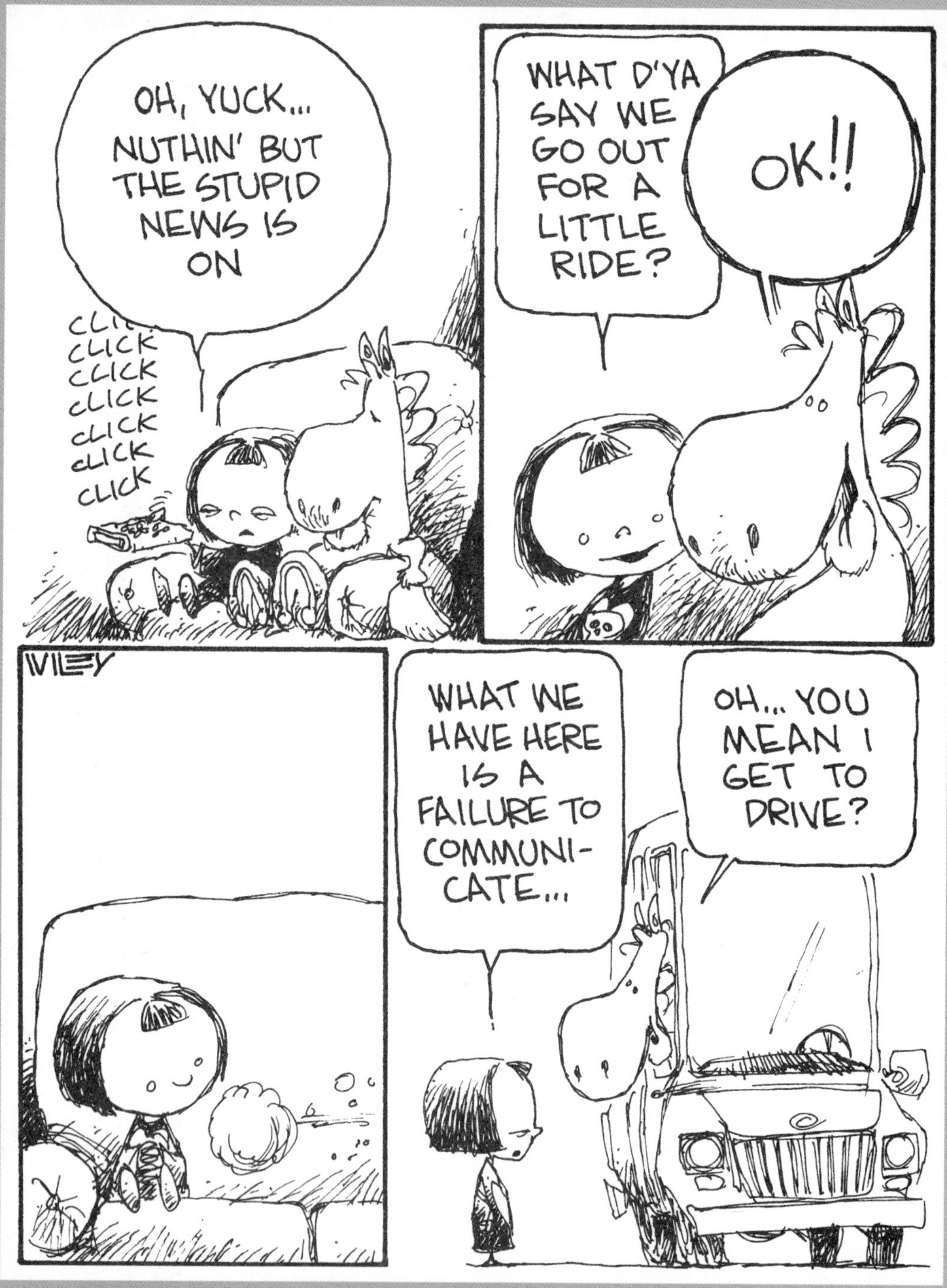
OH, YUCK... NUTHIN' BUT THE STUPID NEWS IS ON
CLICK CLICK CLICK CLICK CLICK CLICK CLICK
WHAT D'YA SAY WE GO OUT FOR A LITTLE RIDE?
OK!!
WILEY
WHAT WE HAVE HERE IS A FAILURE TO COMMUNI-CATE...
OH... YOU MEAN I GET TO DRIVE?

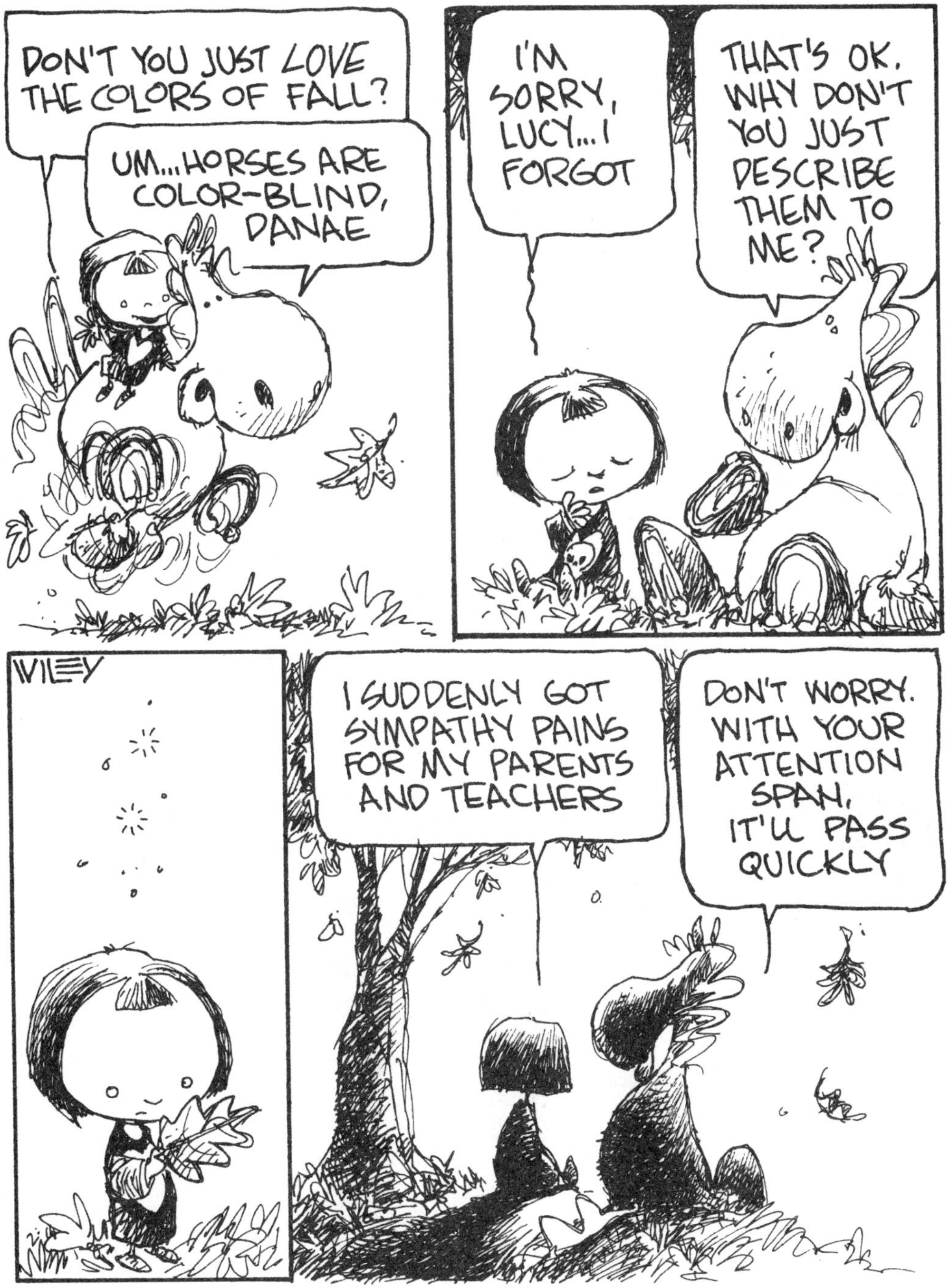
DON'T YOU JUST LOVE THE COLORS OF FALL?
UM...HORSES ARE COLOR-BLIND, DANAE
I'M SORRY, LUCY...I FORGOT
THAT'S OK. WHY DON'T YOU JUST DESCRIBE THEM TO ME?
WILEY
I SUDDENLY GOT SYMPATHY PAINS FOR MY PARENTS AND TEACHERS
DON'T WORRY. WITH YOUR ATTENTION SPAN, IT'LL PASS QUICKLY

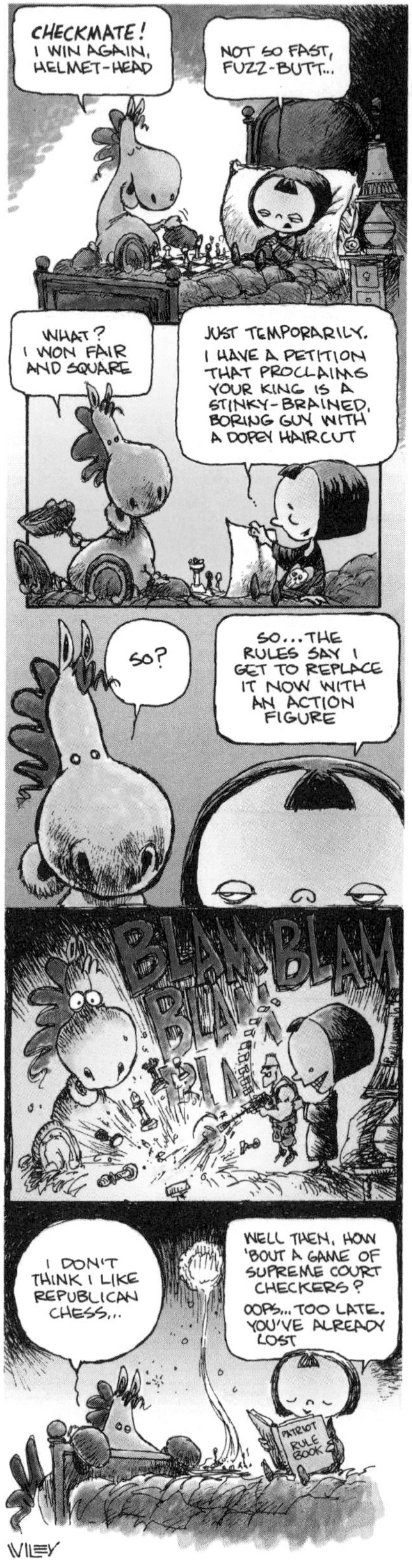
CHECKMATE! I WIN AGAIN, HELMET-HEAD
NOT SO FAST, FUZZ-BUTT...
WHAT? I WON FAIR AND SQUARE
JUST TEMPORARILY. I HAVE A PETITION THAT PROCLAIMS YOUR KING IS A STINKY-BRAINED, BORING GUY WITH A DOPEY HAIRCUT
SO?
SO... THE RULES SAY I GET TO REPLACE IT NOW WITH AN ACTION FIGURE
BLAM BLAM BLAM BLA
I DON'T THINK I LIKE REPUBLICAN CHESS...
WELL THEN, HOW 'BOUT A GAME OF SUPREME COURT CHECKERS?
OOPS... TOO LATE. YOU'VE ALREADY LOST
PATRIOT RULE BOOK
WILEY

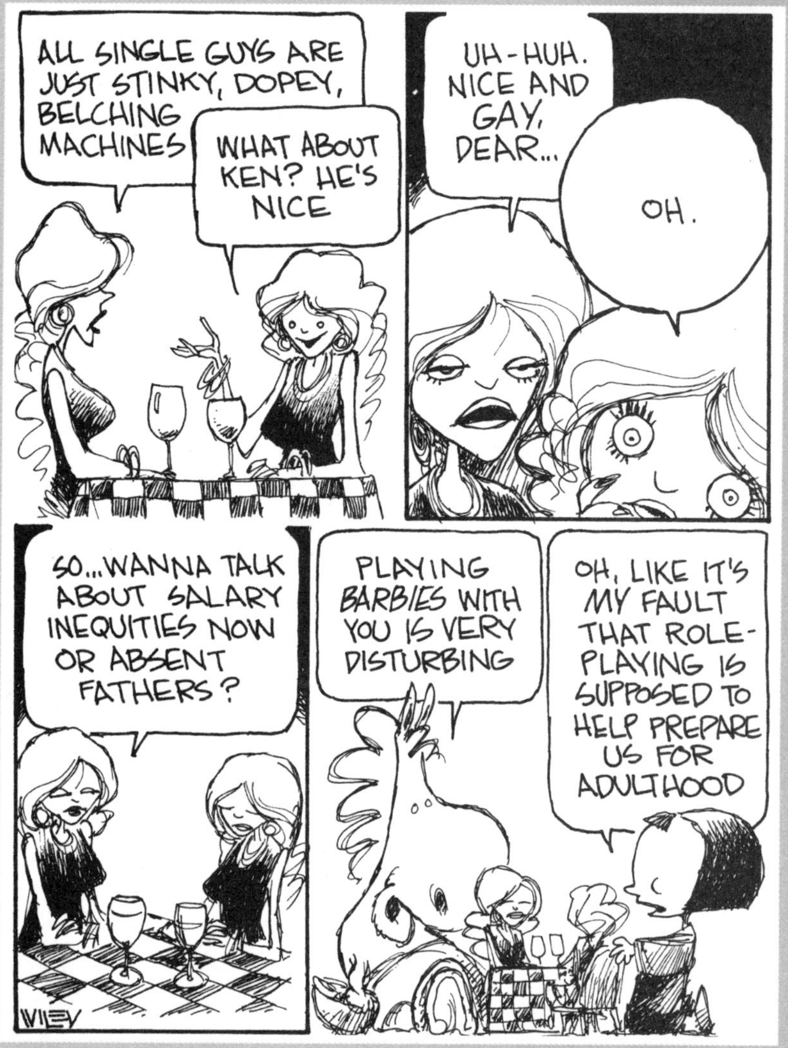
ALL SINGLE GUYS ARE JUST STINKY, DOPEY, BELCHING MACHINES
WHAT ABOUT KEN? HE'S NICE
UH-HUH. NICE AND GAY, DEAR...
OH.
SO... WANNA TALK ABOUT SALARY INEQUITIES NOW OR ABSENT FATHERS?
PLAYING BARBIES WITH YOU IS VERY DISTURBING
OH, LIKE IT'S MY FAULT THAT ROLE-PLAYING IS SUPPOSED TO HELP PREPARE US FOR ADULTHOOD
WILEY

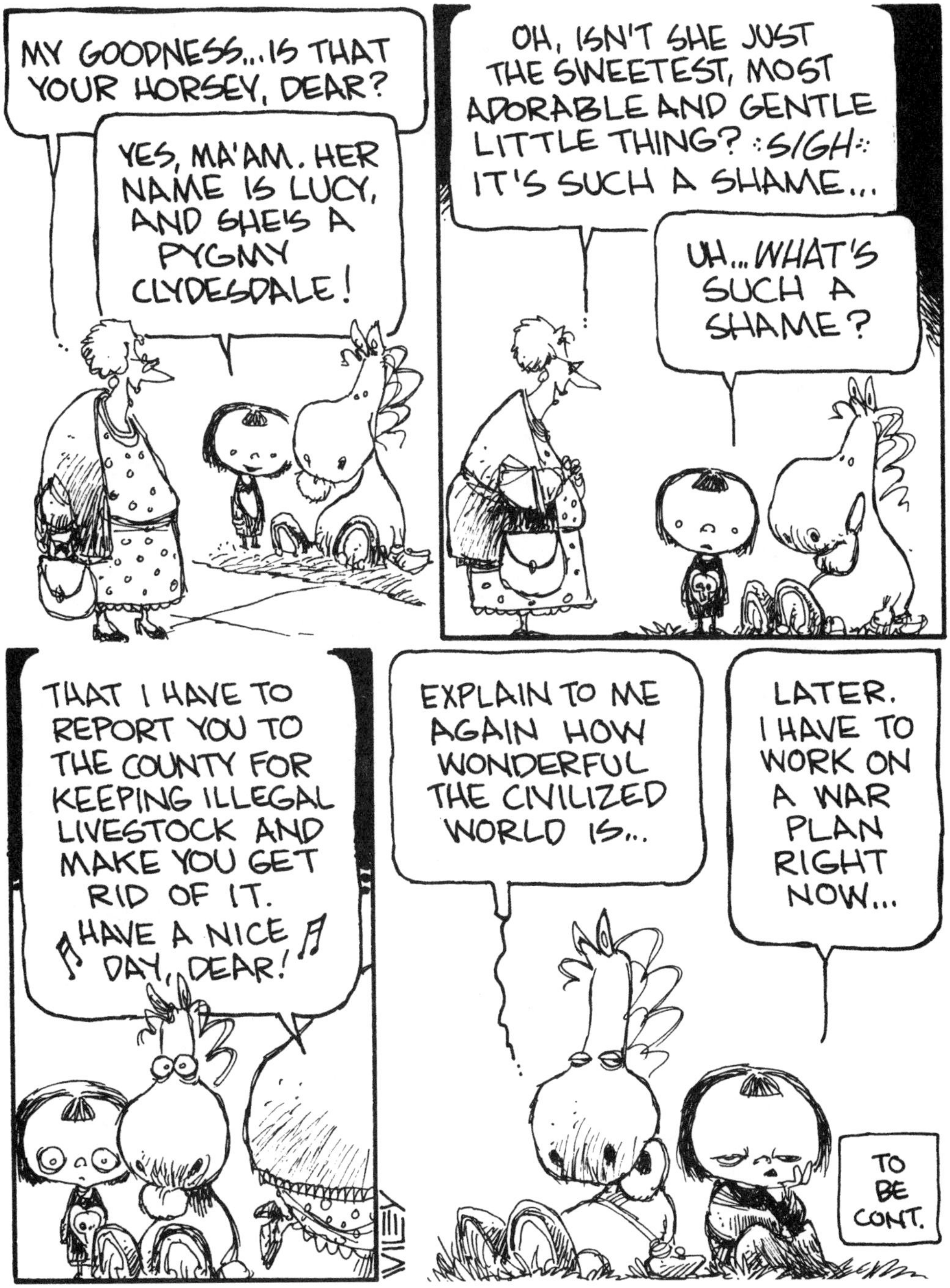
MY GOODNESS...IS THAT YOUR HORSEY, DEAR?
YES, MA'AM. HER NAME IS LUCY, AND SHE'S A PYGMY CLYDESDALE!
OH, ISN'T SHE JUST THE SWEETEST, MOST ADORABLE AND GENTLE LITTLE THING? :SIGH: IT'S SUCH A SHAME...
UH...WHAT'S SUCH A SHAME?
THAT I HAVE TO REPORT YOU TO THE COUNTY FOR KEEPING ILLEGAL LIVESTOCK AND MAKE YOU GET RID OF IT. HAVE A NICE DAY, DEAR!
EXPLAIN TO ME AGAIN HOW WONDERFUL THE CIVILIZED WORLD IS...
LATER. I HAVE TO WORK ON A WAR PLAN RIGHT NOW...
TO BE CONT.

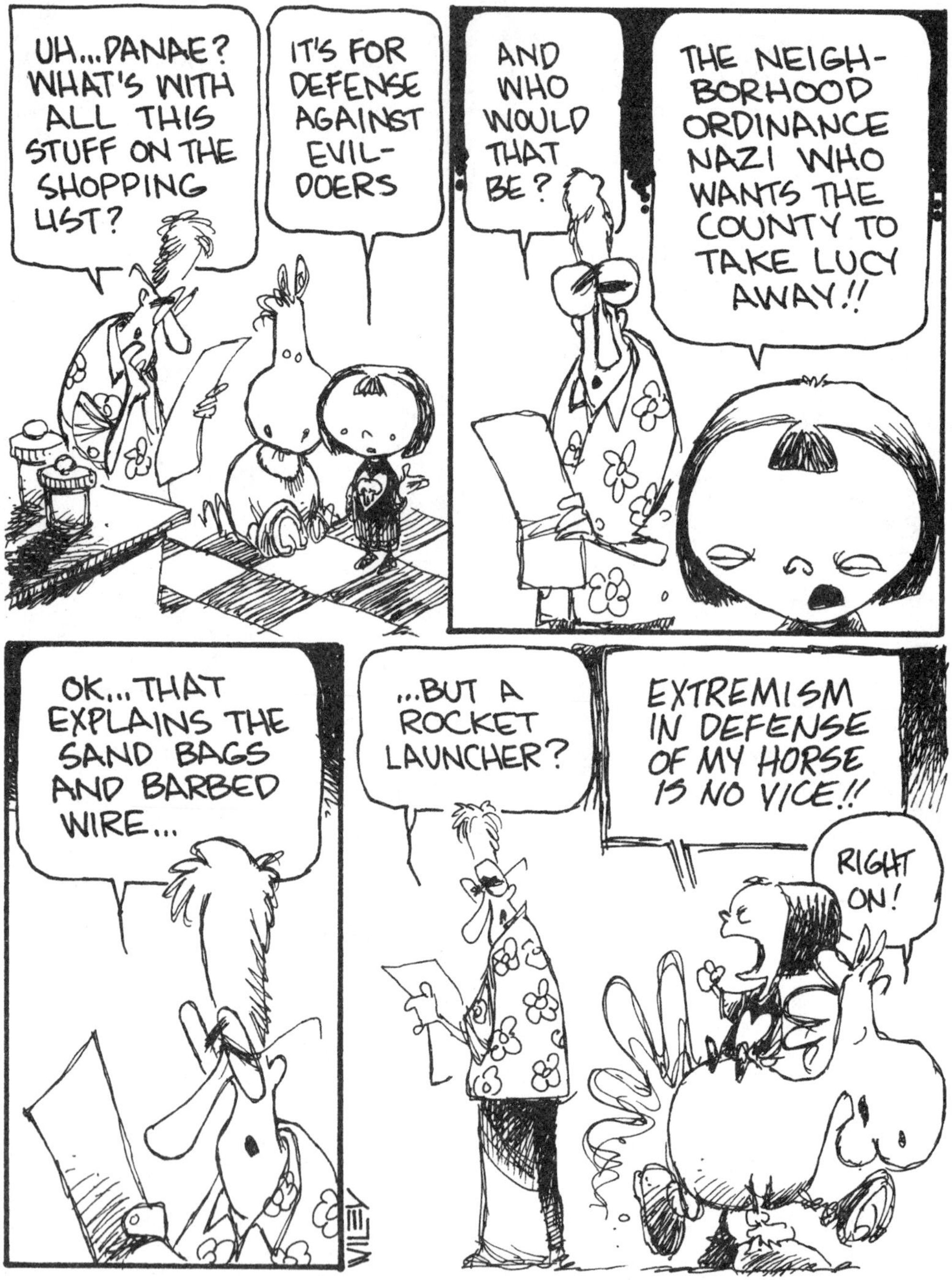
UH...PANAE? WHAT'S WITH ALL THIS STUFF ON THE SHOPPING LIST?
IT'S FOR DEFENSE AGAINST EVIL-DOERS
AND WHO WOULD THAT BE?
THE NEIGH-BORHOOD ORDINANCE NAZI WHO WANTS THE COUNTY TO TAKE LUCY AWAY!!
OK... THAT EXPLAINS THE SAND BAGS AND BARBED WIRE...
...BUT A ROCKET LAUNCHER?
EXTREMISM IN DEFENSE OF MY HORSE IS NO VICE!!
RIGHT ON!
WILEY

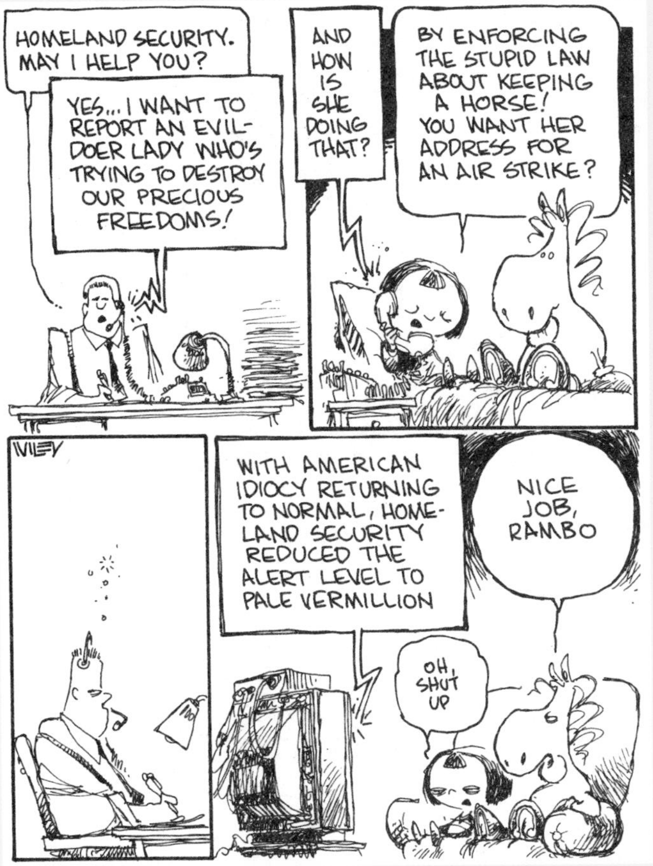
HOMELAND SECURITY. MAY I HELP YOU?
YES... I WANT TO REPORT AN EVIL-DOER LADY WHO'S TRYING TO DESTROY OUR PRECIOUS FREEDOMS!
AND HOW IS SHE DOING THAT?
BY ENFORCING THE STUPID LAW ABOUT KEEPING A HORSE! YOU WANT HER ADDRESS FOR AN AIR STRIKE?
WILEY
WITH AMERICAN IDIOCY RETURNING TO NORMAL, HOMELAND SECURITY REDUCED THE ALERT LEVEL TO PALE VERMILLION
NICE JOB, RAMBO
OH, SHUT UP

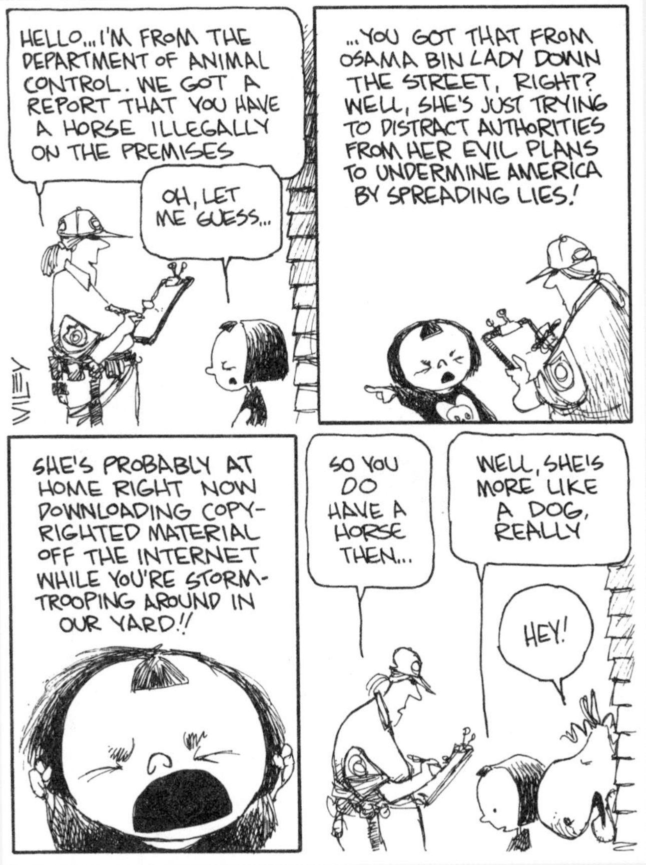
HELLO... I'M FROM THE DEPARTMENT OF ANIMAL CONTROL. WE GOT A REPORT THAT YOU HAVE A HORSE ILLEGALLY ON THE PREMISES
OH, LET ME GUESS...
WILEY
...YOU GOT THAT FROM OSAMA BIN LADY DOWN THE STREET, RIGHT? WELL, SHE'S JUST TRYING TO DISTRACT AUTHORITIES FROM HER EVIL PLANS TO UNDERMINE AMERICA BY SPREADING LIES!
SHE'S PROBABLY AT HOME RIGHT NOW DOWNLOADING COPYRIGHTED MATERIAL OFF THE INTERNET WHILE YOU'RE STORM-TROOPING AROUND IN OUR YARD!!
SO YOU DO HAVE A HORSE THEN...
WELL, SHE'S MORE LIKE A DOG, REALLY
HEY!

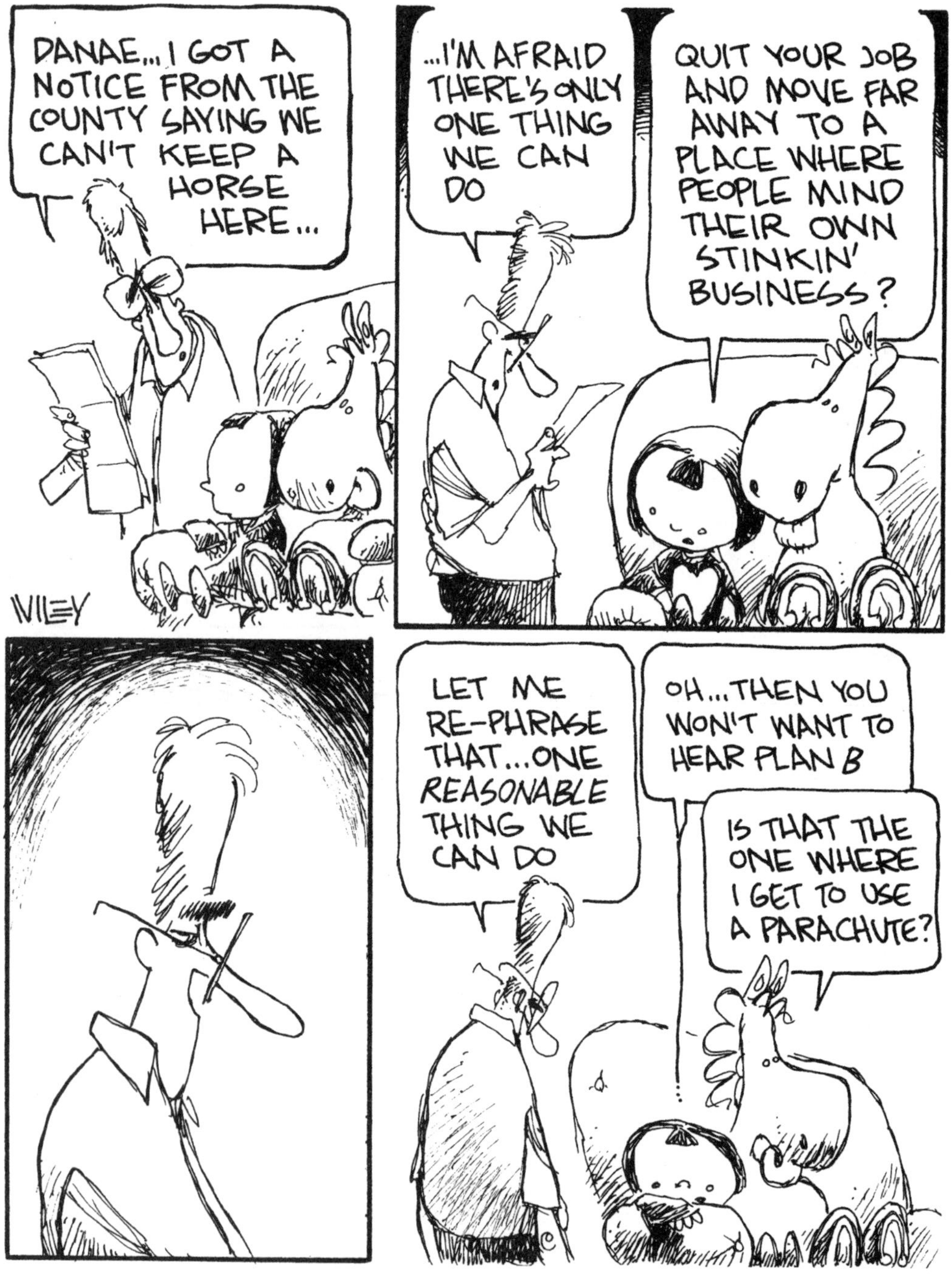
DANAE... I GOT A NOTICE FROM THE COUNTY SAYING WE CAN'T KEEP A HORSE HERE...
WILEY
...I'M AFRAID THERE'S ONLY ONE THING WE CAN DO
QUIT YOUR JOB AND MOVE FAR AWAY TO A PLACE WHERE PEOPLE MIND THEIR OWN STINKIN' BUSINESS?
LET ME RE-PHRASE THAT...ONE *REASONABLE* THING WE CAN DO
OH... THEN YOU WON'T WANT TO HEAR PLAN *B*
IS THAT THE ONE WHERE I GET TO USE A PARACHUTE?

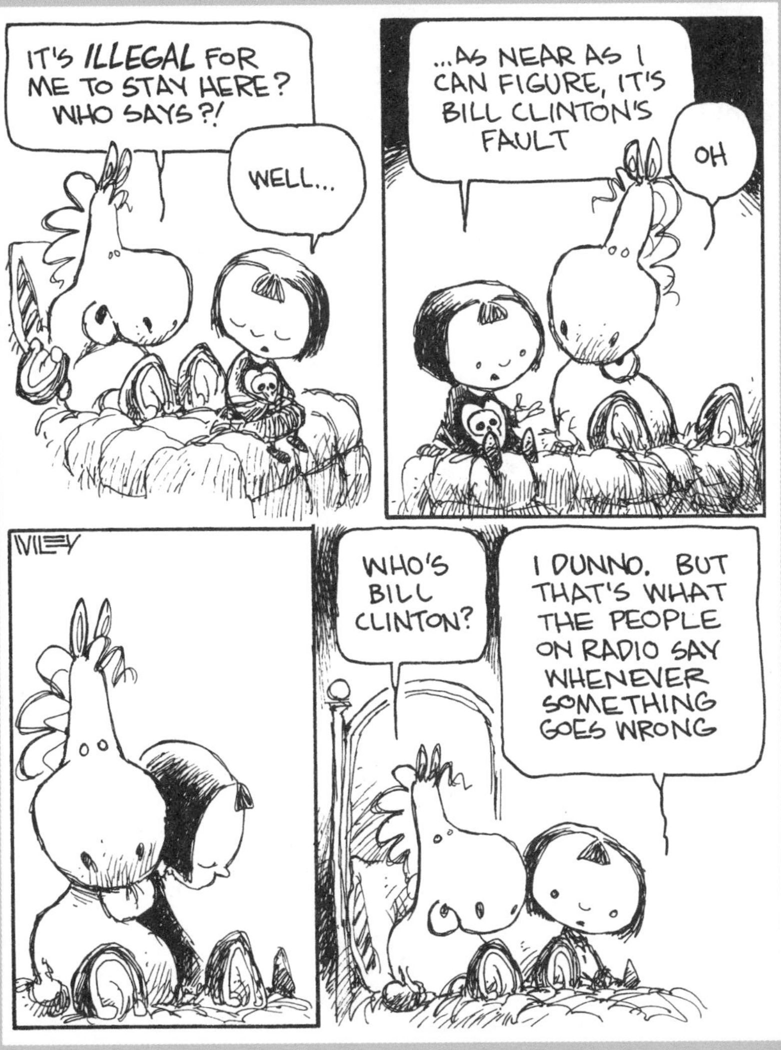
IT'S ILLEGAL FOR ME TO STAY HERE? WHO SAYS?!
WELL...
...AS NEAR AS I CAN FIGURE, IT'S BILL CLINTON'S FAULT
OH
WILEY
WHO'S BILL CLINTON?
I DUNNO. BUT THAT'S WHAT THE PEOPLE ON RADIO SAY WHENEVER SOMETHING GOES WRONG

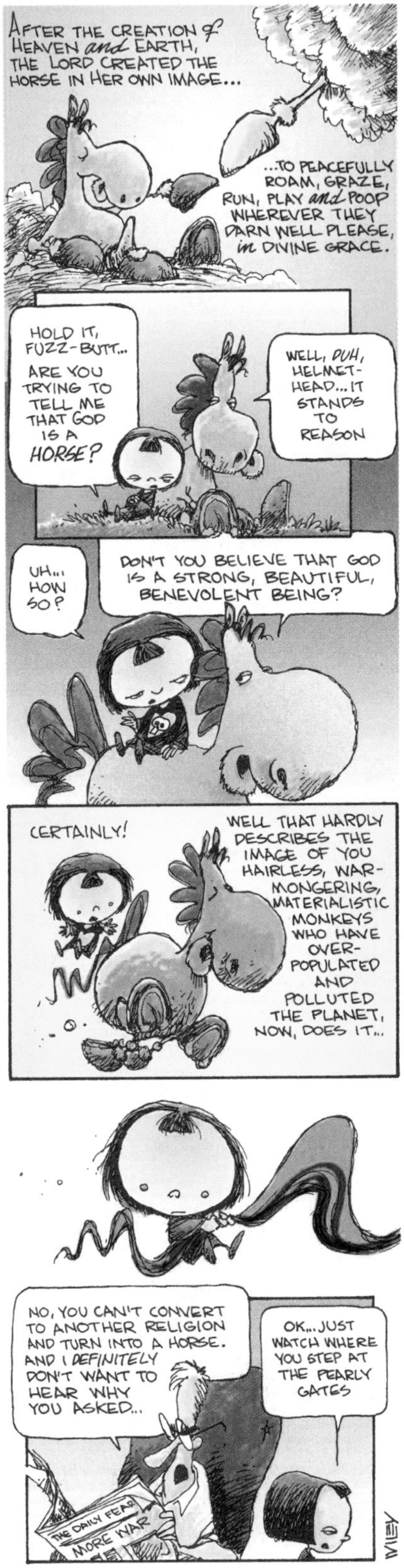
AFTER THE CREATION of HEAVEN and EARTH, THE LORD CREATED THE HORSE IN HER OWN IMAGE...
...TO PEACEFULLY ROAM, GRAZE, RUN, PLAY and POOP WHEREVER THEY DARN WELL PLEASE, in DIVINE GRACE.
HOLD IT, FUZZ-BUTT... ARE YOU TRYING TO TELL ME THAT GOD IS A HORSE?
WELL, DUH, HELMET-HEAD... IT STANDS TO REASON
UH... HOW SO?
DON'T YOU BELIEVE THAT GOD IS A STRONG, BEAUTIFUL, BENEVOLENT BEING?
CERTAINLY!
WELL THAT HARDLY DESCRIBES THE IMAGE OF YOU HAIRLESS, WAR-MONGERING, MATERIALISTIC MONKEYS WHO HAVE OVER-POPULATED AND POLLUTED THE PLANET, NOW, DOES IT...
NO, YOU CAN'T CONVERT TO ANOTHER RELIGION AND TURN INTO A HORSE. AND I DEFINITELY DON'T WANT TO HEAR WHY YOU ASKED...
OK... JUST WATCH WHERE YOU STEP AT THE PEARLY GATES
THE DAILY FEAR
MORE WAR
WILEY

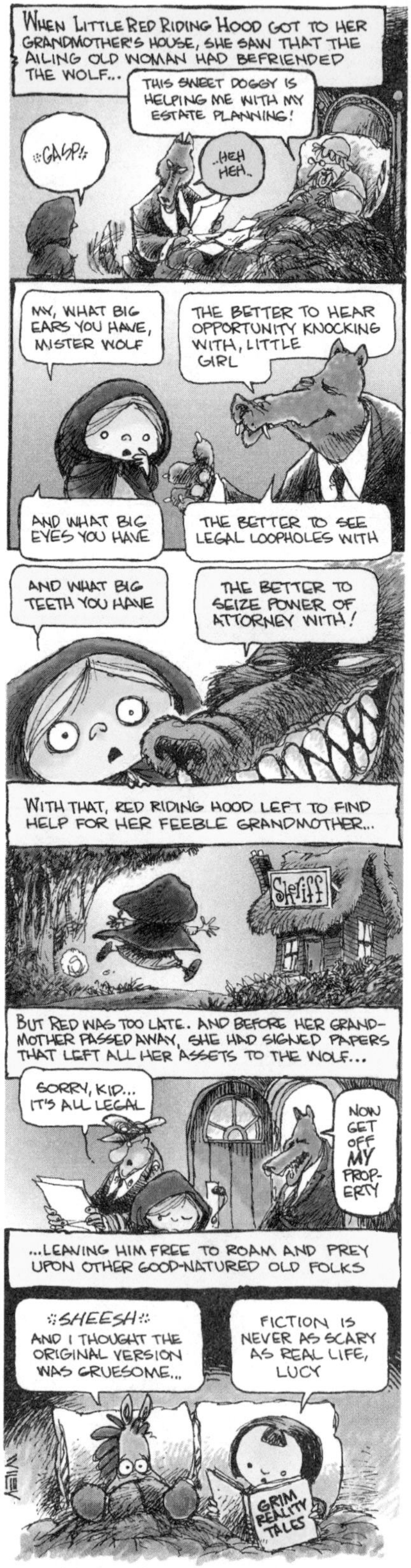
WHEN LITTLE RED RIDING HOOD GOT TO HER GRANDMOTHER'S HOUSE, SHE SAW THAT THE AILING OLD WOMAN HAD BEFRIENDED THE WOLF...
THIS SWEET DOGGY IS HELPING ME WITH MY ESTATE PLANNING!
GASP!
..HEH HEH..
MY, WHAT BIG EARS YOU HAVE, MISTER WOLF
THE BETTER TO HEAR OPPORTUNITY KNOCKING WITH, LITTLE GIRL
AND WHAT BIG EYES YOU HAVE
THE BETTER TO SEE LEGAL LOOPHOLES WITH
AND WHAT BIG TEETH YOU HAVE
THE BETTER TO SEIZE POWER OF ATTORNEY WITH!
WITH THAT, RED RIDING HOOD LEFT TO FIND HELP FOR HER FEEBLE GRANDMOTHER...
SHERIFF
BUT RED WAS TOO LATE. AND BEFORE HER GRANDMOTHER PASSED AWAY, SHE HAD SIGNED PAPERS THAT LEFT ALL HER ASSETS TO THE WOLF...
SORRY, KID... IT'S ALL LEGAL
NOW GET OFF MY PROPERTY
...LEAVING HIM FREE TO ROAM AND PREY UPON OTHER GOOD-NATURED OLD FOLKS
SHEESH
AND I THOUGHT THE ORIGINAL VERSION WAS GRUESOME...
FICTION IS NEVER AS SCARY AS REAL LIFE, LUCY
GRIM REALITY TALES
WILEY

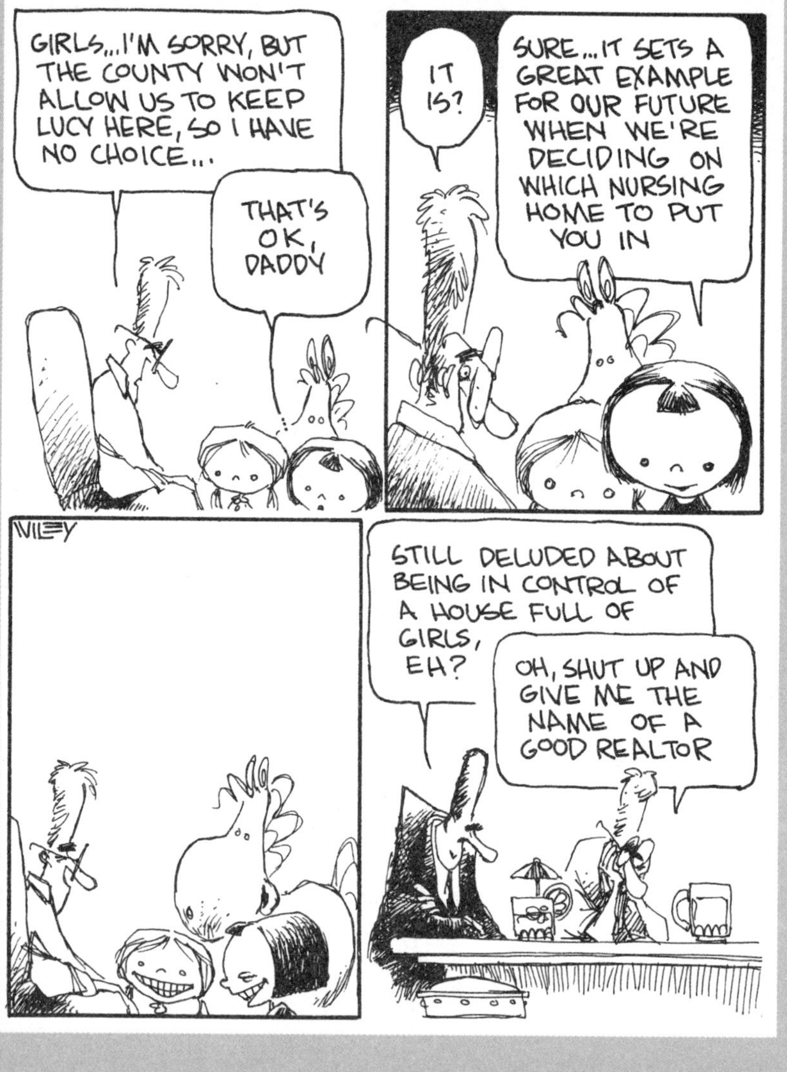
GIRLS... I'M SORRY, BUT THE COUNTY WON'T ALLOW US TO KEEP LUCY HERE, SO I HAVE NO CHOICE...
THAT'S OK, DADDY
IT IS?
SURE... IT SETS A GREAT EXAMPLE FOR OUR FUTURE WHEN WE'RE DECIDING ON WHICH NURSING HOME TO PUT YOU IN
WILEY
STILL DELUDED ABOUT BEING IN CONTROL OF A HOUSE FULL OF GIRLS, EH?
OH, SHUT UP AND GIVE ME THE NAME OF A GOOD REALTOR

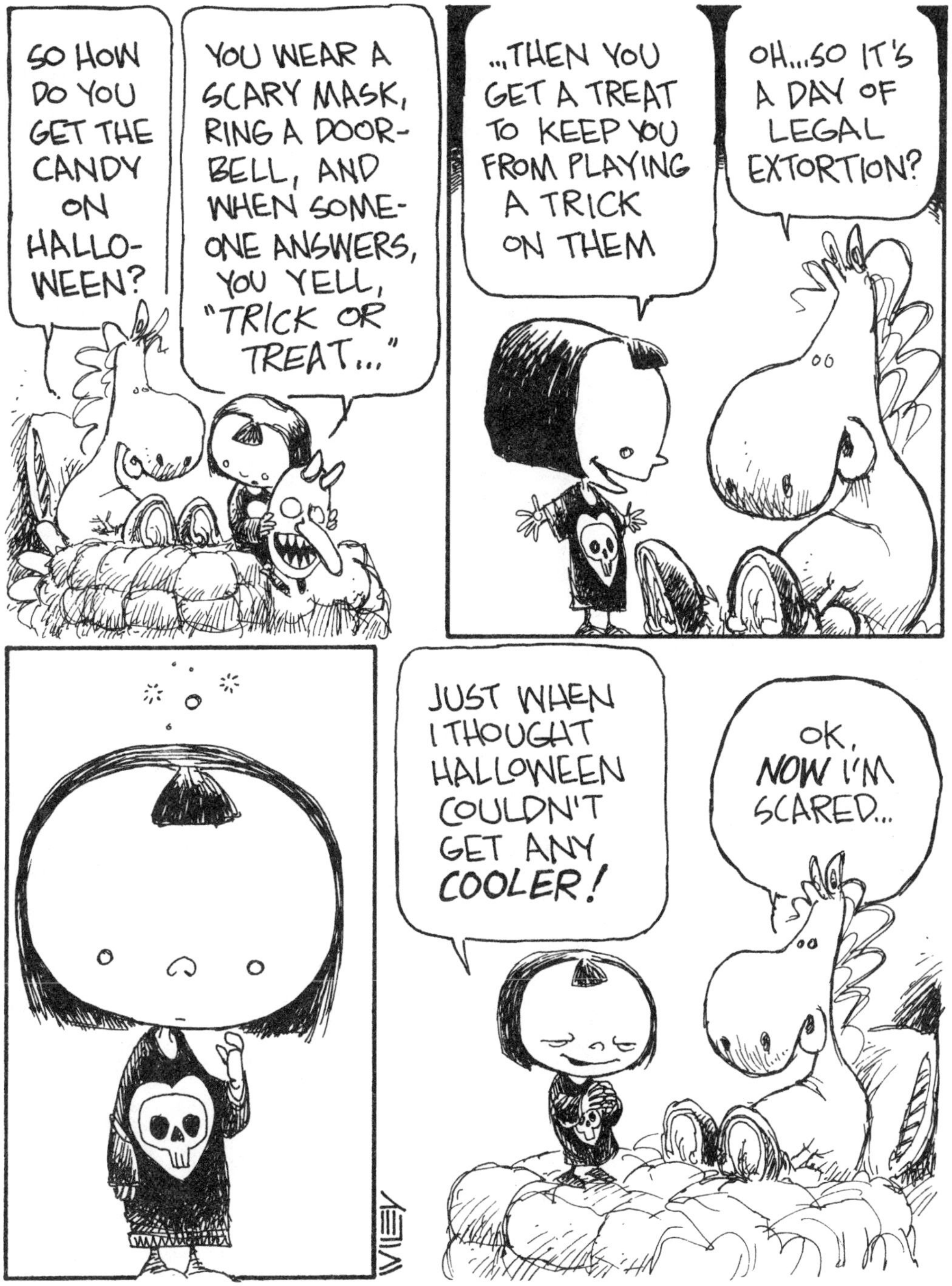
SO HOW DO YOU GET THE CANDY ON HALLO-WEEN?
YOU WEAR A SCARY MASK, RING A DOOR-BELL, AND WHEN SOME-ONE ANSWERS, YOU YELL, "TRICK OR TREAT..."
...THEN YOU GET A TREAT TO KEEP YOU FROM PLAYING A TRICK ON THEM
OH...SO IT'S A DAY OF LEGAL EXTORTION?
JUST WHEN I THOUGHT HALLOWEEN COULDN'T GET ANY COOLER!
OK, NOW I'M SCARED...
WILEY

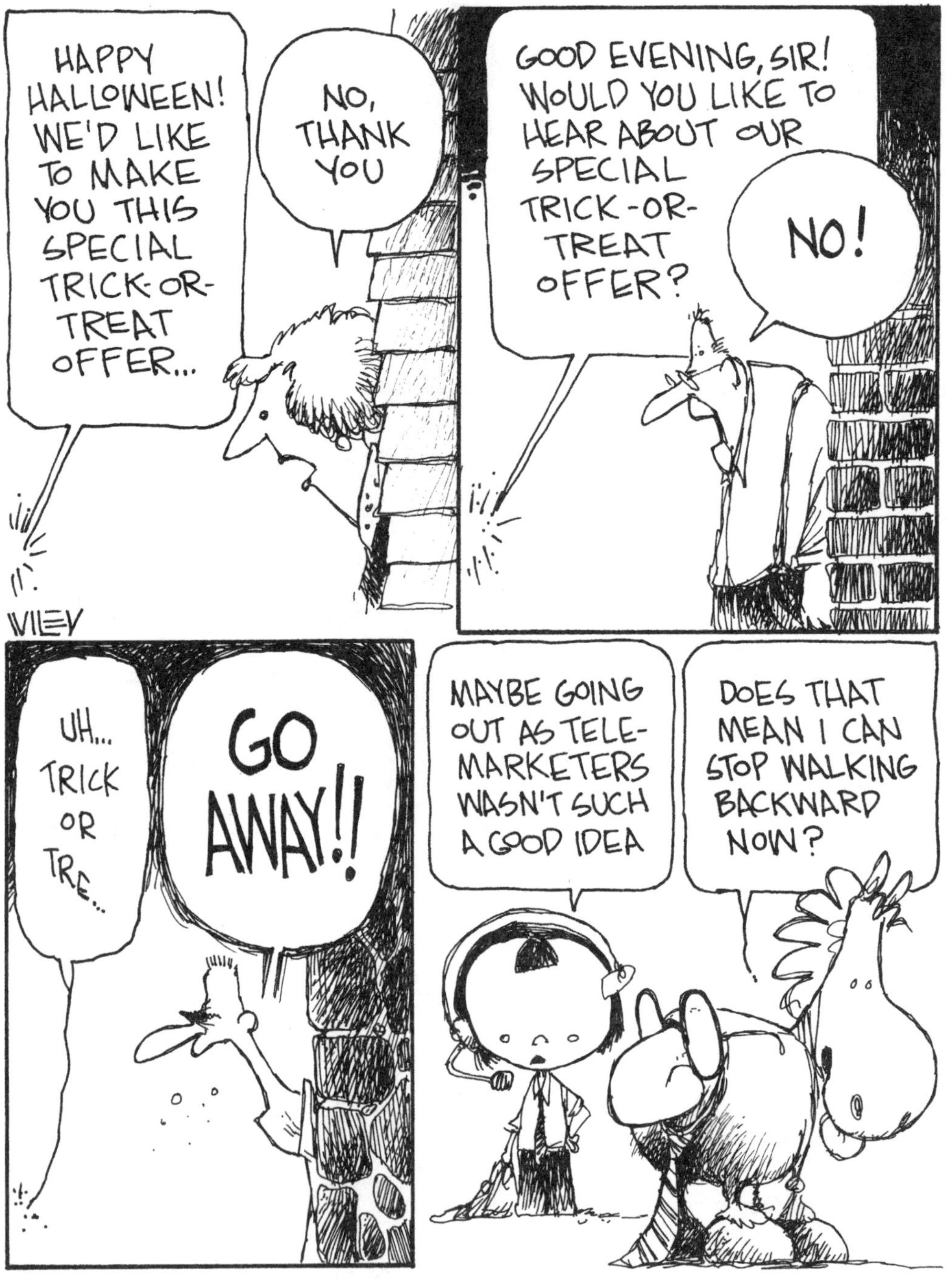
HAPPY HALLOWEEN! WE'D LIKE TO MAKE YOU THIS SPECIAL TRICK-OR-TREAT OFFER...
NO, THANK YOU
WILEY
GOOD EVENING, SIR! WOULD YOU LIKE TO HEAR ABOUT OUR SPECIAL TRICK-OR-TREAT OFFER?
NO!
UH... TRICK OR TRE...
GO AWAY!!
MAYBE GOING OUT AS TELE-MARKETERS WASN'T SUCH A GOOD IDEA
DOES THAT MEAN I CAN STOP WALKING BACKWARD NOW?

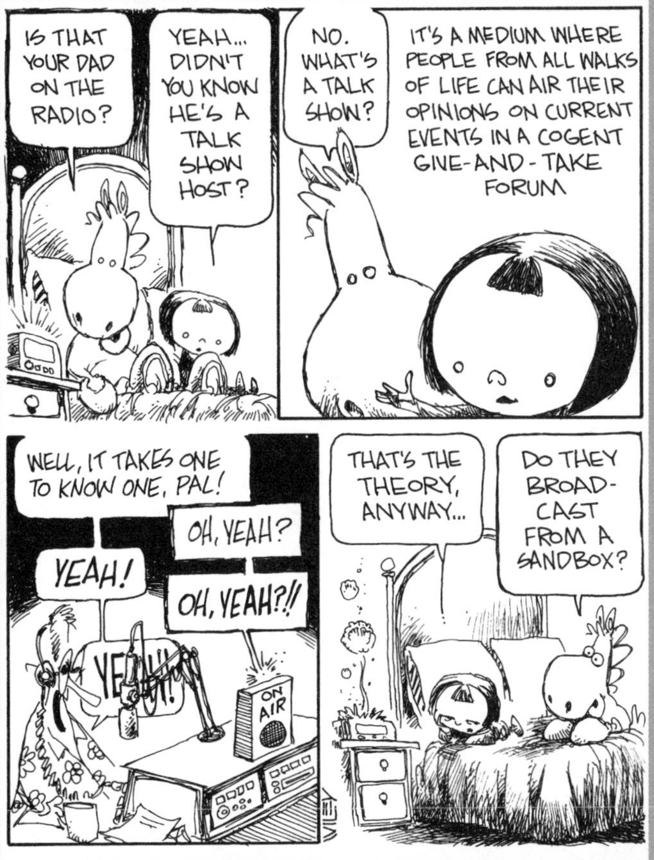
IS THAT YOUR DAD ON THE RADIO?
YEAH... DIDN'T YOU KNOW HE'S A TALK SHOW HOST?
NO. WHAT'S A TALK SHOW?
IT'S A MEDIUM WHERE PEOPLE FROM ALL WALKS OF LIFE CAN AIR THEIR OPINIONS ON CURRENT EVENTS IN A COGENT GIVE-AND-TAKE FORUM
WELL, IT TAKES ONE TO KNOW ONE, PAL!
OH, YEAH?
YEAH!
OH, YEAH?!!
ON AIR
THAT'S THE THEORY, ANYWAY...
DO THEY BROAD-CAST FROM A SANDBOX?

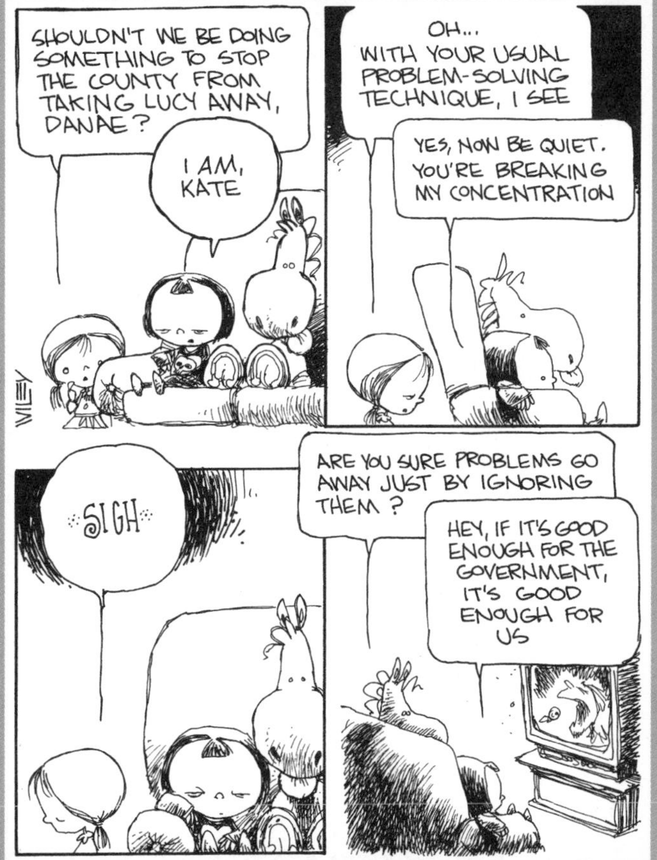
SHOULDN'T WE BE DOING SOMETHING TO STOP THE COUNTY FROM TAKING LUCY AWAY, DANAE?
I AM, KATE
OH... WITH YOUR USUAL PROBLEM-SOLVING TECHNIQUE, I SEE
YES, NOW BE QUIET. YOU'RE BREAKING MY CONCENTRATION
SIGH
ARE YOU SURE PROBLEMS GO AWAY JUST BY IGNORING THEM?
HEY, IF IT'S GOOD ENOUGH FOR THE GOVERNMENT, IT'S GOOD ENOUGH FOR US

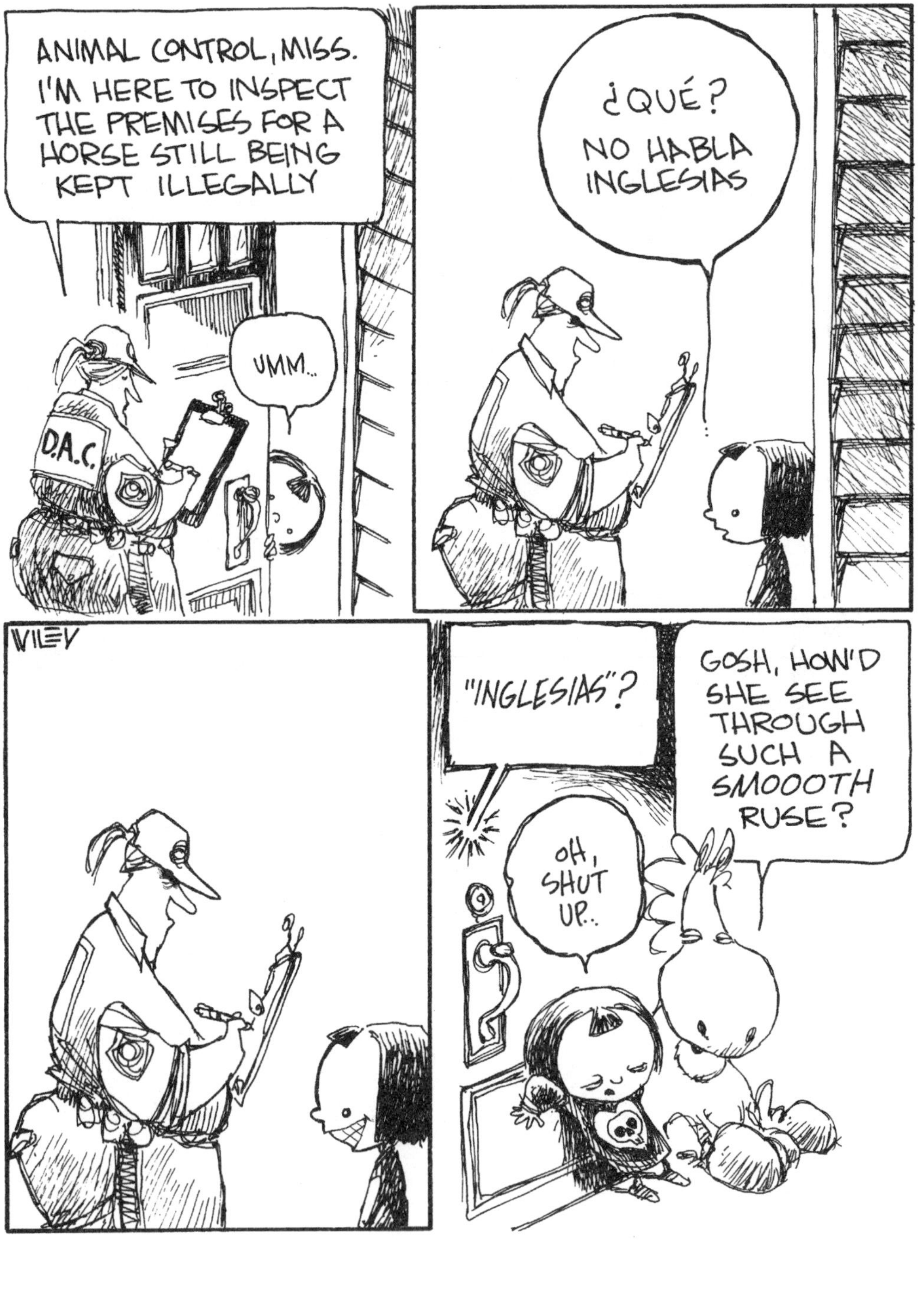
ANIMAL CONTROL, MISS. I'M HERE TO INSPECT THE PREMISES FOR A HORSE STILL BEING KEPT ILLEGALLY
UMM...
D.A.C.
¿QUÉ? NO HABLA INGLESIAS
WILEY
"INGLESIAS"?
GOSH, HOW'D SHE SEE THROUGH SUCH A SMOOOTH RUSE?
OH, SHUT UP..

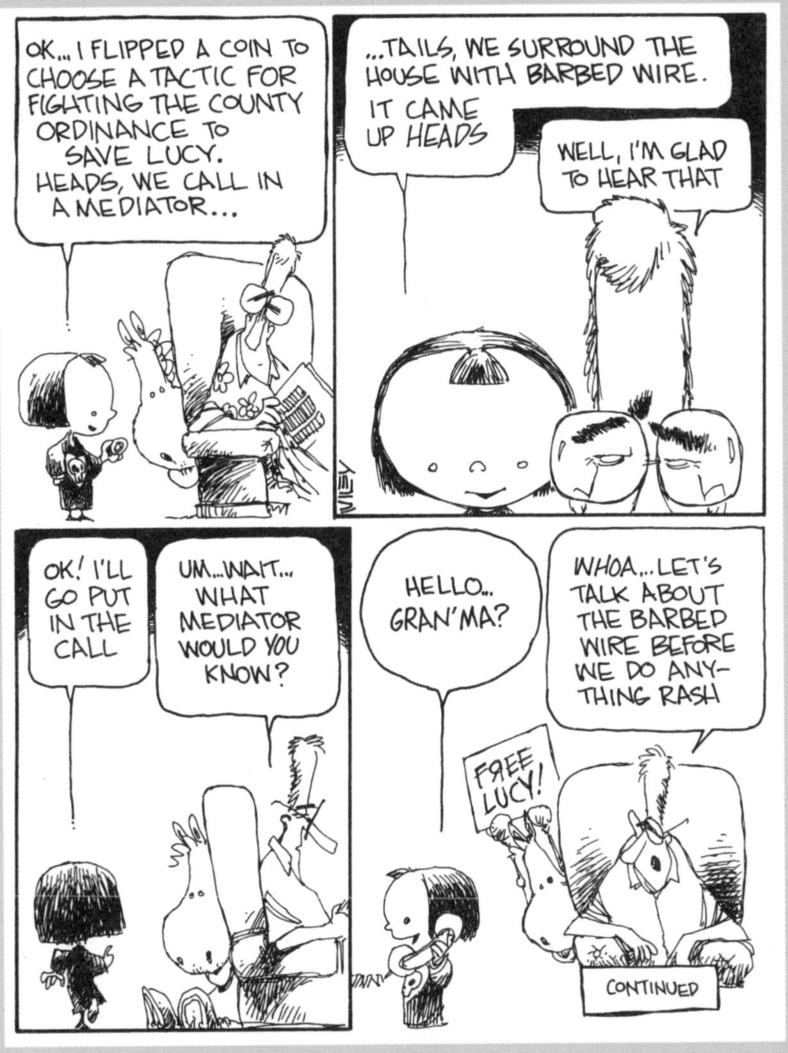

OK... I FLIPPED A COIN TO CHOOSE A TACTIC FOR FIGHTING THE COUNTY ORDINANCE TO SAVE LUCY. HEADS, WE CALL IN A MEDIATOR...
...TAILS, WE SURROUND THE HOUSE WITH BARBED WIRE. IT CAME UP HEADS
WELL, I'M GLAD TO HEAR THAT
OK! I'LL GO PUT IN THE CALL
UM...WAIT... WHAT MEDIATOR WOULD YOU KNOW?
HELLO... GRAN'MA?
FREE LUCY!
WHOA...LET'S TALK ABOUT THE BARBED WIRE BEFORE WE DO ANY-THING RASH
CONTINUED

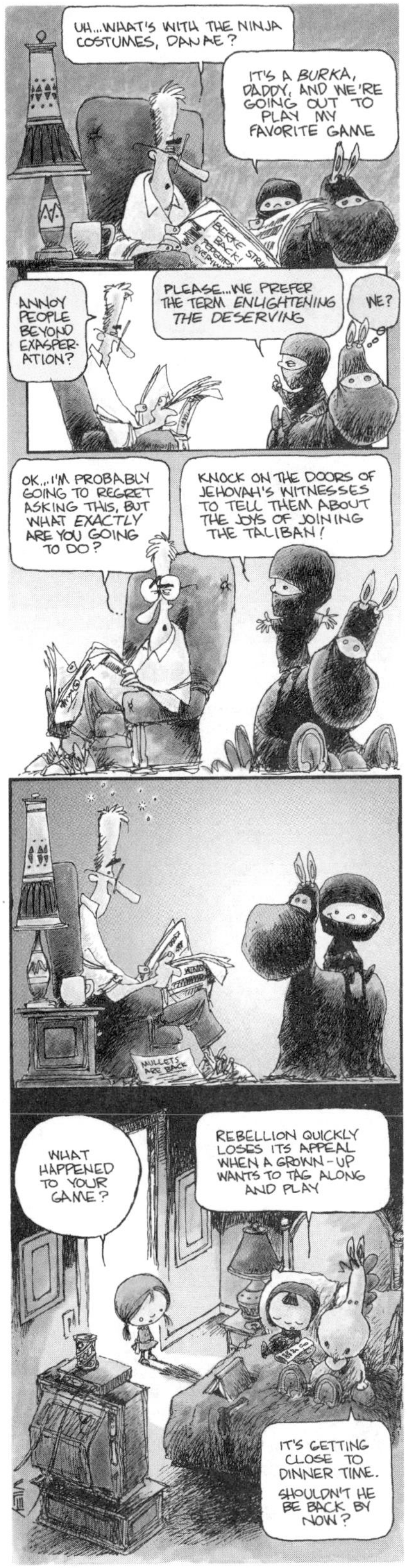

UH...WHAT'S WITH THE NINJA COSTUMES, DANAE?
IT'S A BURKA, DADDY, AND WE'RE GOING OUT TO PLAY MY FAVORITE GAME
ANNOY PEOPLE BEYOND EXASPER-ATION?
PLEASE...WE PREFER THE TERM ENLIGHTENING THE DESERVING
WE?
OK...I'M PROBABLY GOING TO REGRET ASKING THIS, BUT WHAT EXACTLY ARE YOU GOING TO DO?
KNOCK ON THE DOORS OF JEHOVAH'S WITNESSES TO TELL THEM ABOUT THE JOYS OF JOINING THE TALIBAN!
WHAT HAPPENED TO YOUR GAME?
REBELLION QUICKLY LOSES ITS APPEAL WHEN A GROWN-UP WANTS TO TAG ALONG AND PLAY
IT'S GETTING CLOSE TO DINNER TIME. SHOULDN'T HE BE BACK BY NOW?

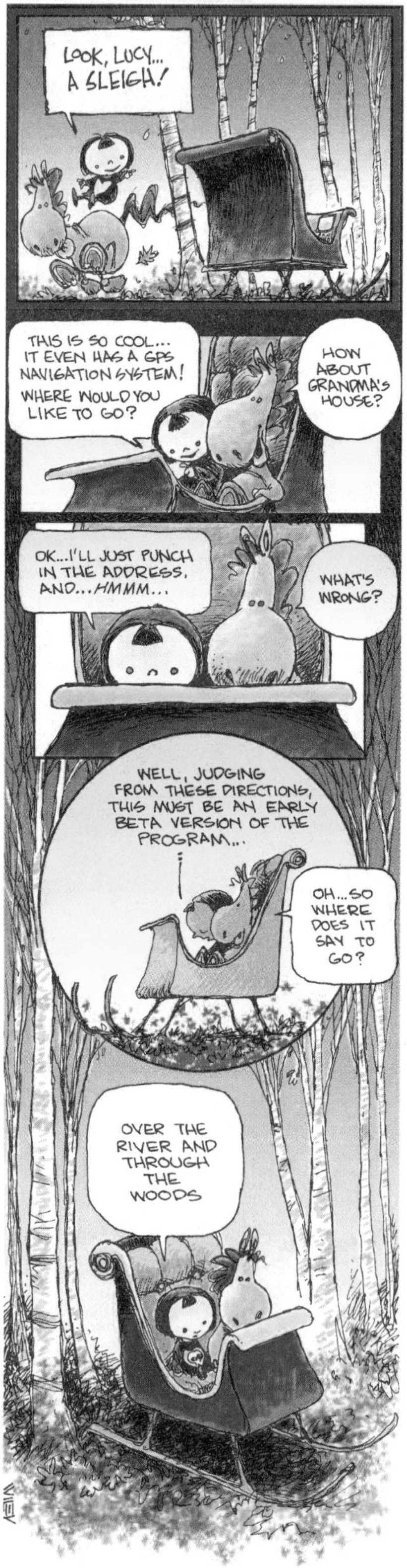
LOOK, LUCY... A SLEIGH!
THIS IS SO COOL... IT EVEN HAS A GPS NAVIGATION SYSTEM! WHERE WOULD YOU LIKE TO GO?
HOW ABOUT GRANDMA'S HOUSE?
OK...I'LL JUST PUNCH IN THE ADDRESS, AND...HMMM...
WHAT'S WRONG?
WELL, JUDGING FROM THESE DIRECTIONS, THIS MUST BE AN EARLY BETA VERSION OF THE PROGRAM...
OH...SO WHERE DOES IT SAY TO GO?
OVER THE RIVER AND THROUGH THE WOODS
WILEY

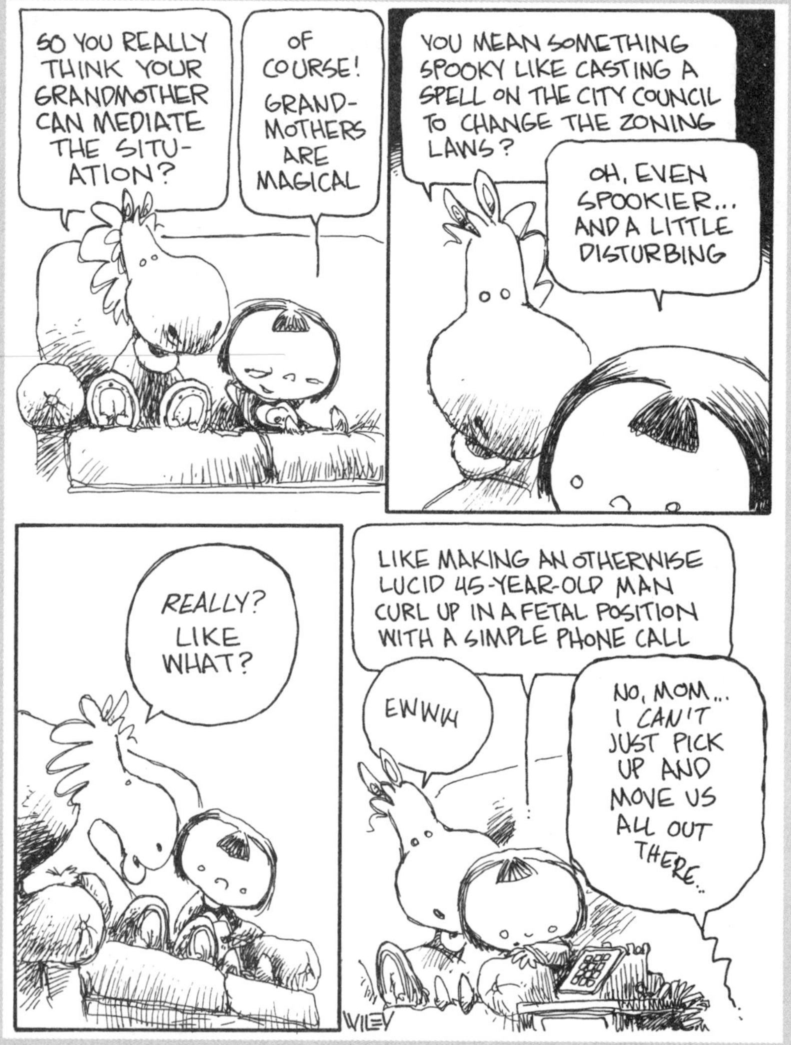
SO YOU REALLY THINK YOUR GRANDMOTHER CAN MEDIATE THE SITU-ATION?
OF COURSE! GRAND-MOTHERS ARE MAGICAL
YOU MEAN SOMETHING SPOOKY LIKE CASTING A SPELL ON THE CITY COUNCIL TO CHANGE THE ZONING LAWS?
OH, EVEN SPOOKIER... AND A LITTLE DISTURBING
REALLY? LIKE WHAT?
LIKE MAKING AN OTHERWISE LUCID 45-YEAR-OLD MAN CURL UP IN A FETAL POSITION WITH A SIMPLE PHONE CALL
EWWW
NO, MOM... I CAN'T JUST PICK UP AND MOVE US ALL OUT THERE...
WILEY

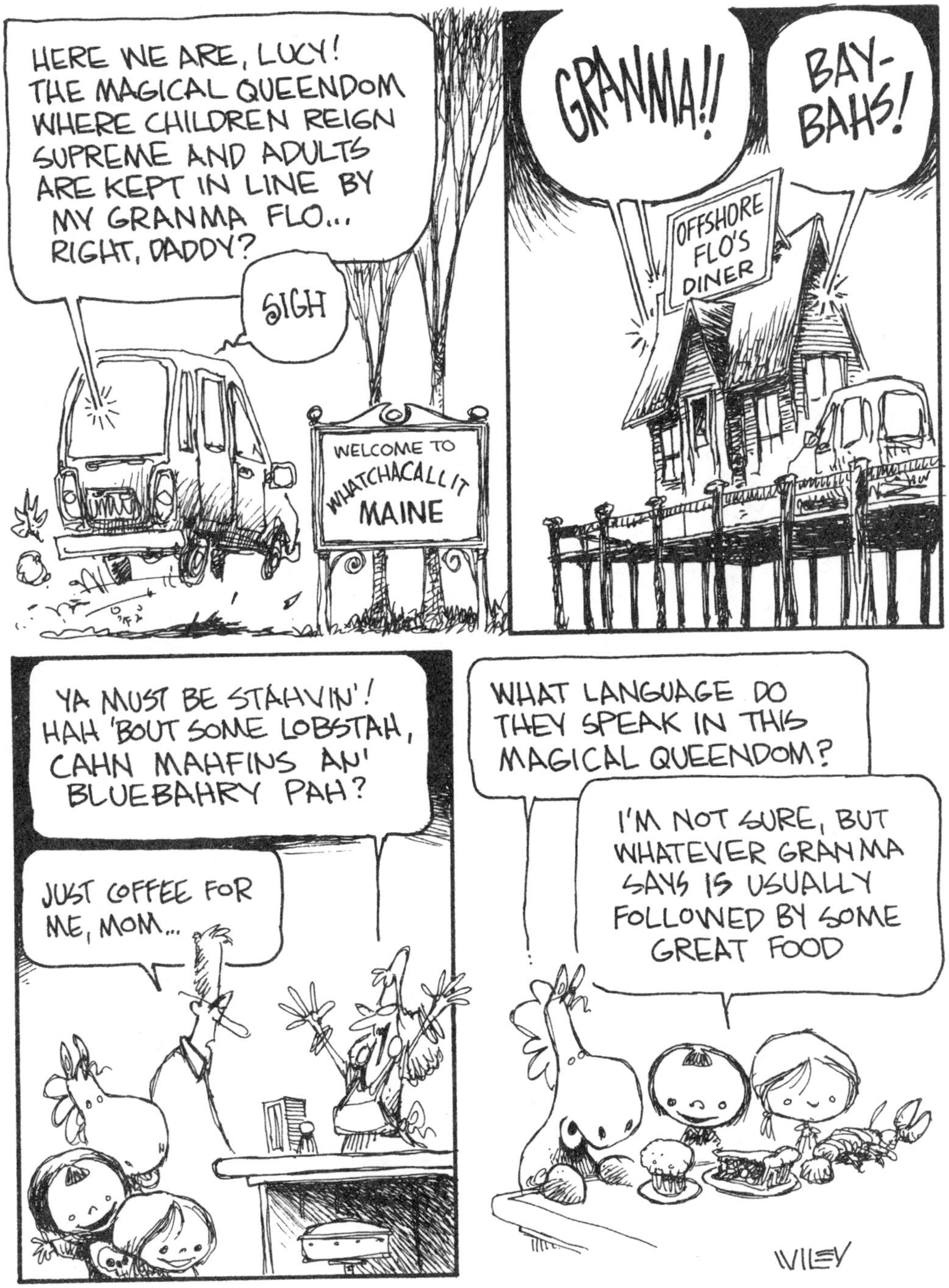
HERE WE ARE, LUCY! THE MAGICAL QUEENDOM WHERE CHILDREN REIGN SUPREME AND ADULTS ARE KEPT IN LINE BY MY GRANMA FLO... RIGHT, DADDY?
SIGH
WELCOME TO WHATCHACALLIT MAINE
GRANMA!!
BAY-BAHS!
OFFSHORE FLO'S DINER
YA MUST BE STAHVIN'! HAH 'BOUT SOME LOBSTAH, CAHN MAHFINS AN' BLUEBAHRY PAH?
JUST COFFEE FOR ME, MOM...
WHAT LANGUAGE DO THEY SPEAK IN THIS MAGICAL QUEENDOM?
I'M NOT SURE, BUT WHATEVER GRANMA SAYS IS USUALLY FOLLOWED BY SOME GREAT FOOD
WILEY

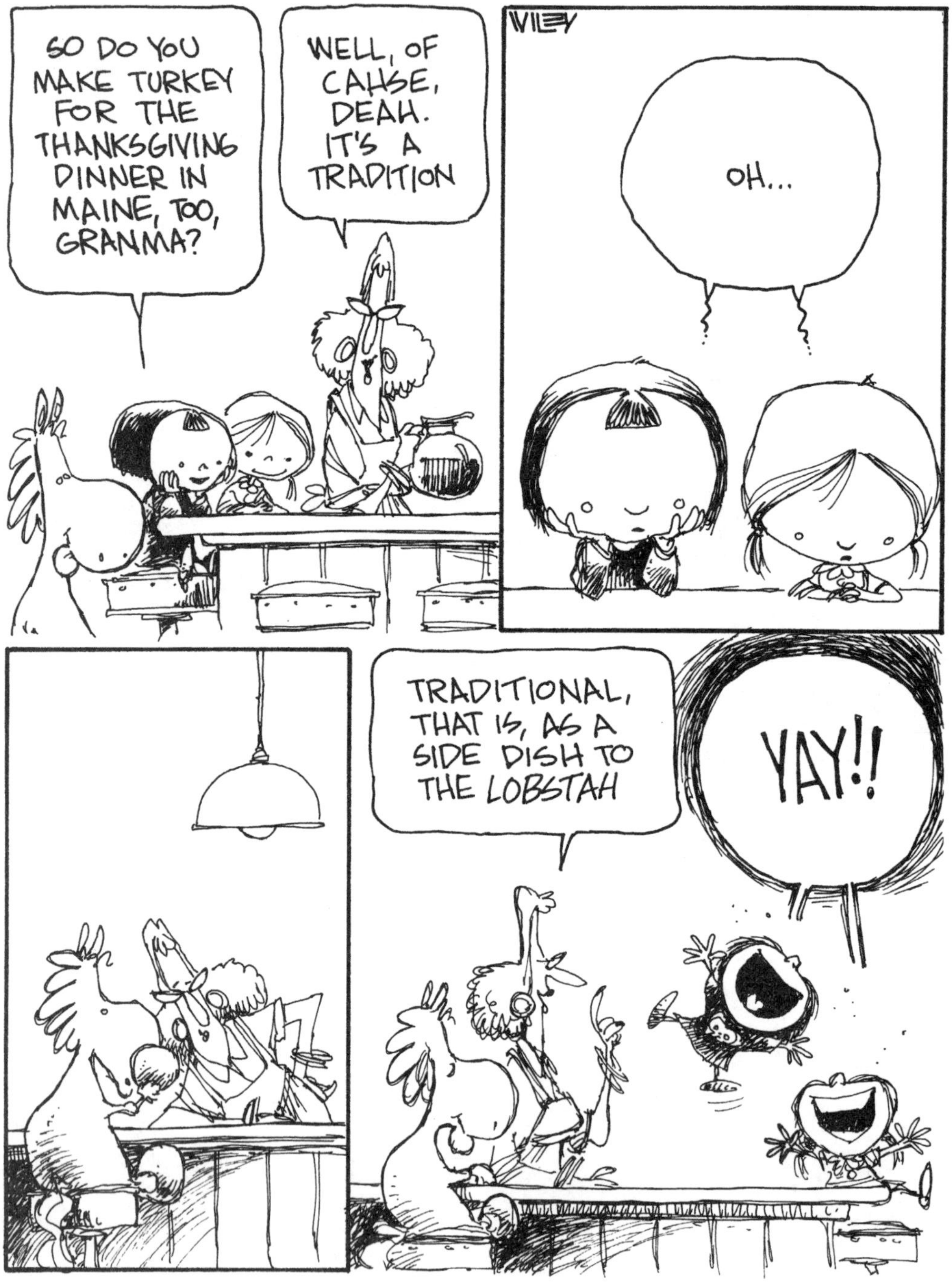
SO DO YOU MAKE TURKEY FOR THE THANKSGIVING DINNER IN MAINE, TOO, GRANMA?
WELL, OF CAHSE, DEAH. IT'S A TRADITION
WILEY
OH...
TRADITIONAL, THAT IS, AS A SIDE DISH TO THE *LOBSTAH*
YAY!!

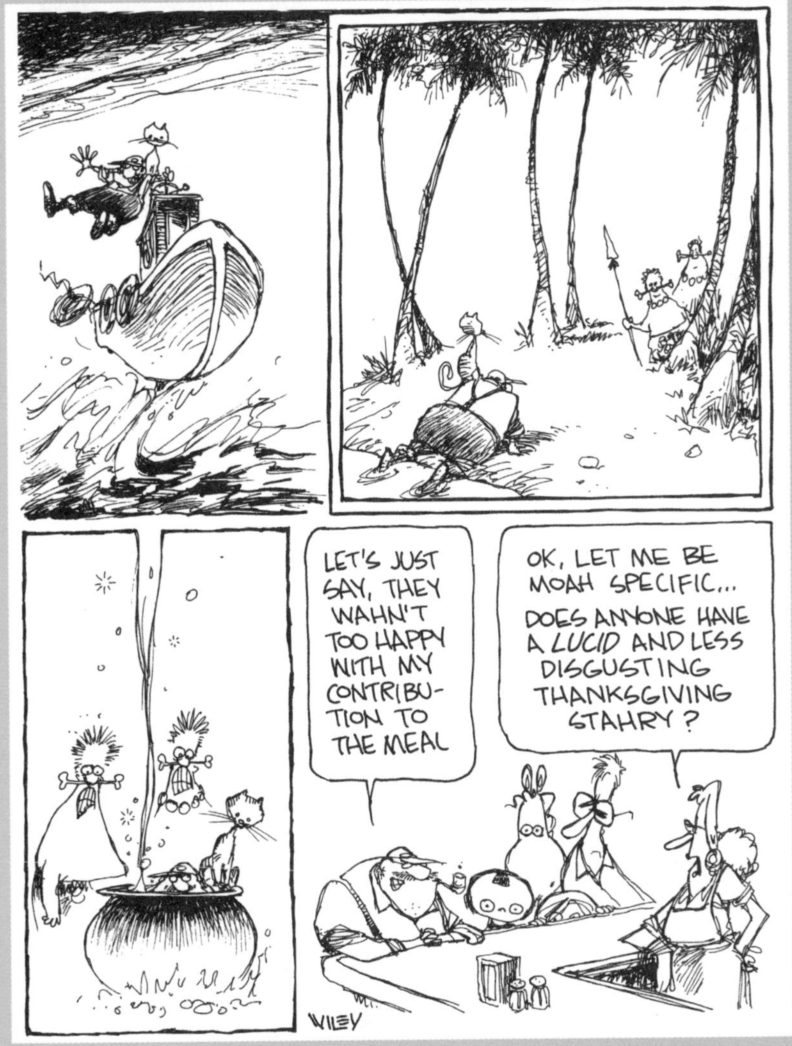
LET'S JUST SAY, THEY WAHN'T TOO HAPPY WITH MY CONTRIBU-TION TO THE MEAL
OK, LET ME BE MOAH SPECIFIC...
DOES ANYONE HAVE A *LUCID* AND LESS DISGUSTING THANKSGIVING STAHRY?
WILEY

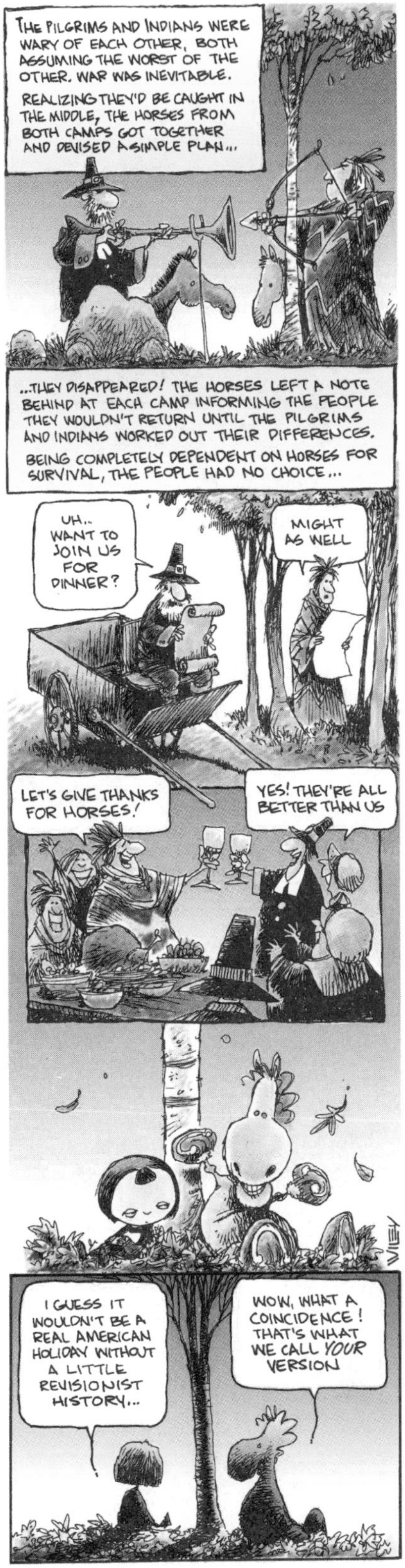
THE PILGRIMS AND INDIANS WERE WARY OF EACH OTHER, BOTH ASSUMING THE WORST OF THE OTHER. WAR WAS INEVITABLE.
REALIZING THEY'D BE CAUGHT IN THE MIDDLE, THE HORSES FROM BOTH CAMPS GOT TOGETHER AND DEVISED A SIMPLE PLAN...
...THEY DISAPPEARED! THE HORSES LEFT A NOTE BEHIND AT EACH CAMP INFORMING THE PEOPLE THEY WOULDN'T RETURN UNTIL THE PILGRIMS AND INDIANS WORKED OUT THEIR DIFFERENCES.
BEING COMPLETELY DEPENDENT ON HORSES FOR SURVIVAL, THE PEOPLE HAD NO CHOICE...
UH.. WANT TO JOIN US FOR DINNER?
MIGHT AS WELL
LET'S GIVE THANKS FOR HORSES!
YES! THEY'RE ALL BETTER THAN US
I GUESS IT WOULDN'T BE A REAL AMERICAN HOLIDAY WITHOUT A LITTLE REVISIONIST HISTORY...
WOW, WHAT A COINCIDENCE! THAT'S WHAT WE CALL *YOUR* VERSION

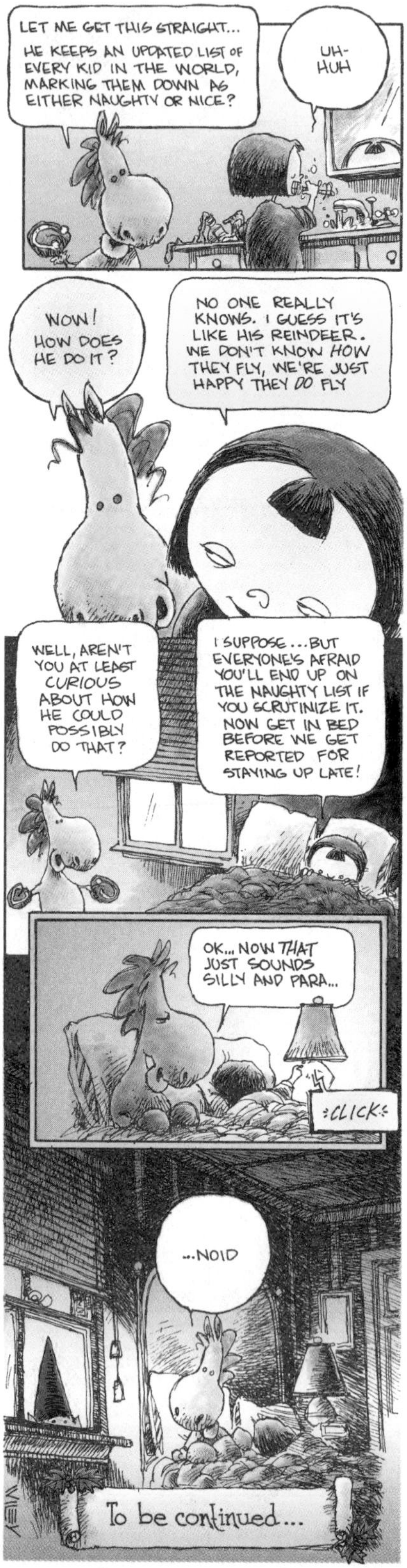
LET ME GET THIS STRAIGHT... HE KEEPS AN UPDATED LIST OF EVERY KID IN THE WORLD, MARKING THEM DOWN AS EITHER NAUGHTY OR NICE?
UH-HUH
WOW! HOW DOES HE DO IT?
NO ONE REALLY KNOWS. I GUESS IT'S LIKE HIS REINDEER. WE DON'T KNOW HOW THEY FLY, WE'RE JUST HAPPY THEY DO FLY
WELL, AREN'T YOU AT LEAST CURIOUS ABOUT HOW HE COULD POSSIBLY DO THAT?
I SUPPOSE...BUT EVERYONE'S AFRAID YOU'LL END UP ON THE NAUGHTY LIST IF YOU SCRUTINIZE IT. NOW GET IN BED BEFORE WE GET REPORTED FOR STAYING UP LATE!
OK... NOW THAT JUST SOUNDS SILLY AND PARA...
CLICK
...NOID
WILEY
To be continued...

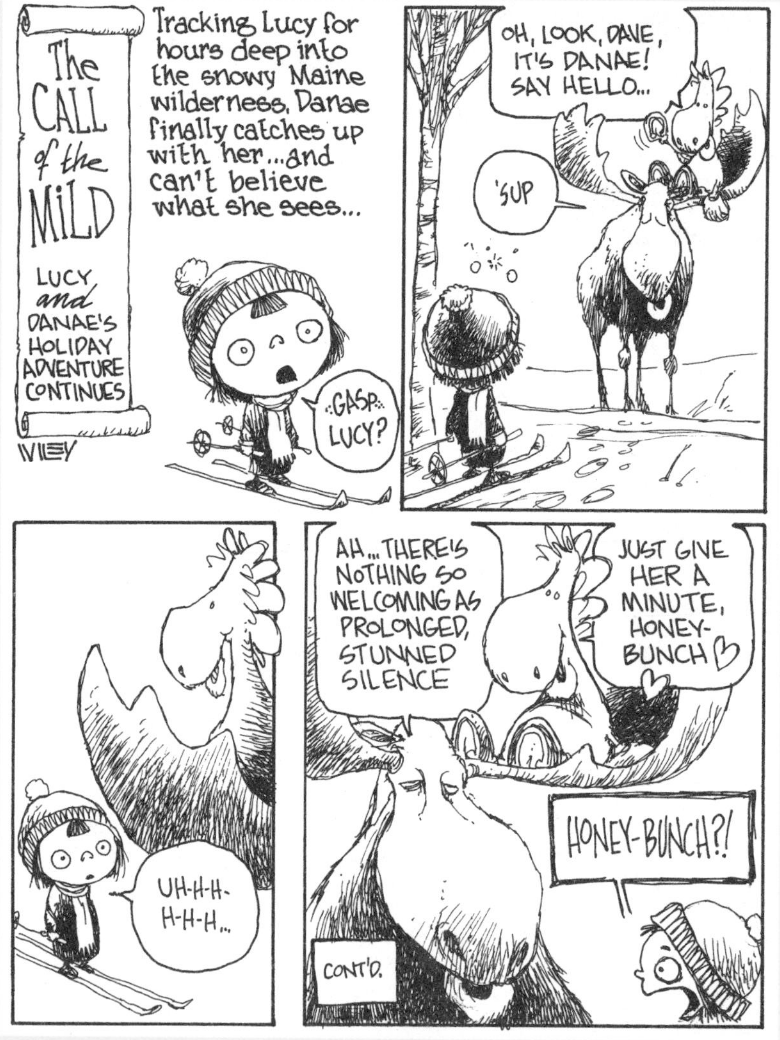
The CALL of the MILD
LUCY and DANAE'S HOLIDAY ADVENTURE CONTINUES
WILEY
Tracking Lucy for hours deep into the snowy Maine wilderness, Danae finally catches up with her...and can't believe what she sees...
GASP. LUCY?
OH, LOOK, DAVE, IT'S DANAE! SAY HELLO...
'SUP
UH-H-H-H-H-H...
AH... THERE'S NOTHING SO WELCOMING AS PROLONGED, STUNNED SILENCE
JUST GIVE HER A MINUTE, HONEY-BUNCH
HONEY-BUNCH?!
CONT'D.

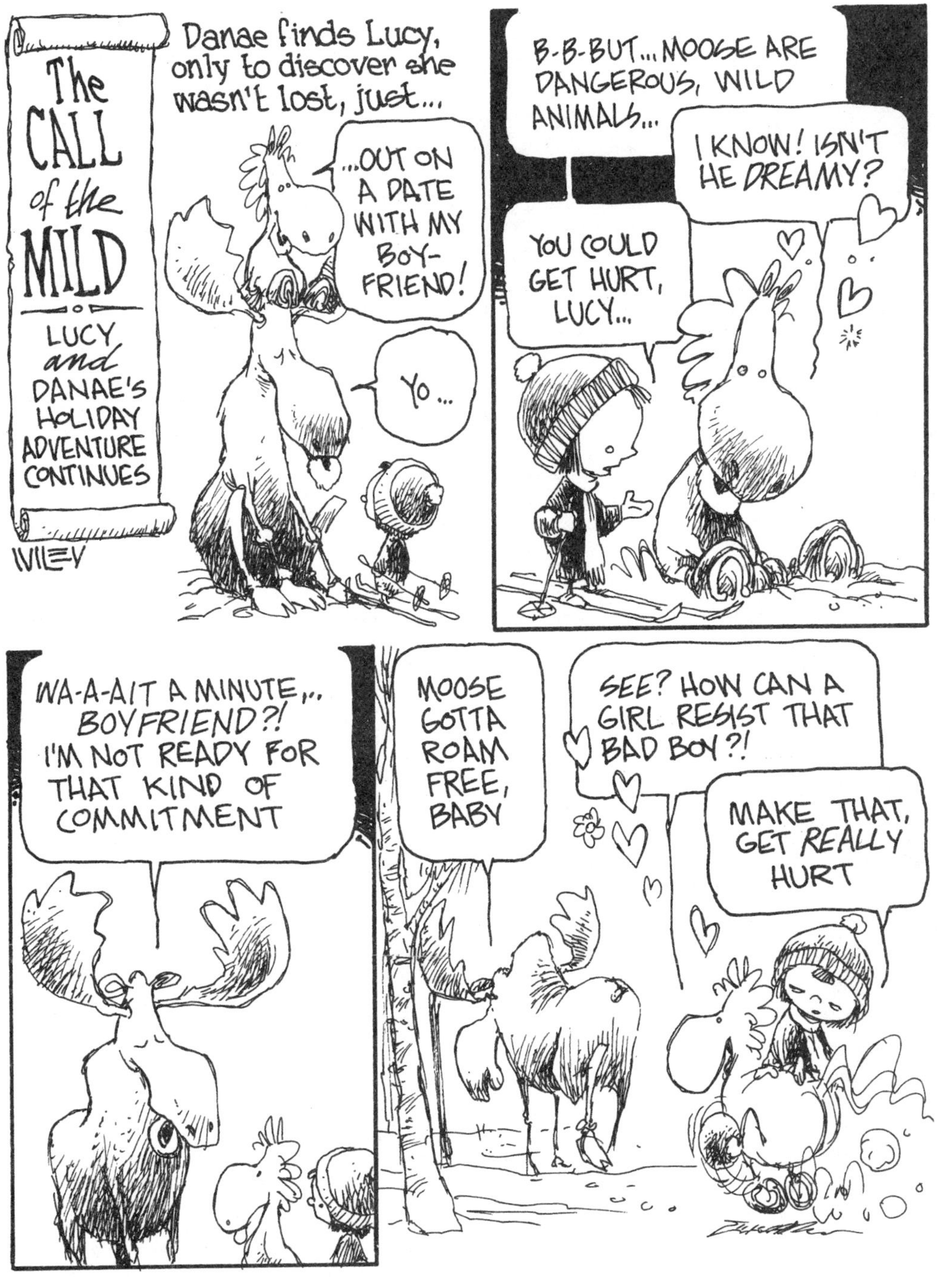
The CALL of the MILD
LUCY and DANAE'S HOLIDAY ADVENTURE CONTINUES
WILEY
Danae finds Lucy, only to discover she wasn't lost, just...
...OUT ON A DATE WITH MY BOY-FRIEND!
YO...
B-B-BUT... MOOSE ARE DANGEROUS, WILD ANIMALS...
YOU COULD GET HURT, LUCY...
I KNOW! ISN'T HE DREAMY?
WA-A-AIT A MINUTE,.. BOYFRIEND?! I'M NOT READY FOR THAT KIND OF COMMITMENT
MOOSE GOTTA ROAM FREE, BABY
SEE? HOW CAN A GIRL RESIST THAT BAD BOY?!
MAKE THAT, GET REALLY HURT

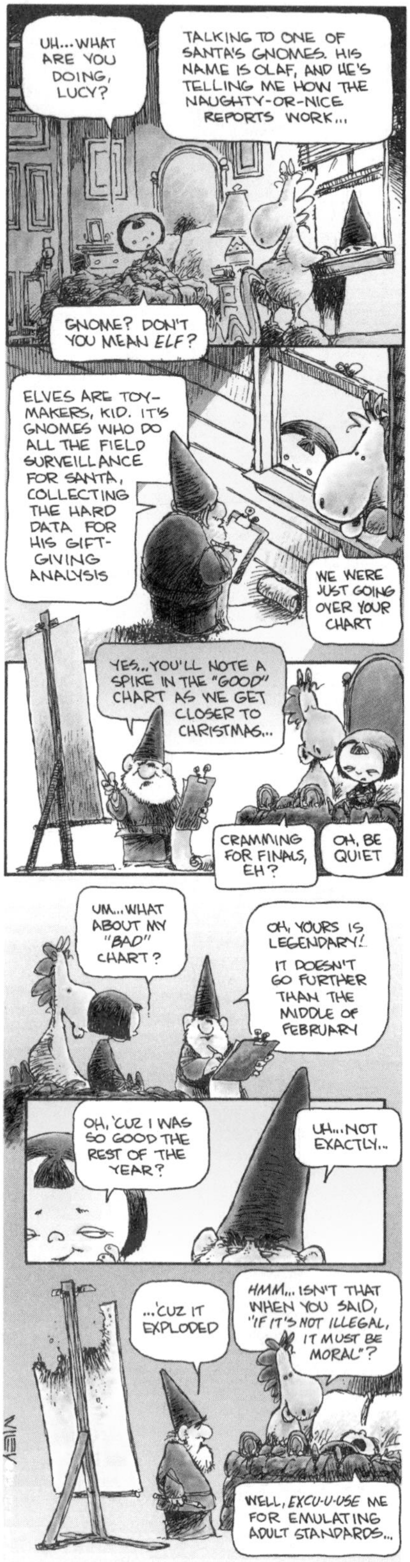
UH... WHAT ARE YOU DOING, LUCY?
TALKING TO ONE OF SANTA'S GNOMES. HIS NAME IS OLAF, AND HE'S TELLING ME HOW THE NAUGHTY-OR-NICE REPORTS WORK...
GNOME? DON'T YOU MEAN ELF?
ELVES ARE TOY-MAKERS, KID. IT'S GNOMES WHO DO ALL THE FIELD SURVEILLANCE FOR SANTA, COLLECTING THE HARD DATA FOR HIS GIFT-GIVING ANALYSIS
WE WERE JUST GOING OVER YOUR CHART
YES... YOU'LL NOTE A SPIKE IN THE "GOOD" CHART AS WE GET CLOSER TO CHRISTMAS...
CRAMMING FOR FINALS, EH?
OH, BE QUIET
UM... WHAT ABOUT MY "BAD" CHART?
OH, YOURS IS LEGENDARY! IT DOESN'T GO FURTHER THAN THE MIDDLE OF FEBRUARY
OH, 'CUZ I WAS SO GOOD THE REST OF THE YEAR?
UH... NOT EXACTLY...
...'CUZ IT EXPLODED
HMM... ISN'T THAT WHEN YOU SAID, "IF IT'S NOT ILLEGAL, IT MUST BE MORAL"?
WELL, EXCU-U-USE ME FOR EMULATING ADULT STANDARDS...
WILEY

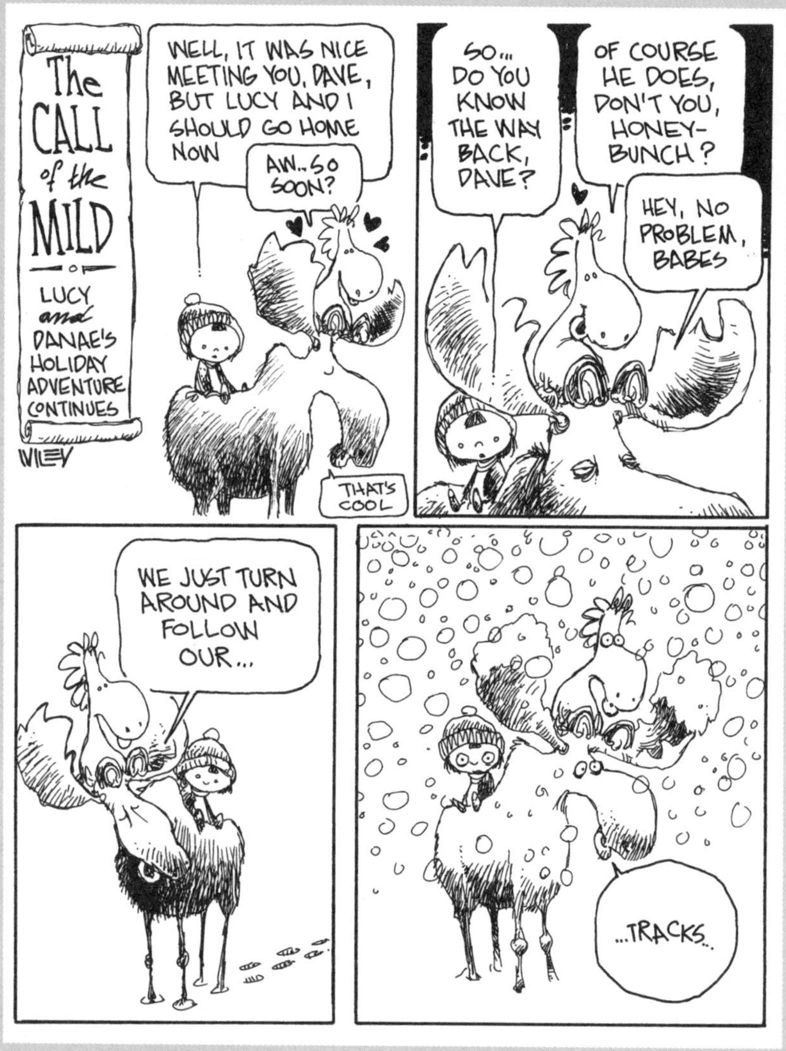
The CALL of the MILD
LUCY and DANAE'S HOLIDAY ADVENTURE CONTINUES
WILEY
WELL, IT WAS NICE MEETING YOU, DAVE, BUT LUCY AND I SHOULD GO HOME NOW
AW.. SO SOON?
THAT'S COOL
SO... DO YOU KNOW THE WAY BACK, DAVE?
OF COURSE HE DOES, DON'T YOU, HONEY-BUNCH?
HEY, NO PROBLEM, BABES
WE JUST TURN AROUND AND FOLLOW OUR...
...TRACKS...

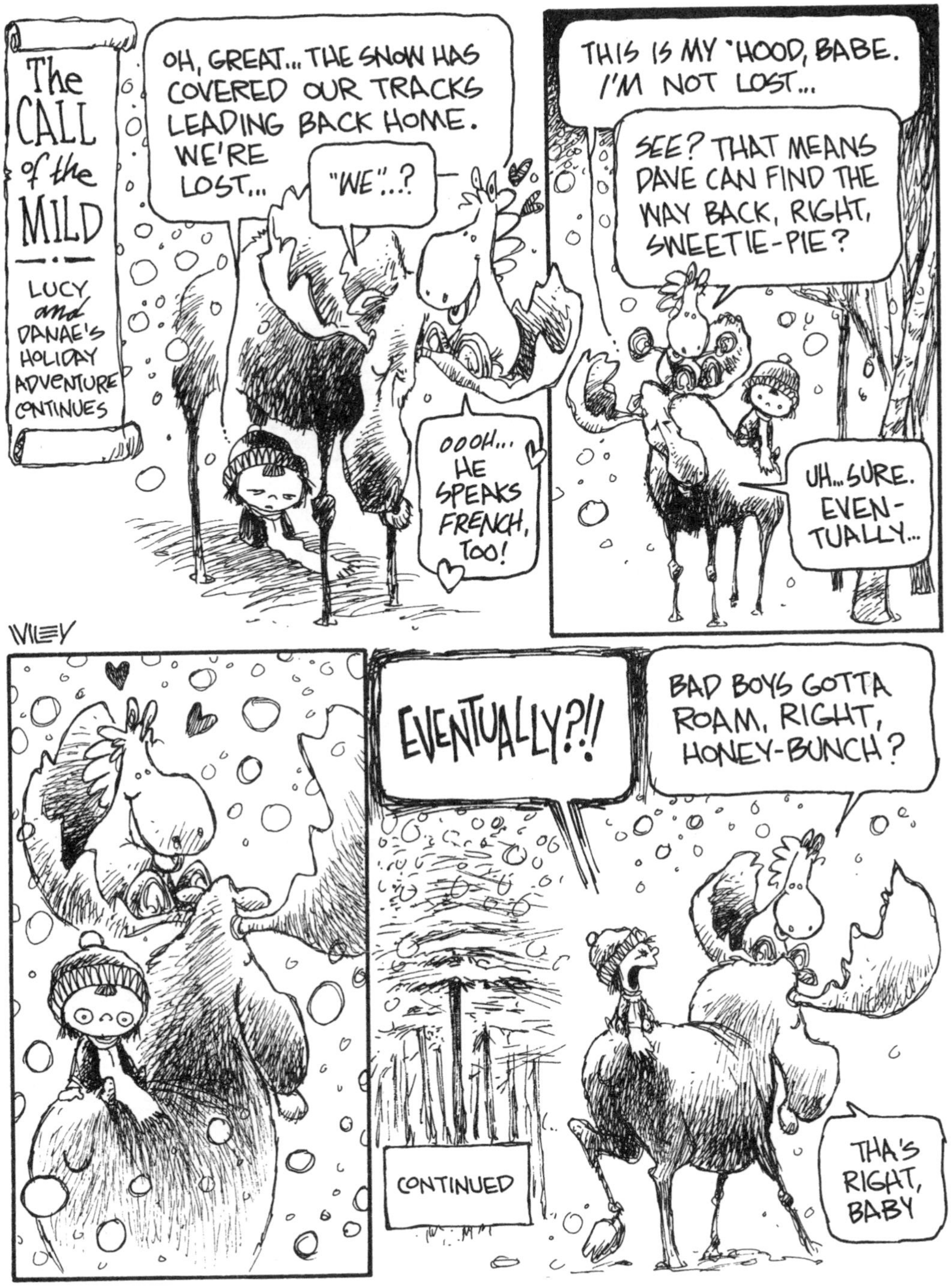
The CALL of the MILD
LUCY and DANAE'S HOLIDAY ADVENTURE CONTINUES
OH, GREAT... THE SNOW HAS COVERED OUR TRACKS LEADING BACK HOME. WE'RE LOST...
"WE"...?
OOOH... HE SPEAKS FRENCH, TOO!
WILEY
THIS IS MY 'HOOD, BABE. I'M NOT LOST...
SEE? THAT MEANS DAVE CAN FIND THE WAY BACK, RIGHT, SWEETIE-PIE?
UH... SURE. EVEN-TUALLY...
EVENTUALLY?!!
BAD BOYS GOTTA ROAM, RIGHT, HONEY-BUNCH?
THA'S RIGHT, BABY
CONTINUED

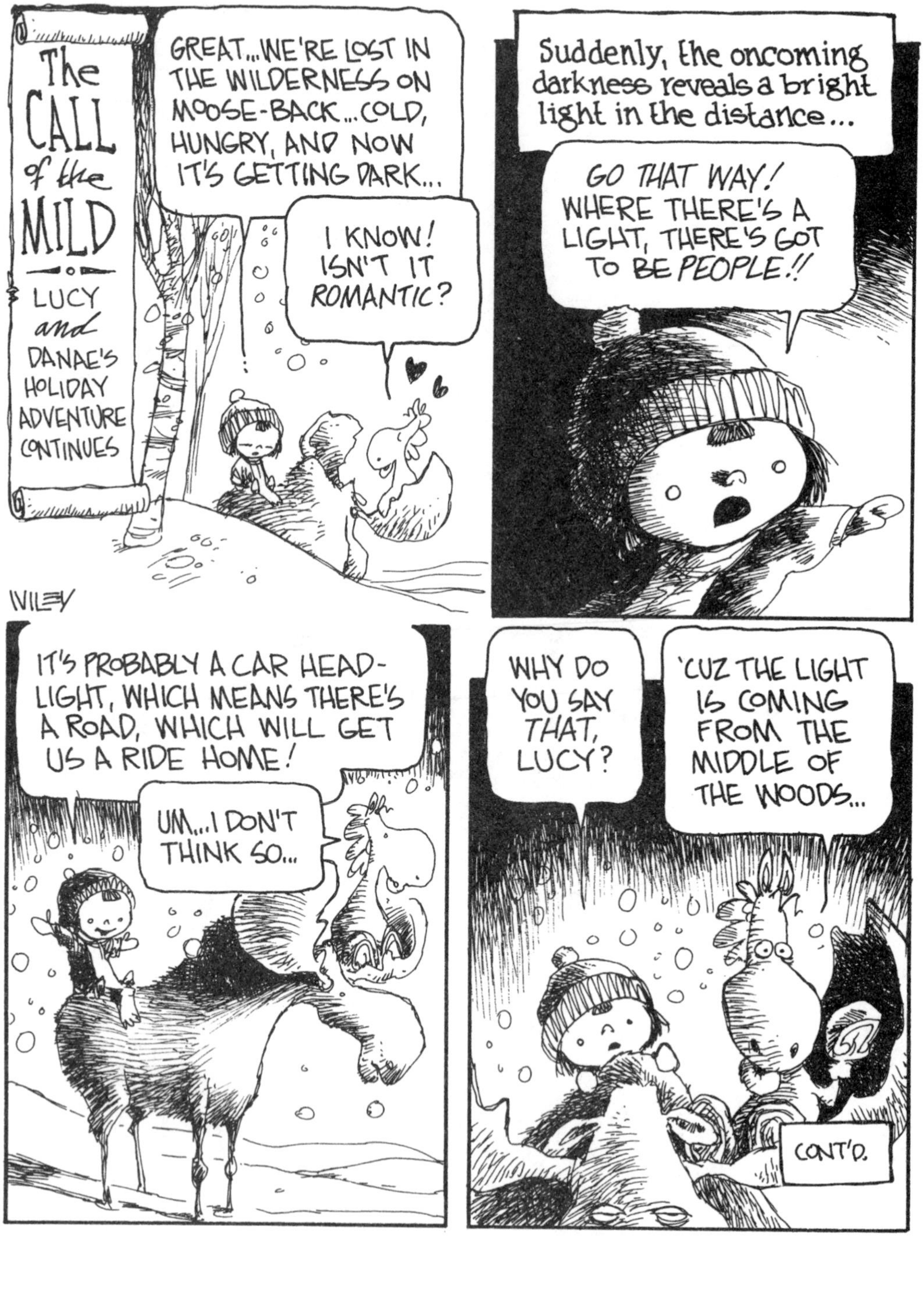
The CALL of the MILD
LUCY and DANAE'S HOLIDAY ADVENTURE CONTINUES
GREAT...WE'RE LOST IN THE WILDERNESS ON MOOSE-BACK...COLD, HUNGRY, AND NOW IT'S GETTING DARK...
I KNOW! ISN'T IT ROMANTIC?
WILEY
Suddenly, the oncoming darkness reveals a bright light in the distance...
GO THAT WAY! WHERE THERE'S A LIGHT, THERE'S GOT TO BE PEOPLE!!
IT'S PROBABLY A CAR HEADLIGHT, WHICH MEANS THERE'S A ROAD, WHICH WILL GET US A RIDE HOME!
UM...I DON'T THINK SO...
WHY DO YOU SAY THAT, LUCY?
'CUZ THE LIGHT IS COMING FROM THE MIDDLE OF THE WOODS...
CONT'D.

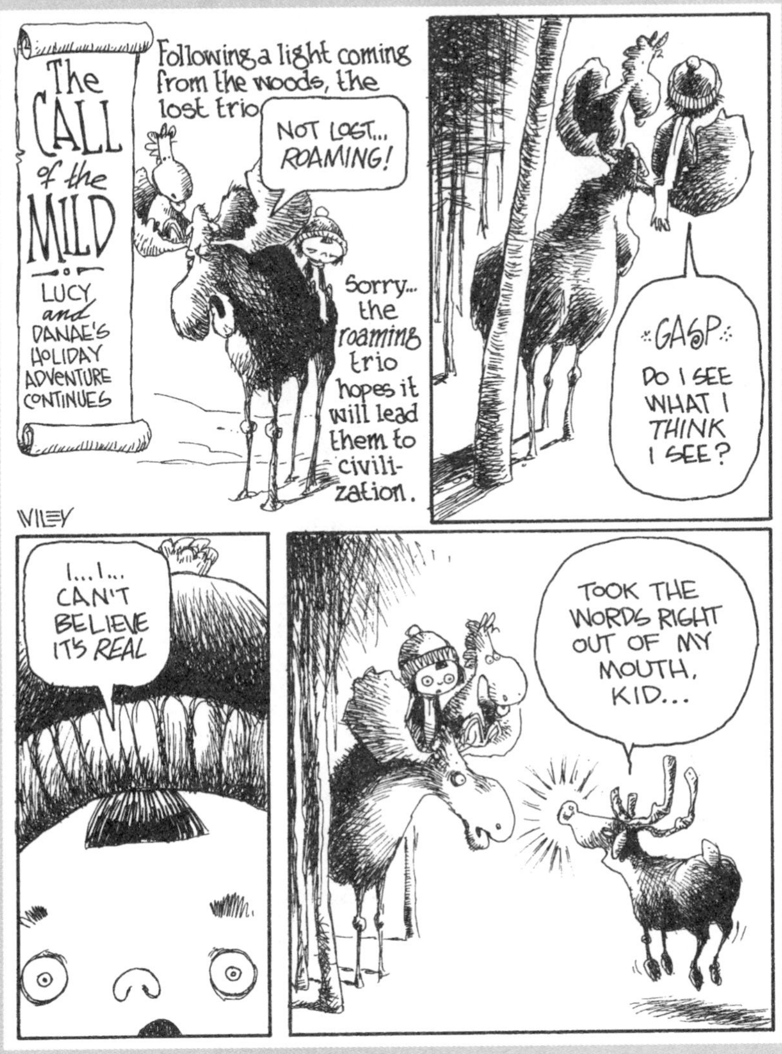
The CALL of the MILD
LUCY and DANAE'S HOLIDAY ADVENTURE CONTINUES
Following a light coming from the woods, the lost trio
NOT LOST... ROAMING!
Sorry... the roaming trio hopes it will lead them to civilization.
GASP
DO I SEE WHAT I THINK I SEE?
WILEY
I... I... CAN'T BELIEVE IT'S REAL
TOOK THE WORDS RIGHT OUT OF MY MOUTH, KID...

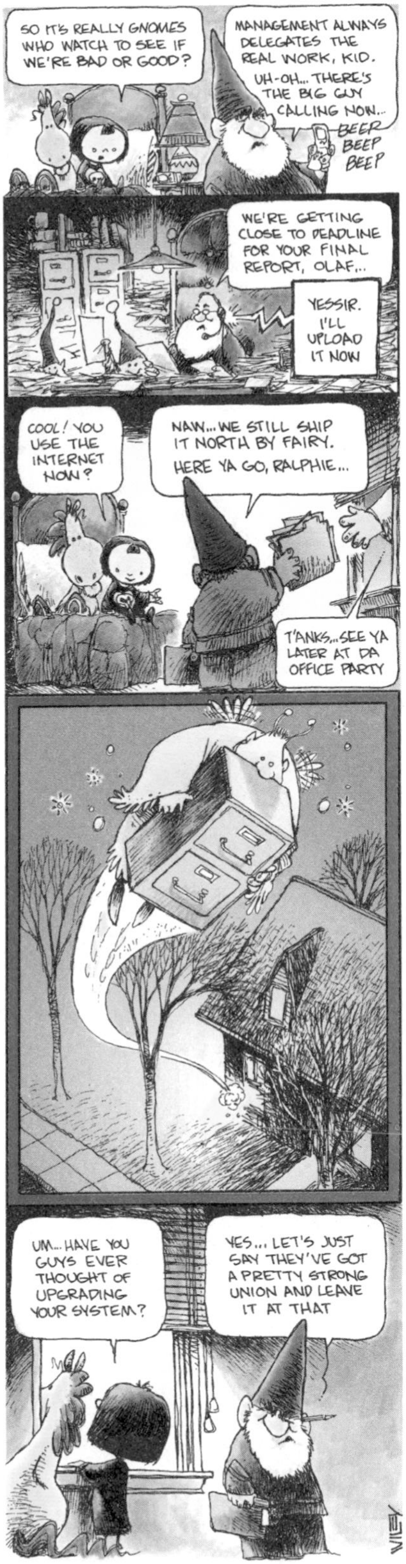
SO IT'S REALLY GNOMES WHO WATCH TO SEE IF WE'RE BAD OR GOOD?
MANAGEMENT ALWAYS DELEGATES THE REAL WORK, KID.
UH-OH... THERE'S THE BIG GUY CALLING NOW...
BEEP BEEP BEEP
WE'RE GETTING CLOSE TO DEADLINE FOR YOUR FINAL REPORT, OLAF...
YESSIR. I'LL UPLOAD IT NOW
COOL! YOU USE THE INTERNET NOW?
NAW... WE STILL SHIP IT NORTH BY FAIRY. HERE YA GO, RALPHIE...
T'ANKS... SEE YA LATER AT DA OFFICE PARTY
UM... HAVE YOU GUYS EVER THOUGHT OF UPGRADING YOUR SYSTEM?
YES... LET'S JUST SAY THEY'VE GOT A PRETTY STRONG UNION AND LEAVE IT AT THAT
WILEY

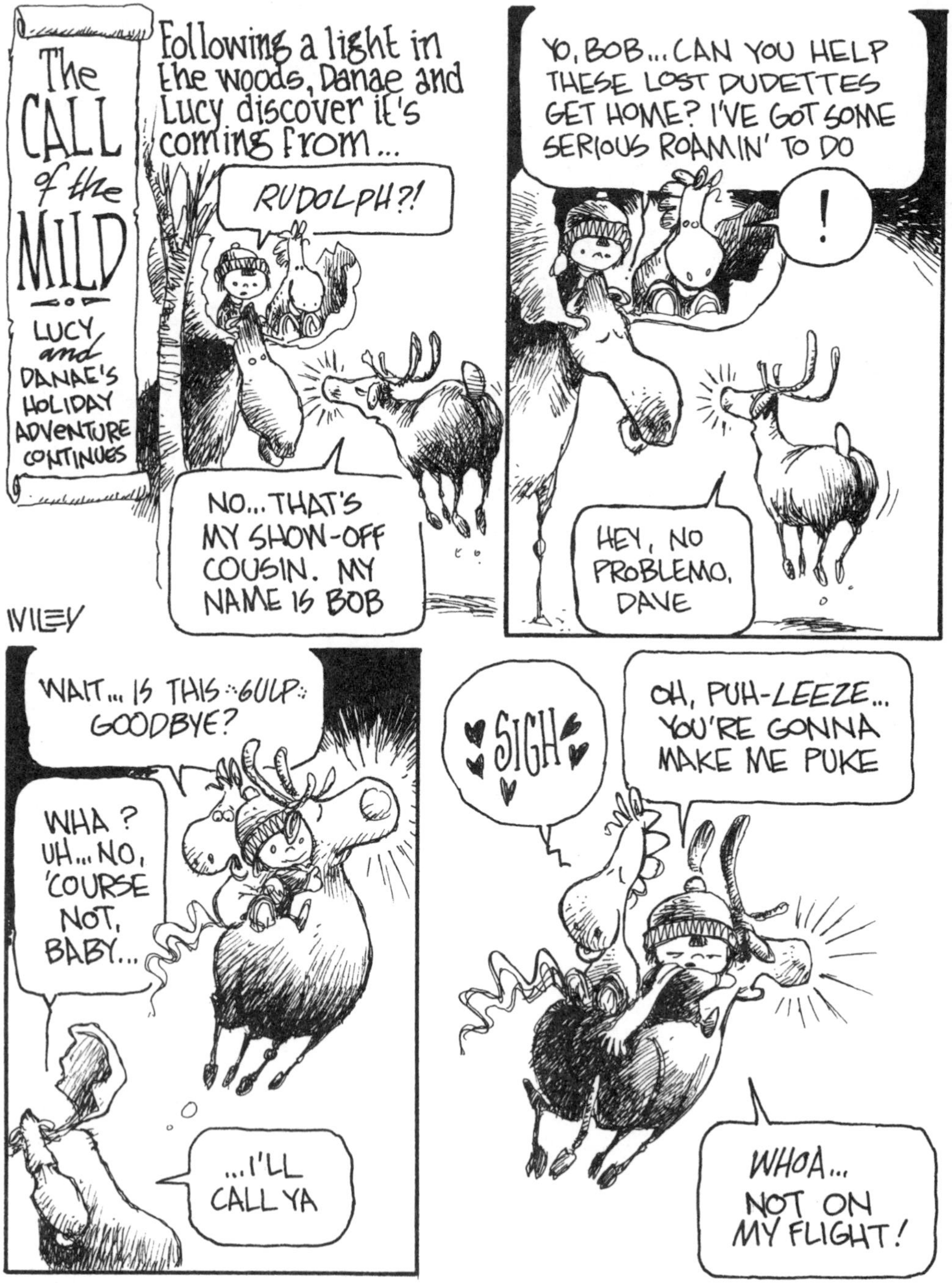
The CALL of the MILD
LUCY and DANAE'S HOLIDAY ADVENTURE CONTINUES
Following a light in the woods, Danae and Lucy discover it's coming from...
RUDOLPH?!
NO... THAT'S MY SHOW-OFF COUSIN. MY NAME IS BOB
WILEY
YO, BOB... CAN YOU HELP THESE LOST DUDETTES GET HOME? I'VE GOT SOME SERIOUS ROAMIN' TO DO
!
HEY, NO PROBLEMO, DAVE
WAIT... IS THIS GULP GOODBYE?
WHA? UH... NO, 'COURSE NOT, BABY...
...I'LL CALL YA
SIGH
OH, PUH-LEEZE... YOU'RE GONNA MAKE ME PUKE
WHOA... NOT ON MY FLIGHT!

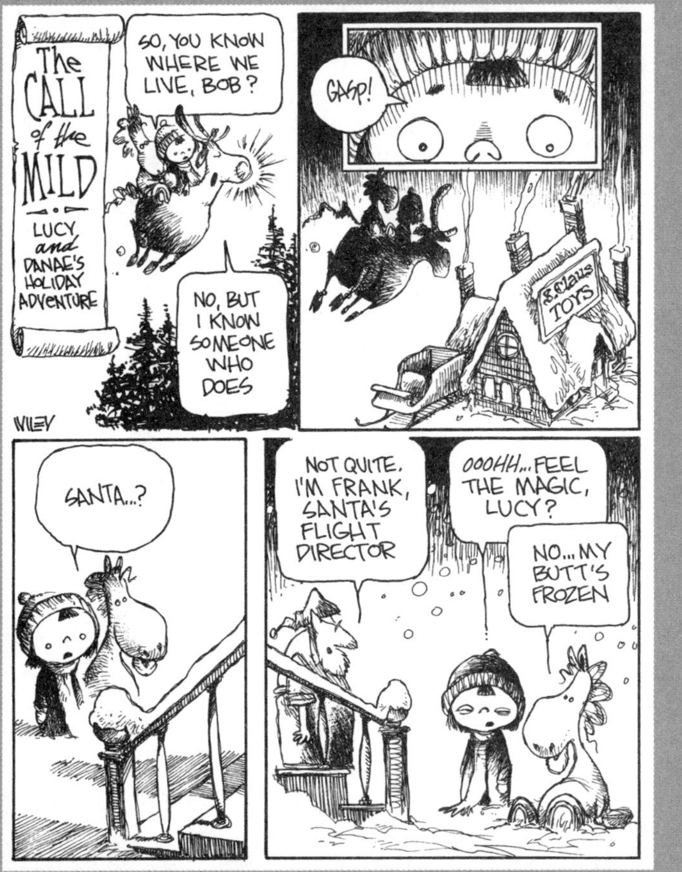
The CALL of the MILD
LUCY and DANAE'S HOLIDAY ADVENTURE
SO, YOU KNOW WHERE WE LIVE, BOB?
NO, BUT I KNOW SOMEONE WHO DOES
WILEY
GASP!
S. Claus TOYS
SANTA...?
NOT QUITE. I'M FRANK, SANTA'S FLIGHT DIRECTOR
OOOHH... FEEL THE MAGIC, LUCY?
NO... MY BUTT'S FROZEN

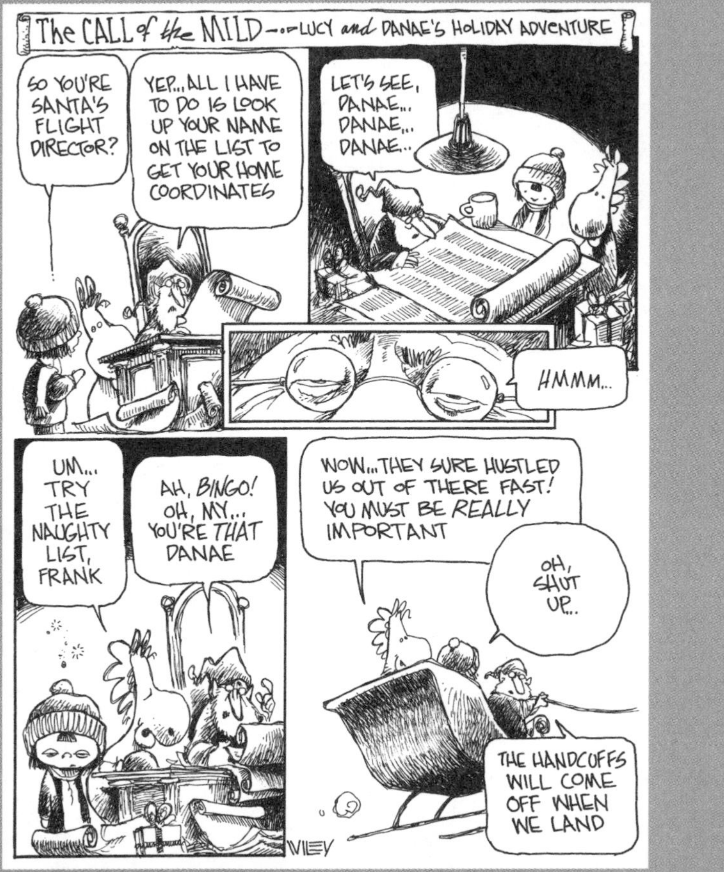
The CALL of the MILD — LUCY and DANAE'S HOLIDAY ADVENTURE
SO YOU'RE SANTA'S FLIGHT DIRECTOR?
YEP... ALL I HAVE TO DO IS LOOK UP YOUR NAME ON THE LIST TO GET YOUR HOME COORDINATES
LET'S SEE, DANAE... DANAE... DANAE...
HMMM...
UM... TRY THE NAUGHTY LIST, FRANK
AH, BINGO! OH, MY... YOU'RE THAT DANAE
WOW... THEY SURE HUSTLED US OUT OF THERE FAST! YOU MUST BE REALLY IMPORTANT
OH, SHUT UP...
THE HANDCUFFS WILL COME OFF WHEN WE LAND
WILEY

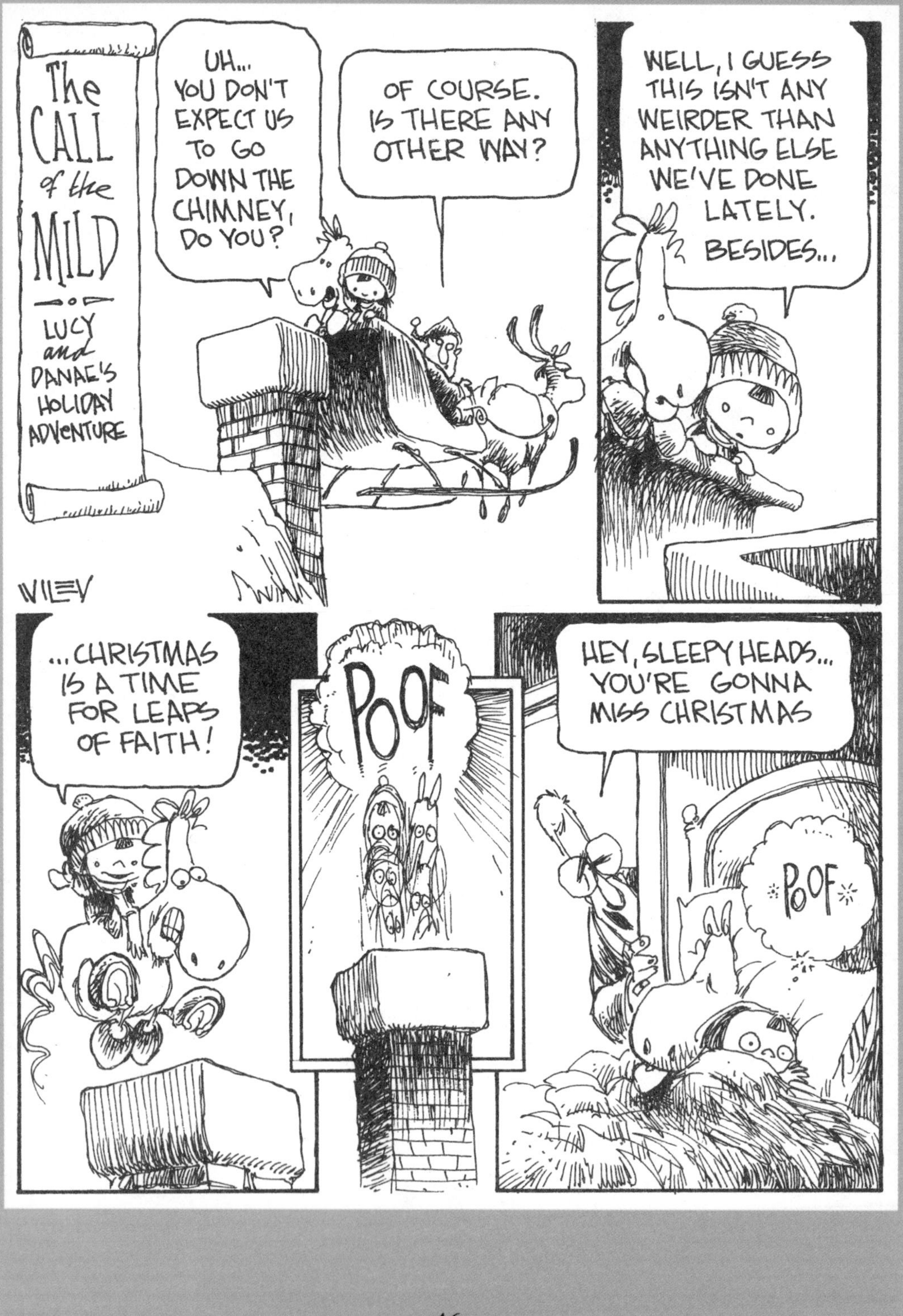
The CALL of the MILD
LUCY and DANAE'S HOLIDAY ADVENTURE
WILEY
UH... YOU DON'T EXPECT US TO GO DOWN THE CHIMNEY, DO YOU?
OF COURSE. IS THERE ANY OTHER WAY?
WELL, I GUESS THIS ISN'T ANY WEIRDER THAN ANYTHING ELSE WE'VE DONE LATELY. BESIDES...
...CHRISTMAS IS A TIME FOR LEAPS OF FAITH!
POOF
HEY, SLEEPY HEADS... YOU'RE GONNA MISS CHRISTMAS
POOF

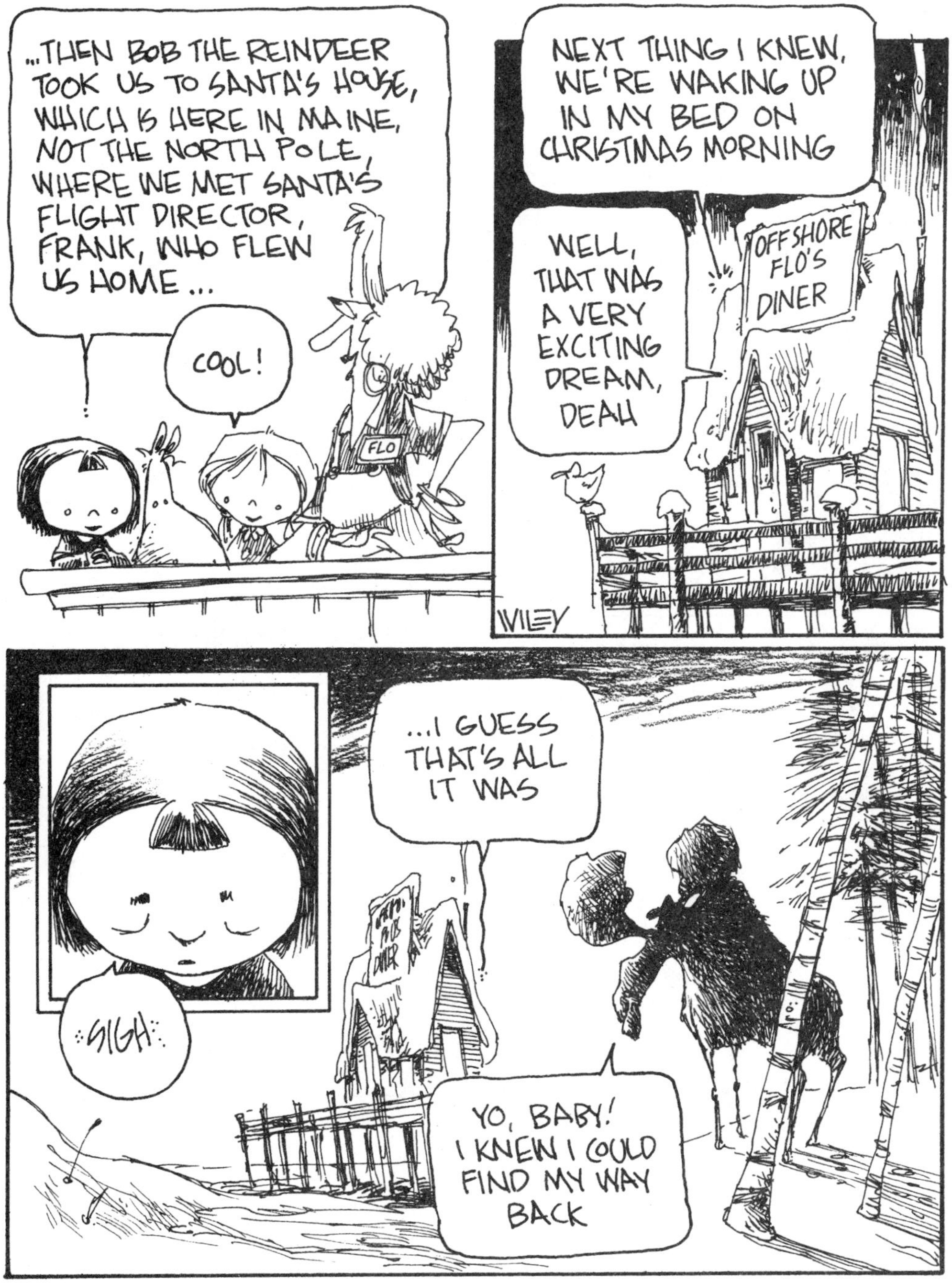
...THEN BOB THE REINDEER TOOK US TO SANTA'S HOUSE, WHICH IS HERE IN MAINE, NOT THE NORTH POLE, WHERE WE MET SANTA'S FLIGHT DIRECTOR, FRANK, WHO FLEW US HOME...
COOL!
FLO
NEXT THING I KNEW, WE'RE WAKING UP IN MY BED ON CHRISTMAS MORNING
WELL, THAT WAS A VERY EXCITING DREAM, DEAH
OFF SHORE FLO'S DINER
WILEY
...I GUESS THAT'S ALL IT WAS
SIGH
YO, BABY! I KNEW I COULD FIND MY WAY BACK

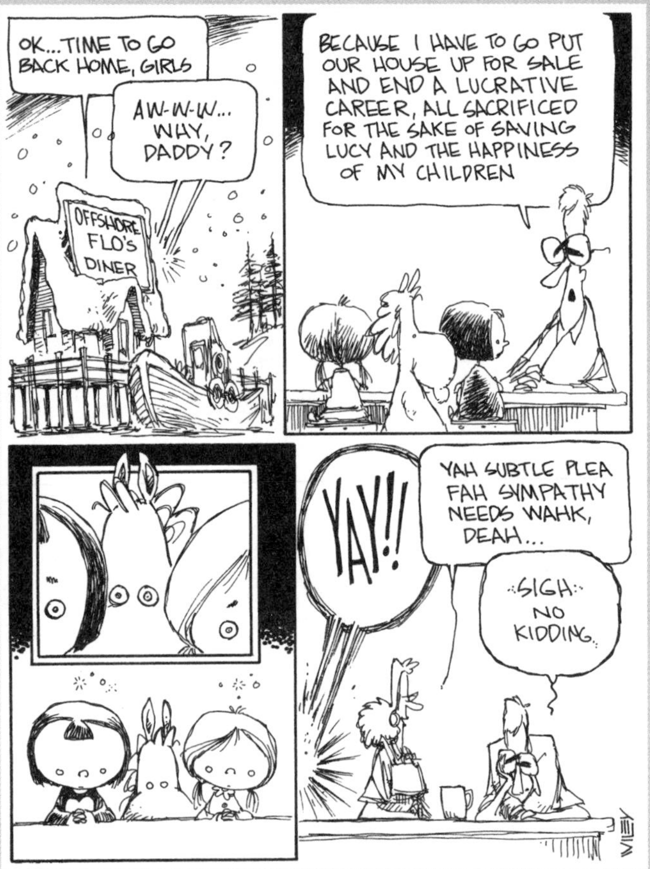
OK...TIME TO GO BACK HOME, GIRLS
AW-W-W... WHY, DADDY?
OFFSHORE FLO'S DINER
BECAUSE I HAVE TO GO PUT OUR HOUSE UP FOR SALE AND END A LUCRATIVE CAREER, ALL SACRIFICED FOR THE SAKE OF SAVING LUCY AND THE HAPPINESS OF MY CHILDREN
YAY!!
YAH SUBTLE PLEA FAH SYMPATHY NEEDS WAHK, DEAH...
SIGH NO KIDDING.
WILEY

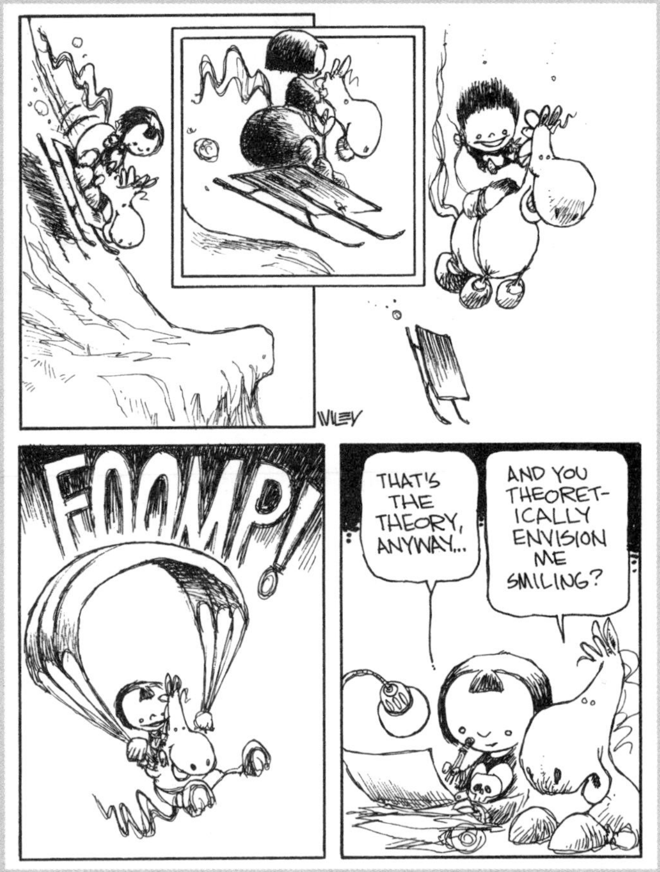
WILEY
FOOMP!
THAT'S THE THEORY, ANYWAY...
AND YOU THEORET-ICALLY ENVISION ME SMILING?

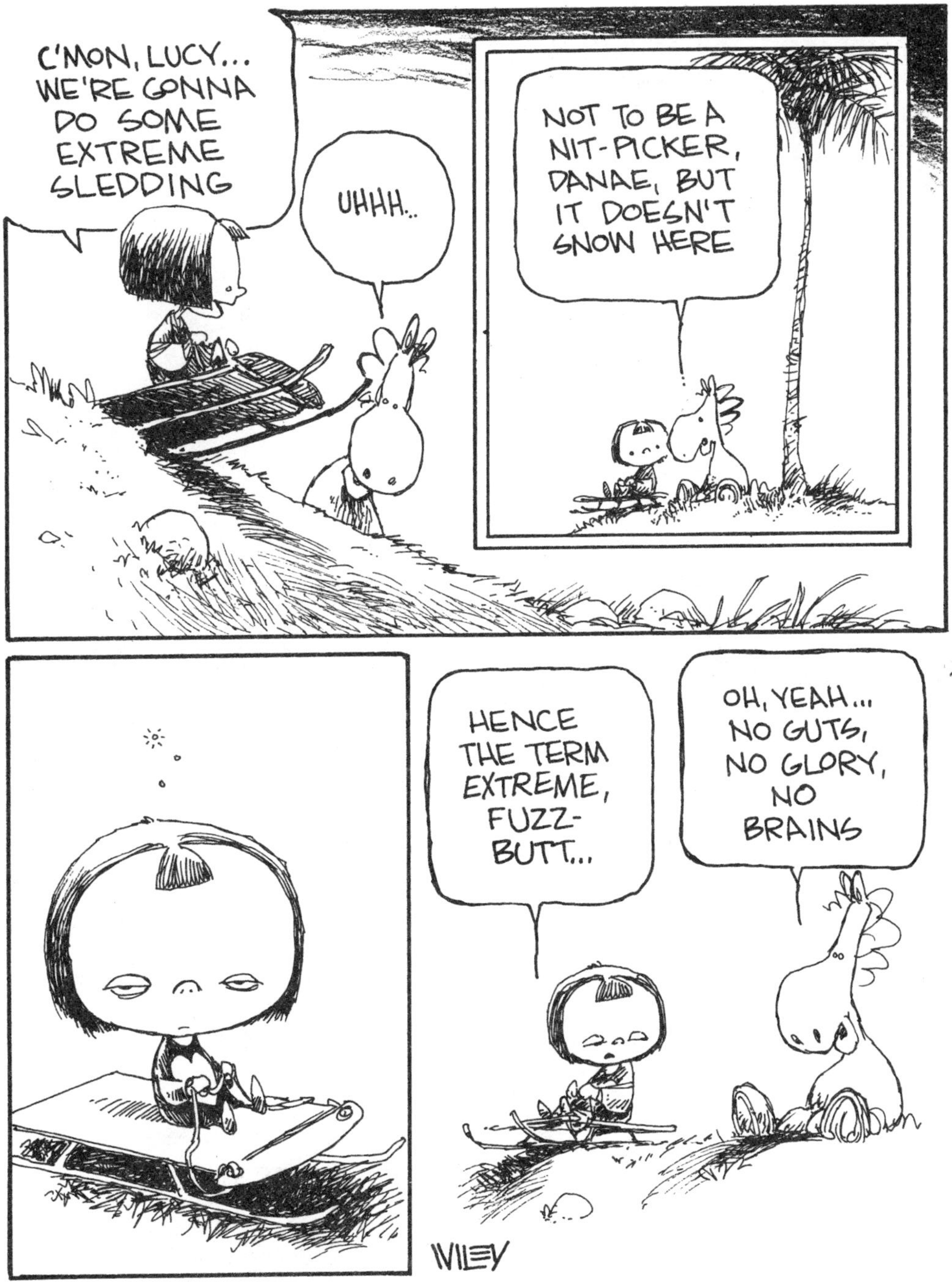
C'MON, LUCY... WE'RE GONNA DO SOME EXTREME SLEDDING
UHHH..
NOT TO BE A NIT-PICKER, DANAE, BUT IT DOESN'T SNOW HERE
HENCE THE TERM EXTREME, FUZZ-BUTT...
OH, YEAH... NO GUTS, NO GLORY, NO BRAINS
WILEY

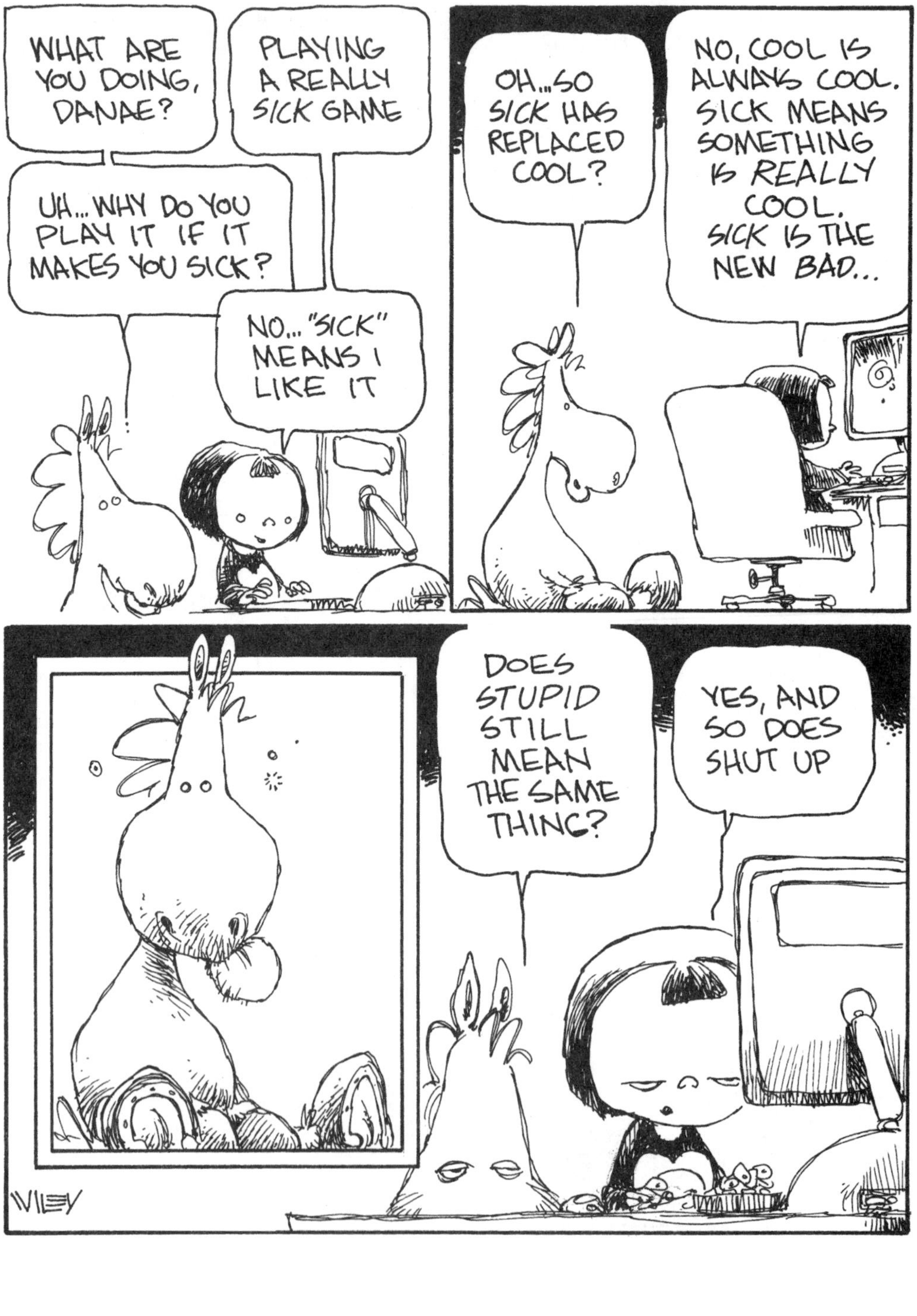
WHAT ARE YOU DOING, DANAE?
PLAYING A REALLY SICK GAME
UH... WHY DO YOU PLAY IT IF IT MAKES YOU SICK?
NO... "SICK" MEANS I LIKE IT
OH...SO SICK HAS REPLACED COOL?
NO, COOL IS ALWAYS COOL. SICK MEANS SOMETHING IS REALLY COOL. SICK IS THE NEW BAD...
DOES STUPID STILL MEAN THE SAME THING?
YES, AND SO DOES SHUT UP
WILEY

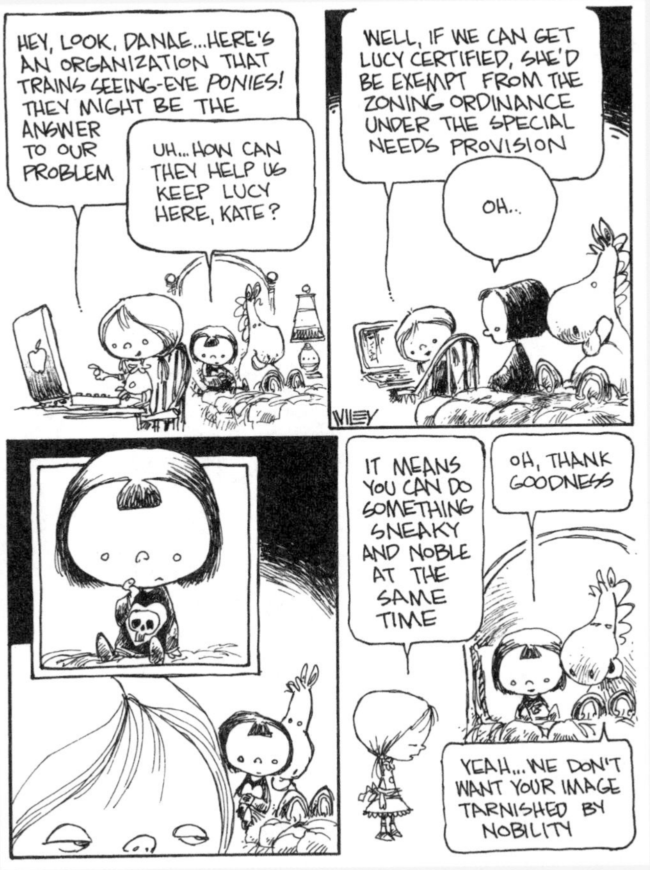
HEY, LOOK, DANAE...HERE'S AN ORGANIZATION THAT TRAINS SEEING-EYE PONIES! THEY MIGHT BE THE ANSWER TO OUR PROBLEM
UH...HOW CAN THEY HELP US KEEP LUCY HERE, KATE?
WELL, IF WE CAN GET LUCY CERTIFIED, SHE'D BE EXEMPT FROM THE ZONING ORDINANCE UNDER THE SPECIAL NEEDS PROVISION
OH...
WILEY
IT MEANS YOU CAN DO SOMETHING SNEAKY AND NOBLE AT THE SAME TIME
OH, THANK GOODNESS
YEAH... WE DON'T WANT YOUR IMAGE TARNISHED BY NOBILITY

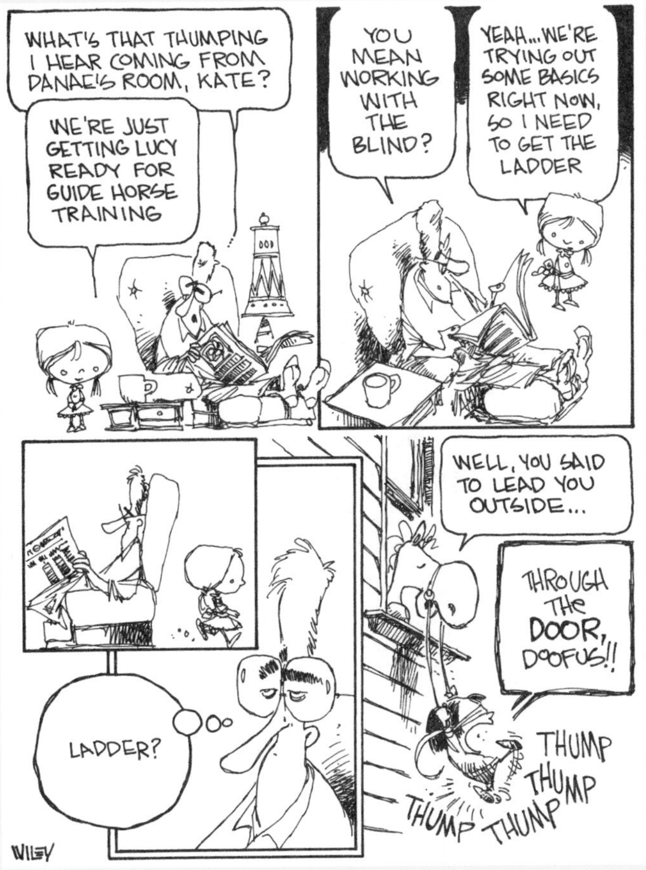
WHAT'S THAT THUMPING I HEAR COMING FROM DANAE'S ROOM, KATE?
WE'RE JUST GETTING LUCY READY FOR GUIDE HORSE TRAINING
YOU MEAN WORKING WITH THE BLIND?
YEAH... WE'RE TRYING OUT SOME BASICS RIGHT NOW, SO I NEED TO GET THE LADDER
LADDER?
WELL, YOU SAID TO LEAD YOU OUTSIDE...
THROUGH THE DOOR, DOOFUS!!
THUMP THUMP THUMP THUMP
WILEY

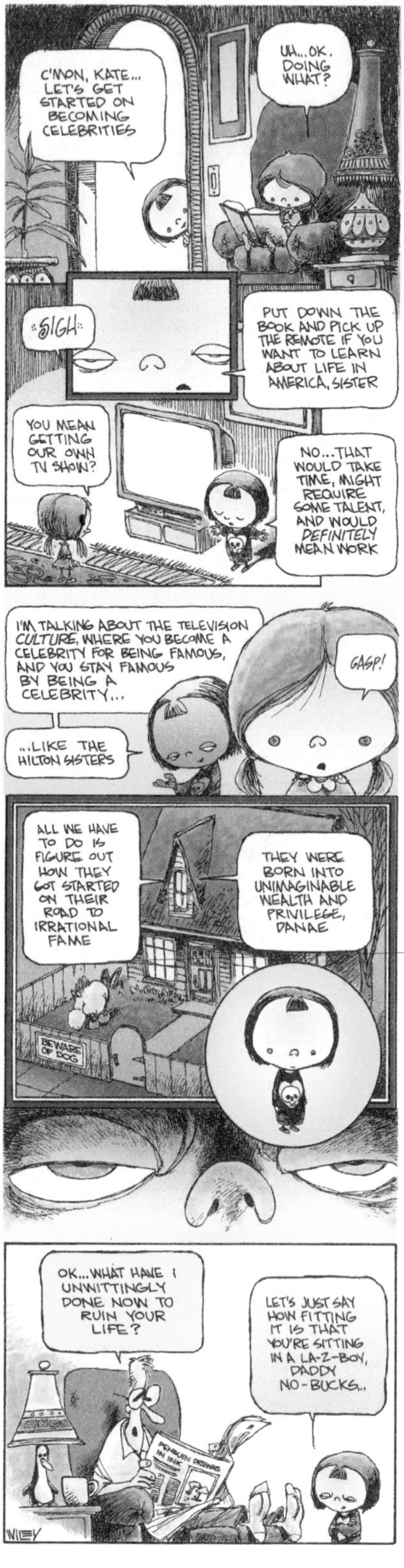
C'MON, KATE... LET'S GET STARTED ON BECOMING CELEBRITIES
UH...OK. DOING WHAT?
SIGH
PUT DOWN THE BOOK AND PICK UP THE REMOTE IF YOU WANT TO LEARN ABOUT LIFE IN AMERICA, SISTER
YOU MEAN GETTING OUR OWN TV SHOW?
NO...THAT WOULD TAKE TIME, MIGHT REQUIRE SOME TALENT, AND WOULD DEFINITELY MEAN WORK
I'M TALKING ABOUT THE TELEVISION CULTURE, WHERE YOU BECOME A CELEBRITY FOR BEING FAMOUS, AND YOU STAY FAMOUS BY BEING A CELEBRITY...
GASP!
...LIKE THE HILTON SISTERS
ALL WE HAVE TO DO IS FIGURE OUT HOW THEY GOT STARTED ON THEIR ROAD TO IRRATIONAL FAME
THEY WERE BORN INTO UNIMAGINABLE WEALTH AND PRIVILEGE, DANAE
BEWARE OF DOG
OK...WHAT HAVE I UNWITTINGLY DONE NOW TO RUIN YOUR LIFE?
LET'S JUST SAY HOW FITTING IT IS THAT YOU'RE SITTING IN A LA-Z-BOY, DADDY NO-BUCKS..
WILEY

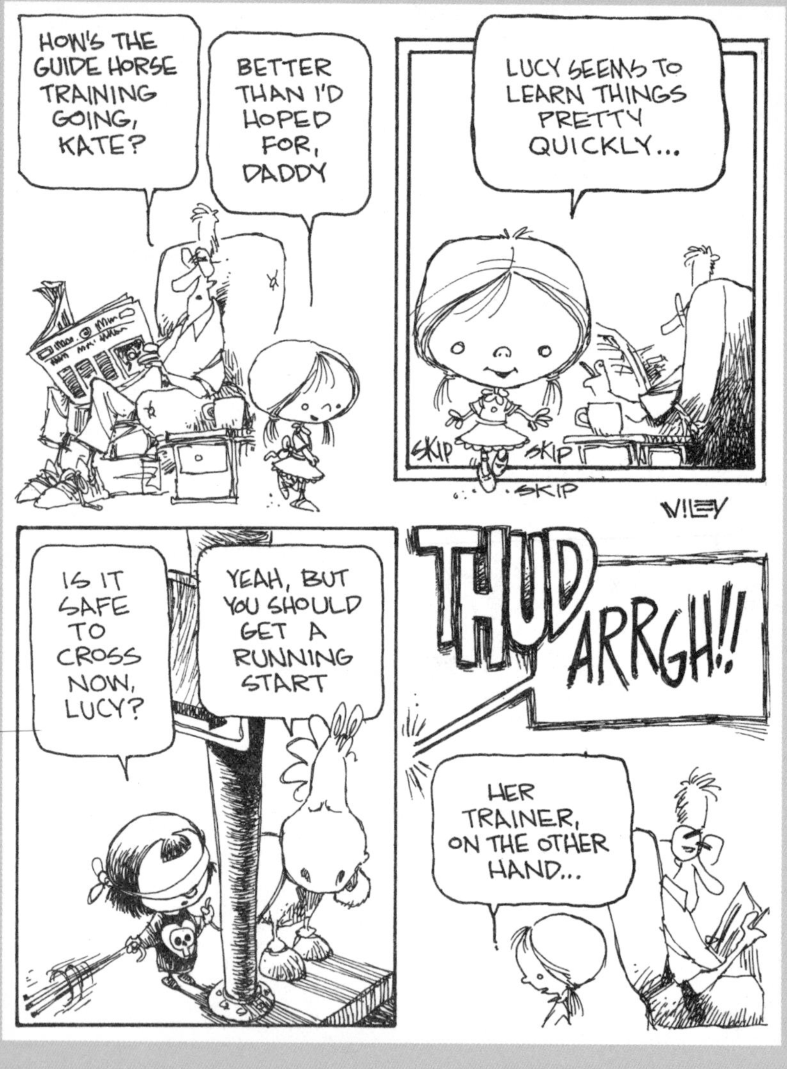
HOW'S THE GUIDE HORSE TRAINING GOING, KATE?
BETTER THAN I'D HOPED FOR, DADDY
LUCY SEEMS TO LEARN THINGS PRETTY QUICKLY...
SKIP SKIP SKIP
WILEY
IS IT SAFE TO CROSS NOW, LUCY?
YEAH, BUT YOU SHOULD GET A RUNNING START
THUD
ARRGH!!
HER TRAINER, ON THE OTHER HAND...

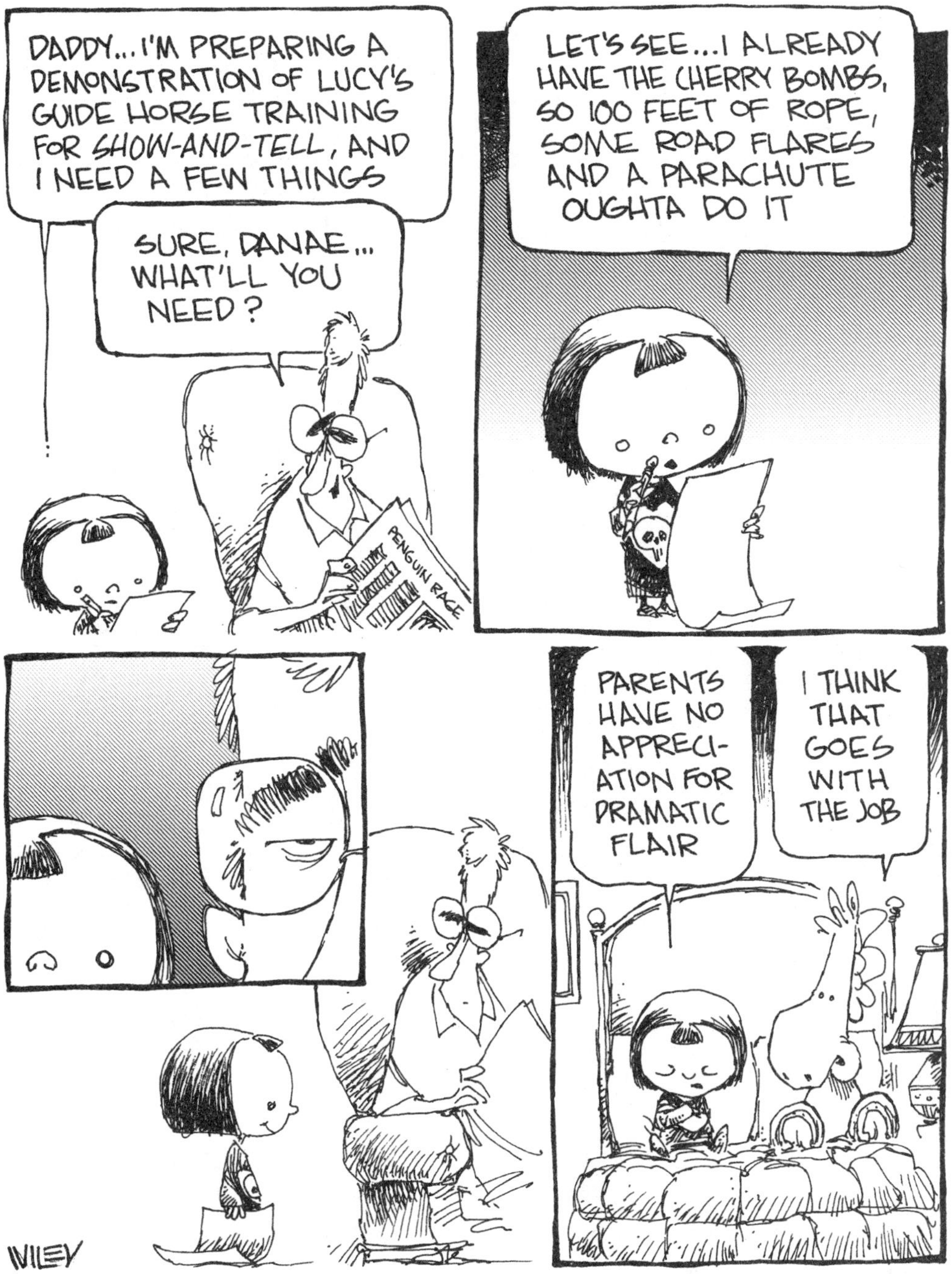
DADDY... I'M PREPARING A DEMONSTRATION OF LUCY'S GUIDE HORSE TRAINING FOR SHOW-AND-TELL, AND I NEED A FEW THINGS
SURE, DANAE... WHAT'LL YOU NEED?
PENGUIN RACE
LET'S SEE... I ALREADY HAVE THE CHERRY BOMBS, SO 100 FEET OF ROPE, SOME ROAD FLARES AND A PARACHUTE OUGHTA DO IT
WILEY
PARENTS HAVE NO APPRECIATION FOR DRAMATIC FLAIR
I THINK THAT GOES WITH THE JOB

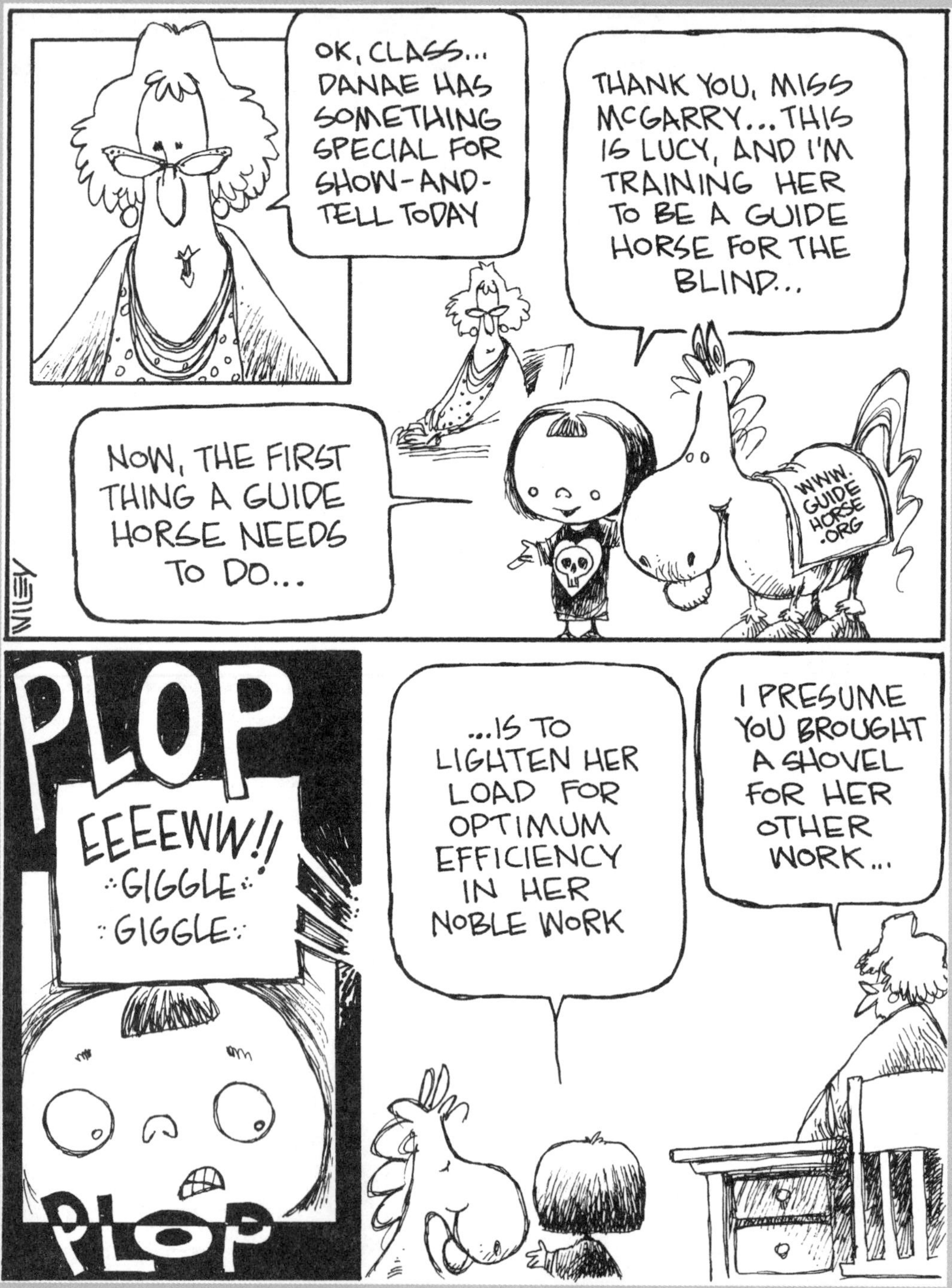
OK, CLASS... DANAE HAS SOMETHING SPECIAL FOR SHOW-AND-TELL TODAY
THANK YOU, MISS McGARRY... THIS IS LUCY, AND I'M TRAINING HER TO BE A GUIDE HORSE FOR THE BLIND...
NOW, THE FIRST THING A GUIDE HORSE NEEDS TO DO...
WWW. GUIDE HORSE .ORG
WILEY
PLOP
EEEEWW!!
GIGGLE
GIGGLE
PLOP
...IS TO LIGHTEN HER LOAD FOR OPTIMUM EFFICIENCY IN HER NOBLE WORK
I PRESUME YOU BROUGHT A SHOVEL FOR HER OTHER WORK...

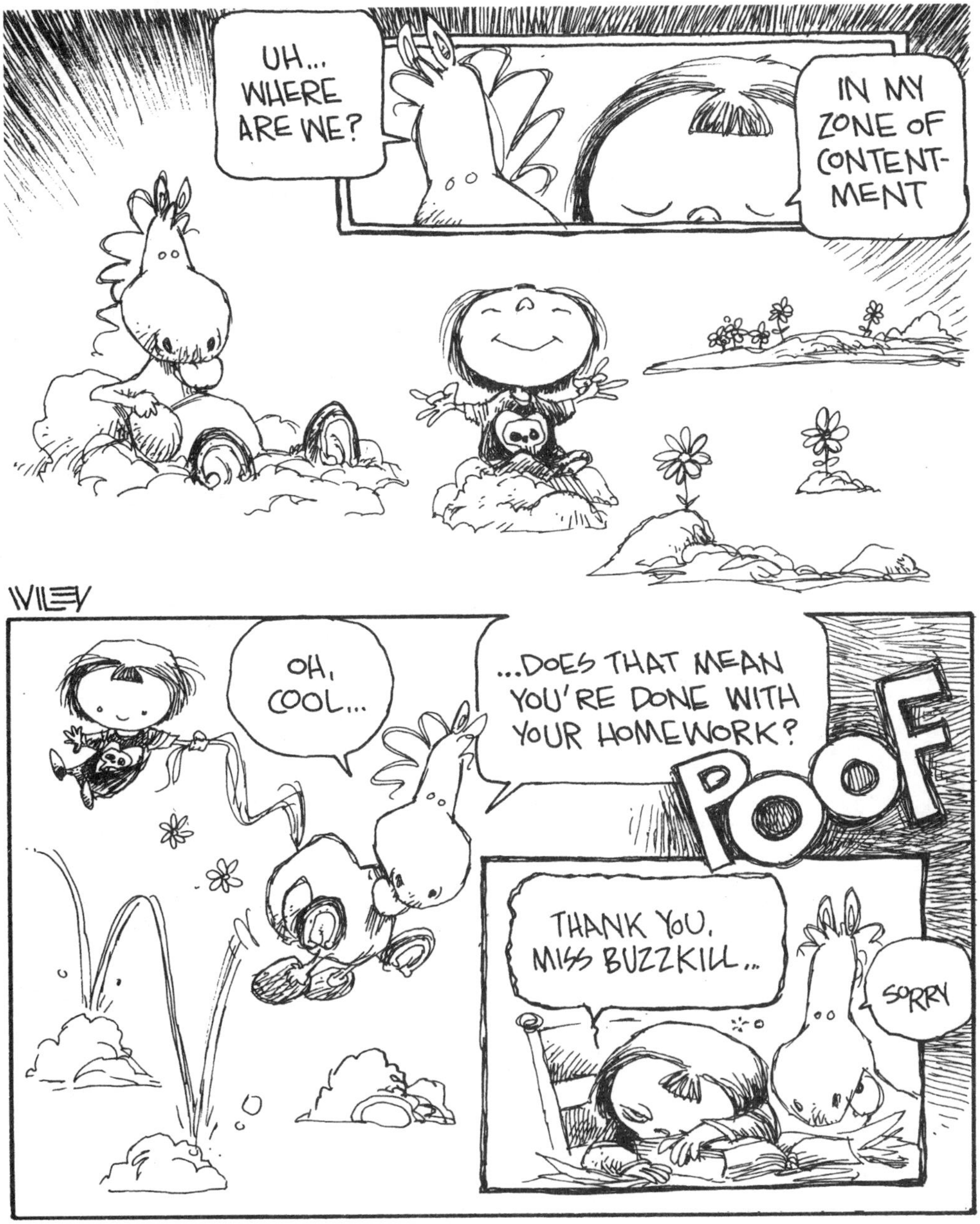
UH... WHERE ARE WE?
IN MY ZONE OF CONTENT-MENT
WILEY
OH, COOL...
...DOES THAT MEAN YOU'RE DONE WITH YOUR HOMEWORK?
POOF
THANK YOU, MISS BUZZKILL...
SORRY

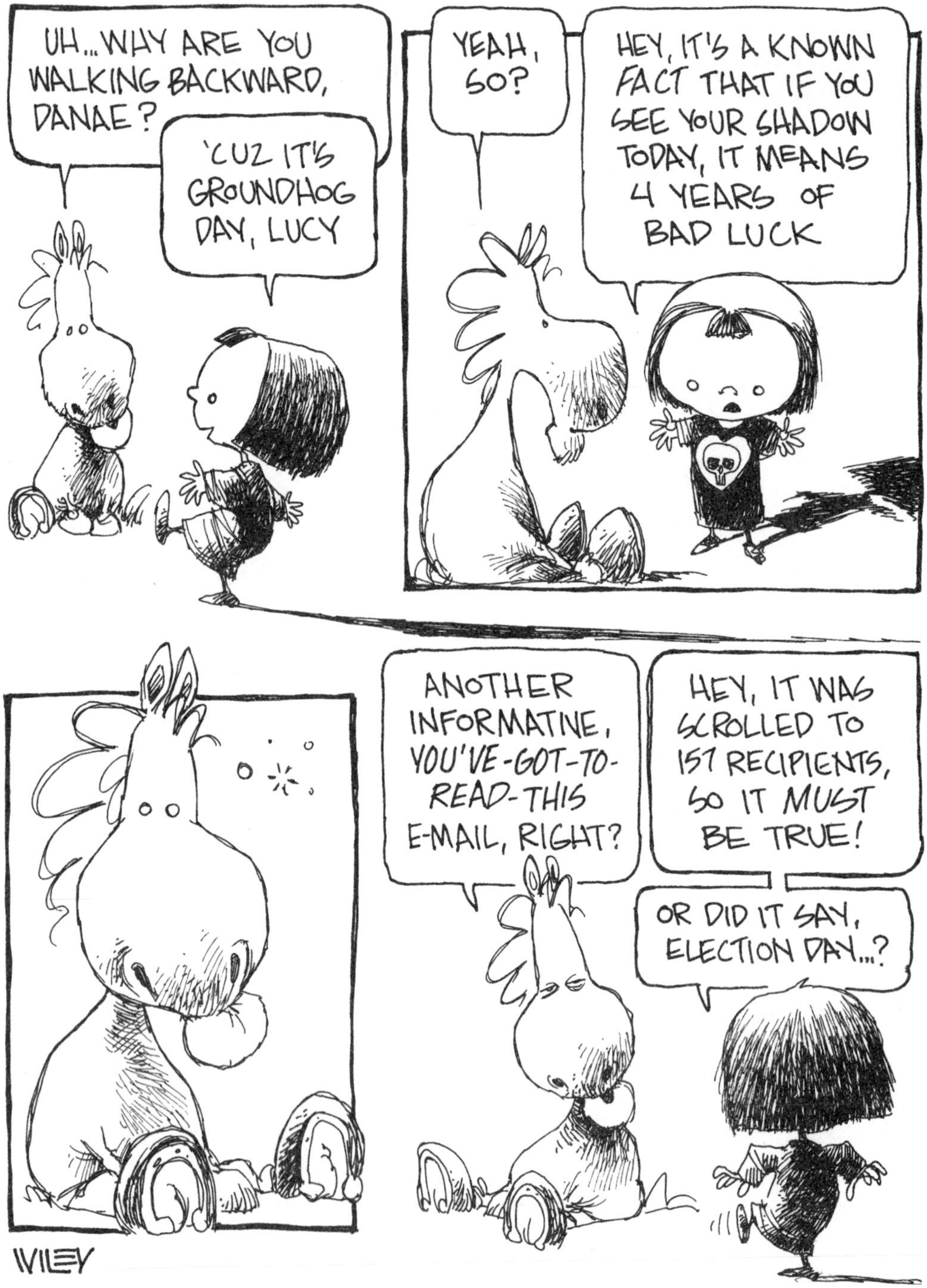
UH... WHY ARE YOU WALKING BACKWARD, DANAE?
'CUZ IT'S GROUNDHOG DAY, LUCY
YEAH, SO?
HEY, IT'S A KNOWN FACT THAT IF YOU SEE YOUR SHADOW TODAY, IT MEANS 4 YEARS OF BAD LUCK
ANOTHER INFORMATIVE, YOU'VE-GOT-TO-READ-THIS E-MAIL, RIGHT?
HEY, IT WAS SCROLLED TO 157 RECIPIENTS, SO IT MUST BE TRUE!
OR DID IT SAY, ELECTION DAY...?
WILEY

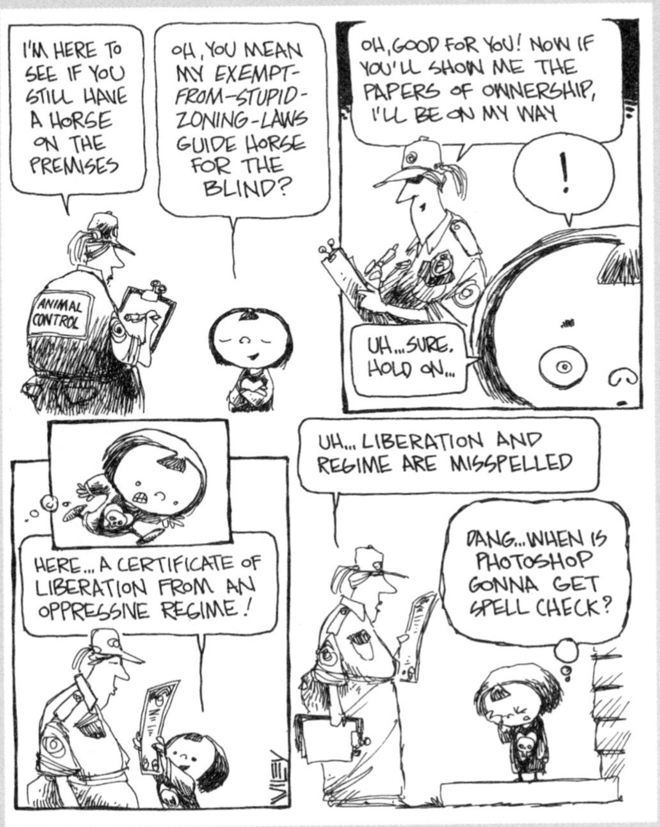
I'M HERE TO SEE IF YOU STILL HAVE A HORSE ON THE PREMISES
ANIMAL CONTROL
OH, YOU MEAN MY EXEMPT-FROM-STUPID-ZONING-LAWS GUIDE HORSE FOR THE BLIND?
OH, GOOD FOR YOU! NOW IF YOU'LL SHOW ME THE PAPERS OF OWNERSHIP, I'LL BE ON MY WAY
!
UH...SURE. HOLD ON...
HERE... A CERTIFICATE OF LIBERATION FROM AN OPPRESSIVE REGIME!
UH... LIBERATION AND REGIME ARE MISSPELLED
DANG...WHEN IS PHOTOSHOP GONNA GET SPELL CHECK?
WILEY

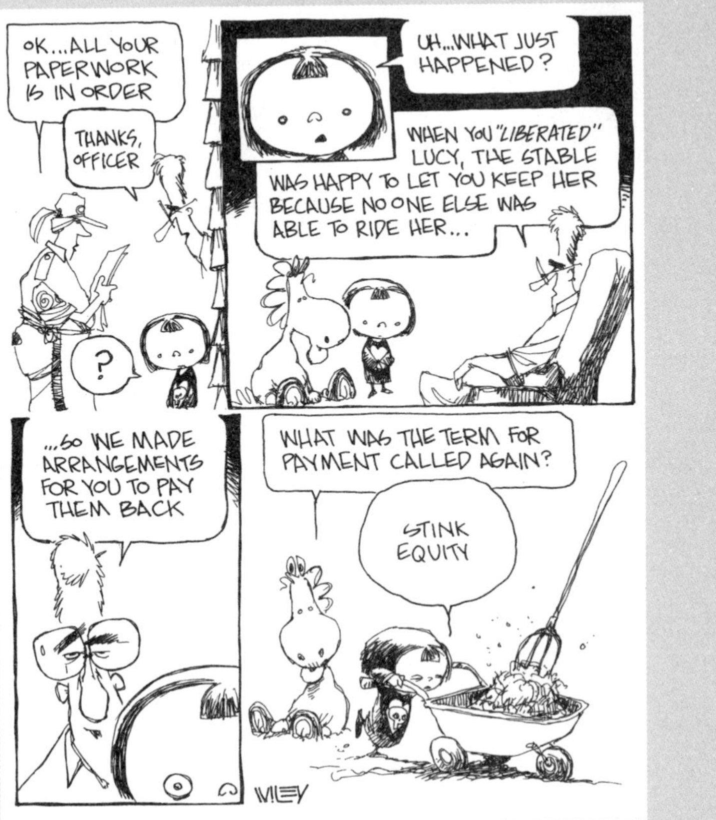
OK...ALL YOUR PAPERWORK IS IN ORDER
THANKS, OFFICER
?
UH...WHAT JUST HAPPENED?
WHEN YOU "LIBERATED" LUCY, THE STABLE WAS HAPPY TO LET YOU KEEP HER BECAUSE NO ONE ELSE WAS ABLE TO RIDE HER...
...SO WE MADE ARRANGEMENTS FOR YOU TO PAY THEM BACK
WHAT WAS THE TERM FOR PAYMENT CALLED AGAIN?
STINK EQUITY
WILEY

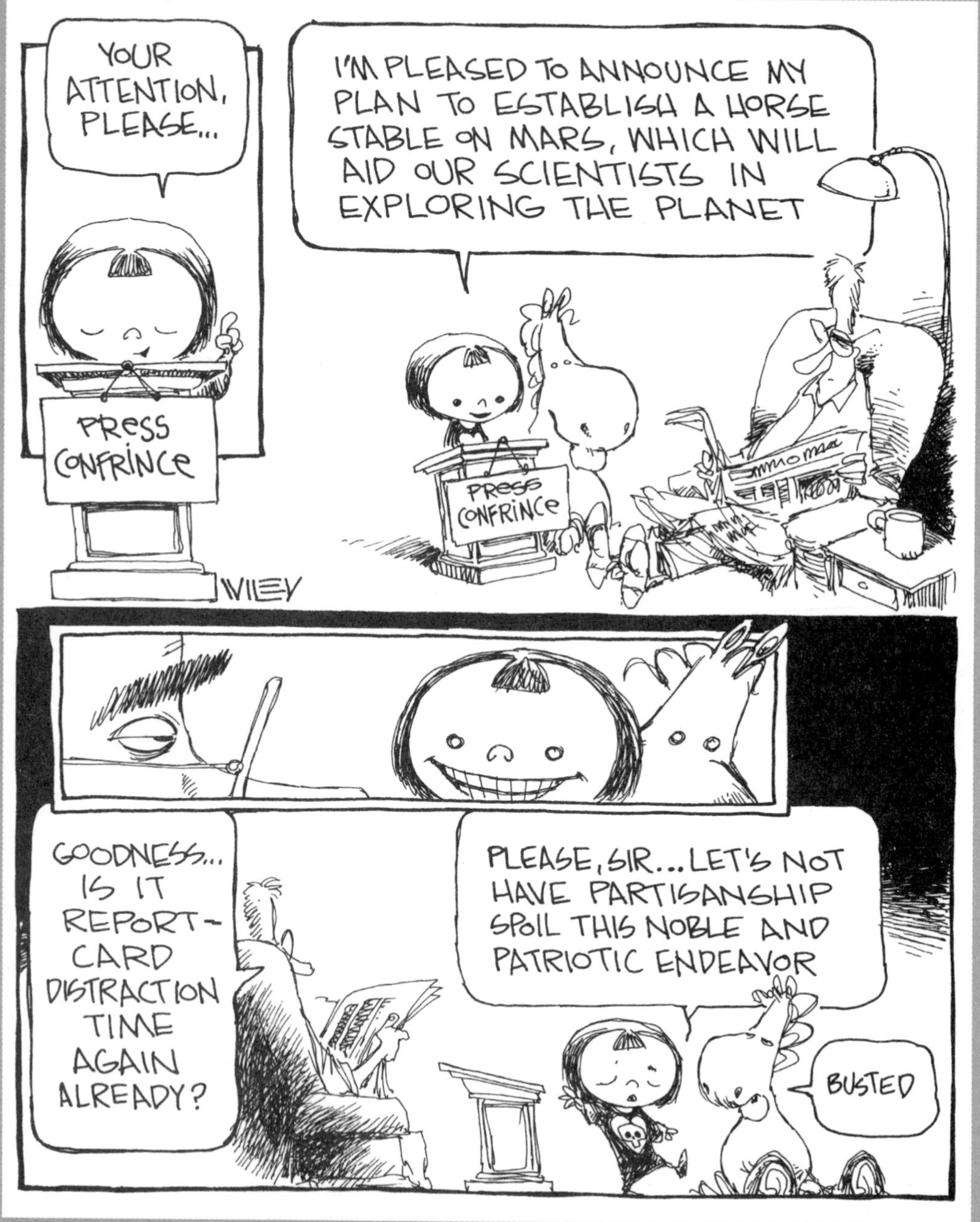
YOUR ATTENTION, PLEASE...
PRESS CONFRINCE
I'M PLEASED TO ANNOUNCE MY PLAN TO ESTABLISH A HORSE STABLE ON MARS, WHICH WILL AID OUR SCIENTISTS IN EXPLORING THE PLANET
PRESS CONFRINCE
WILEY
GOODNESS... IS IT REPORT-CARD DISTRACTION TIME AGAIN ALREADY?
PLEASE, SIR... LET'S NOT HAVE PARTISANSHIP SPOIL THIS NOBLE AND PATRIOTIC ENDEAVOR
BUSTED

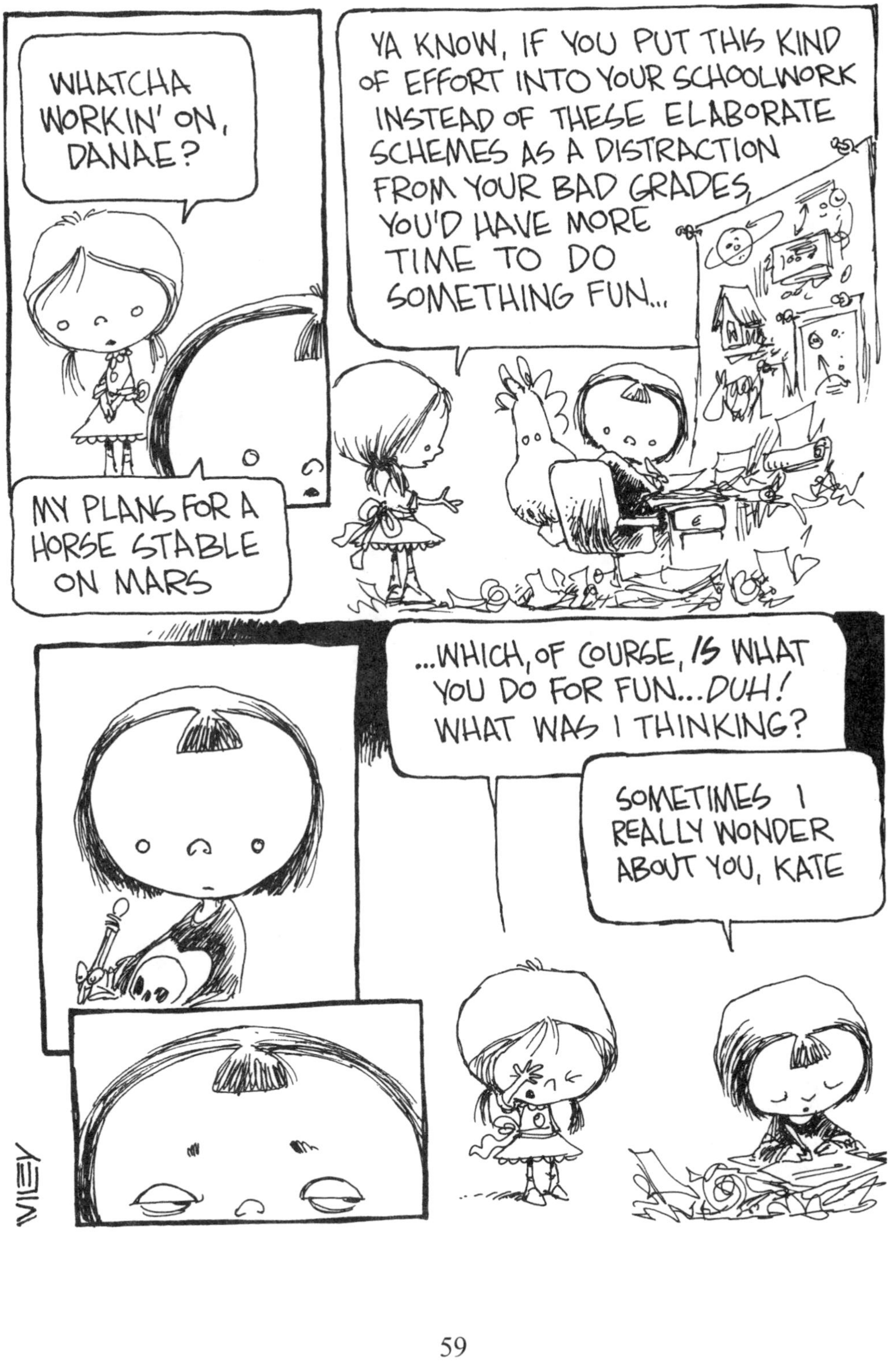
WHATCHA WORKIN' ON, DANAE?
MY PLANS FOR A HORSE STABLE ON MARS
YA KNOW, IF YOU PUT THIS KIND OF EFFORT INTO YOUR SCHOOLWORK INSTEAD OF THESE ELABORATE SCHEMES AS A DISTRACTION FROM YOUR BAD GRADES, YOU'D HAVE MORE TIME TO DO SOMETHING FUN...
...WHICH, OF COURSE, IS WHAT YOU DO FOR FUN...DUH! WHAT WAS I THINKING?
SOMETIMES I REALLY WONDER ABOUT YOU, KATE
WILEY

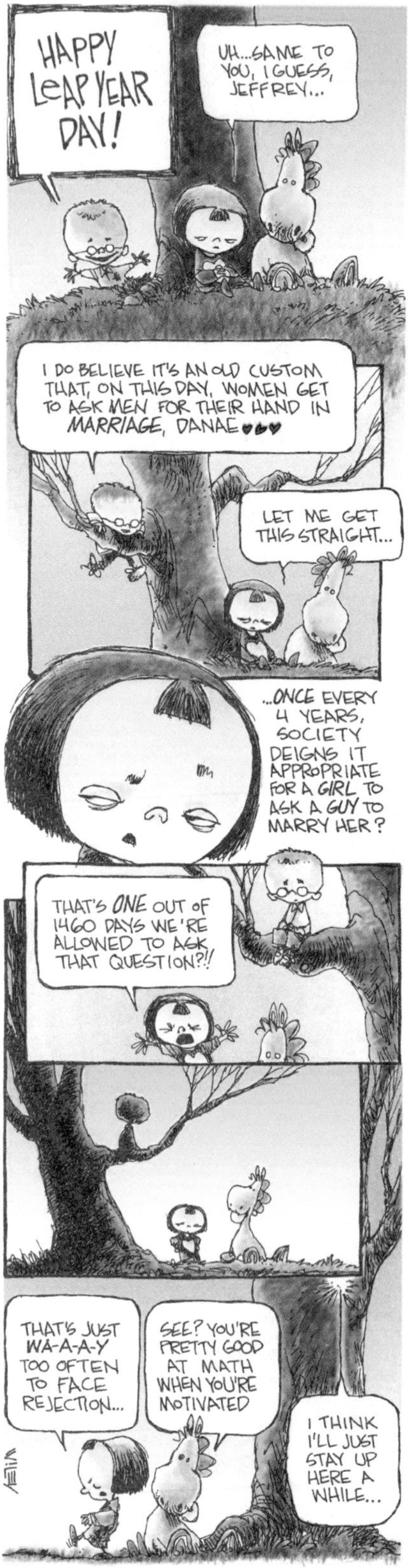
HAPPY LEAP YEAR DAY!
UH...SAME TO YOU, I GUESS, JEFFREY...
I DO BELIEVE IT'S AN OLD CUSTOM THAT, ON THIS DAY, WOMEN GET TO ASK MEN FOR THEIR HAND IN MARRIAGE, DANAE
LET ME GET THIS STRAIGHT...
...ONCE EVERY 4 YEARS, SOCIETY DEIGNS IT APPROPRIATE FOR A GIRL TO ASK A GUY TO MARRY HER?
THAT'S ONE OUT OF 1460 DAYS WE'RE ALLOWED TO ASK THAT QUESTION?!
THAT'S JUST WA-A-A-Y TOO OFTEN TO FACE REJECTION...
SEE? YOU'RE PRETTY GOOD AT MATH WHEN YOU'RE MOTIVATED
I THINK I'LL JUST STAY UP HERE A WHILE...
WILEY

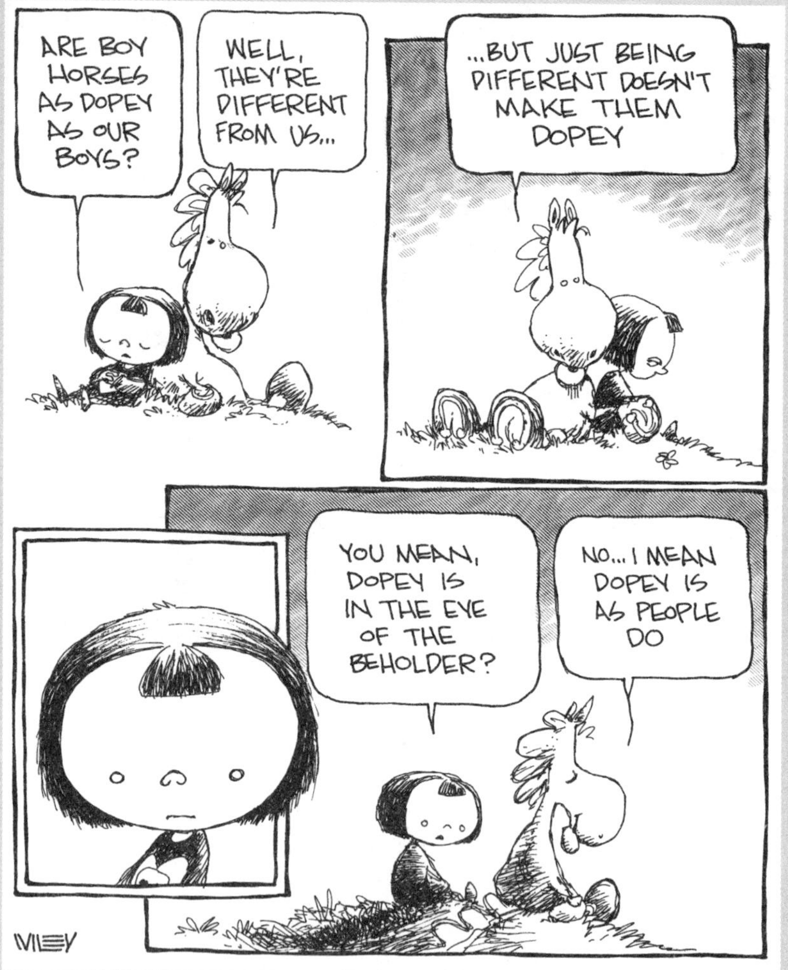
ARE BOY HORSES AS DOPEY AS OUR BOYS?
WELL, THEY'RE DIFFERENT FROM US...
...BUT JUST BEING DIFFERENT DOESN'T MAKE THEM DOPEY
YOU MEAN, DOPEY IS IN THE EYE OF THE BEHOLDER?
NO...I MEAN DOPEY IS AS PEOPLE DO
WILEY

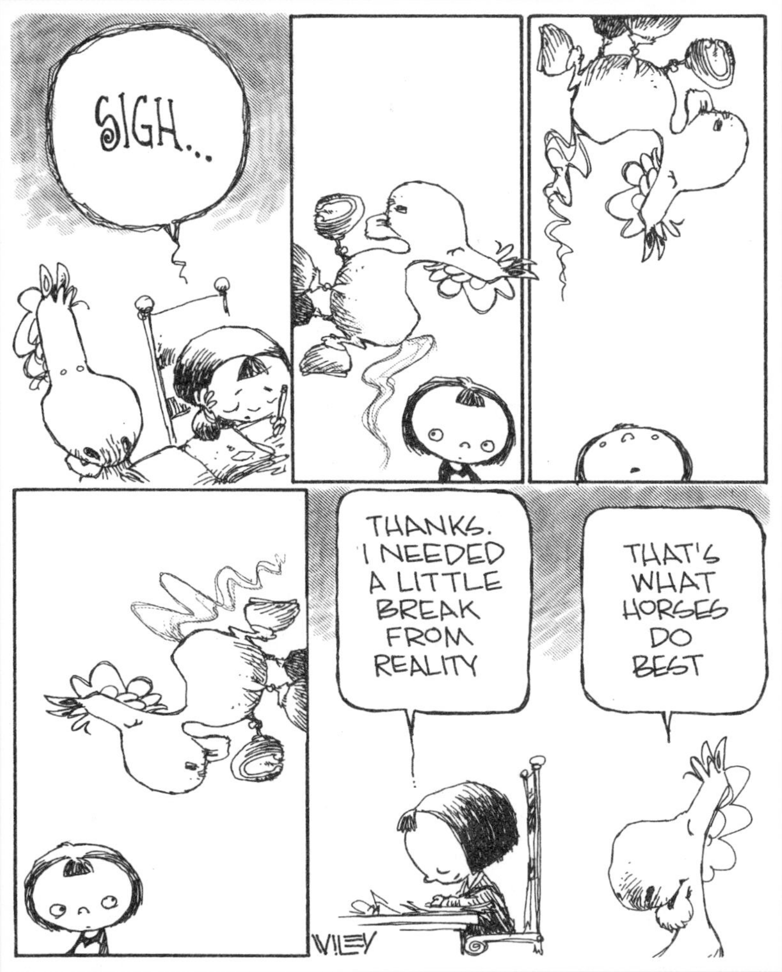
SIGH...
THANKS. I NEEDED A LITTLE BREAK FROM REALITY
THAT'S WHAT HORSES DO BEST
WILEY

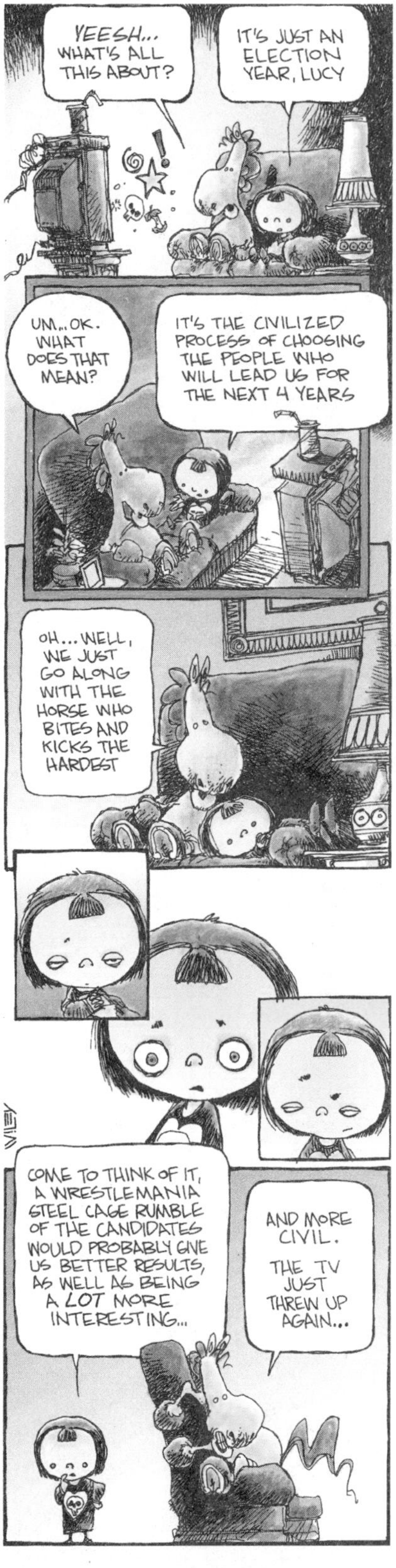
YEESH... WHAT'S ALL THIS ABOUT?
IT'S JUST AN ELECTION YEAR, LUCY
UM...OK. WHAT DOES THAT MEAN?
IT'S THE CIVILIZED PROCESS OF CHOOSING THE PEOPLE WHO WILL LEAD US FOR THE NEXT 4 YEARS
OH... WELL, WE JUST GO ALONG WITH THE HORSE WHO BITES AND KICKS THE HARDEST
WILEY
COME TO THINK OF IT, A WRESTLEMANIA STEEL CAGE RUMBLE OF THE CANDIDATES WOULD PROBABLY GIVE US BETTER RESULTS, AS WELL AS BEING A LOT MORE INTERESTING...
AND MORE CIVIL.
THE TV JUST THREW UP AGAIN...

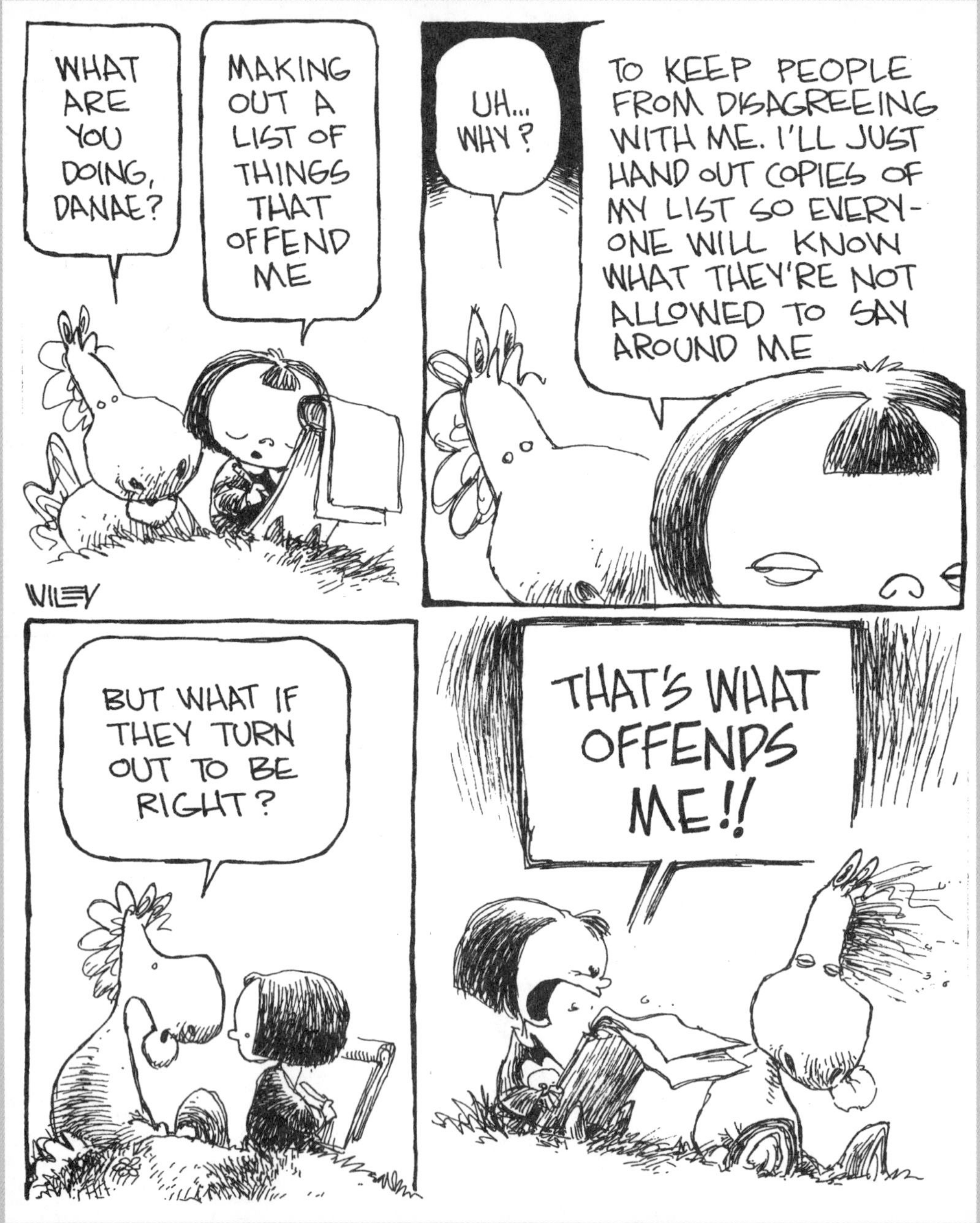
WHAT ARE YOU DOING, DANAE?
MAKING OUT A LIST OF THINGS THAT OFFEND ME
WILEY
UH... WHY?
TO KEEP PEOPLE FROM DISAGREEING WITH ME. I'LL JUST HAND OUT COPIES OF MY LIST SO EVERY-ONE WILL KNOW WHAT THEY'RE NOT ALLOWED TO SAY AROUND ME
BUT WHAT IF THEY TURN OUT TO BE RIGHT?
THAT'S WHAT OFFENDS ME!!

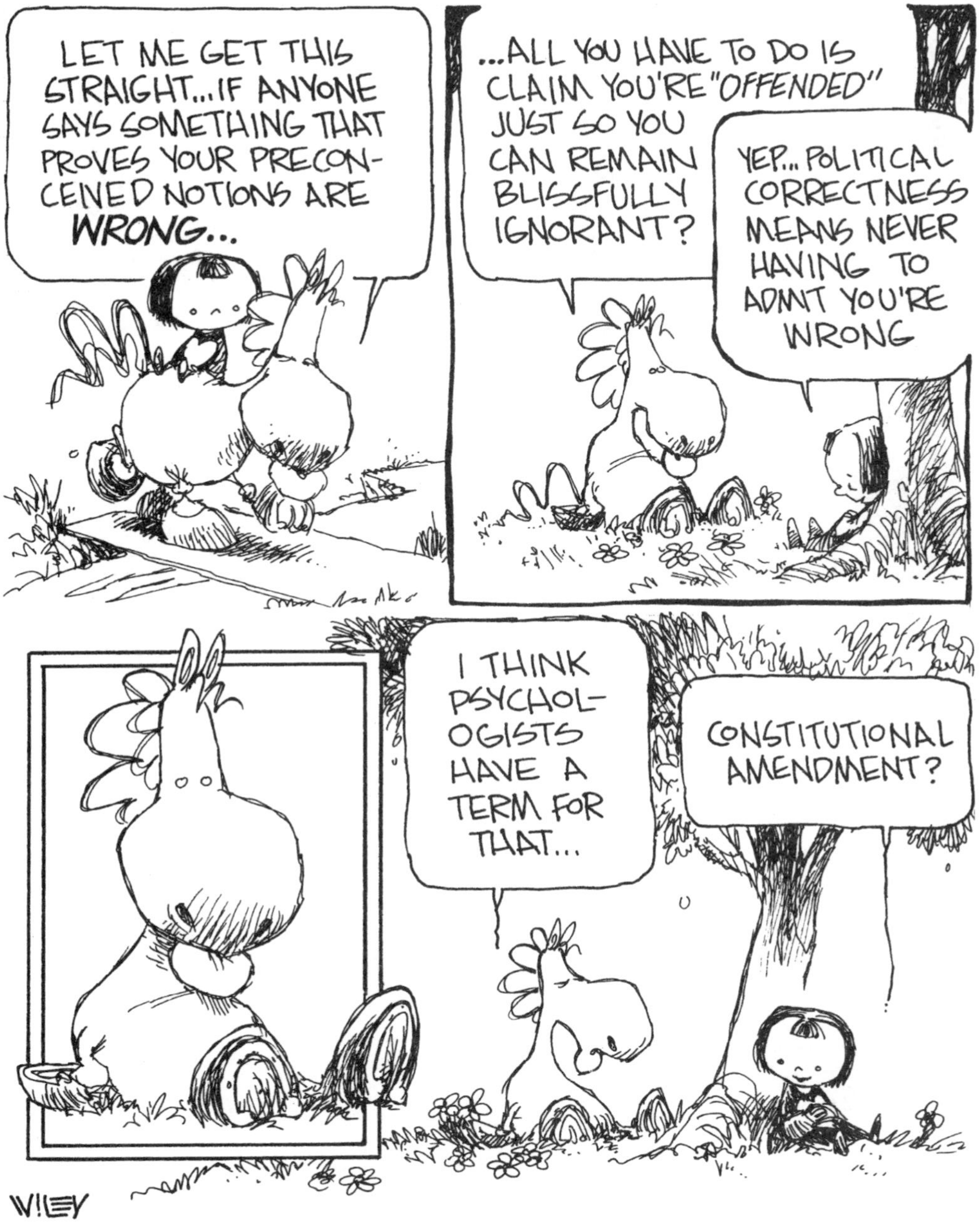
LET ME GET THIS STRAIGHT...IF ANYONE SAYS SOMETHING THAT PROVES YOUR PRECON-CEIVED NOTIONS ARE **WRONG...**
...ALL YOU HAVE TO DO IS CLAIM YOU'RE "OFFENDED" JUST SO YOU CAN REMAIN BLISSFULLY IGNORANT?
YEP... POLITICAL CORRECTNESS MEANS NEVER HAVING TO ADMIT YOU'RE WRONG
I THINK PSYCHOL-OGISTS HAVE A TERM FOR THAT...
CONSTITUTIONAL AMENDMENT?
WILEY

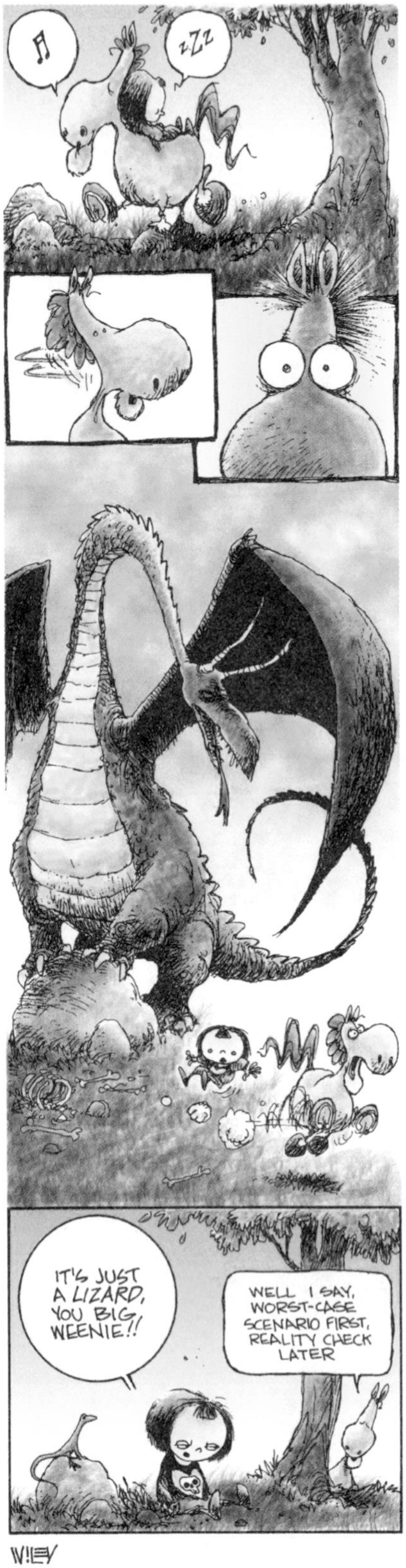
♫
zZz
IT'S JUST A LIZARD, YOU BIG WEENIE!!
WELL I SAY, WORST-CASE SCENARIO FIRST, REALITY CHECK LATER
W!LEY

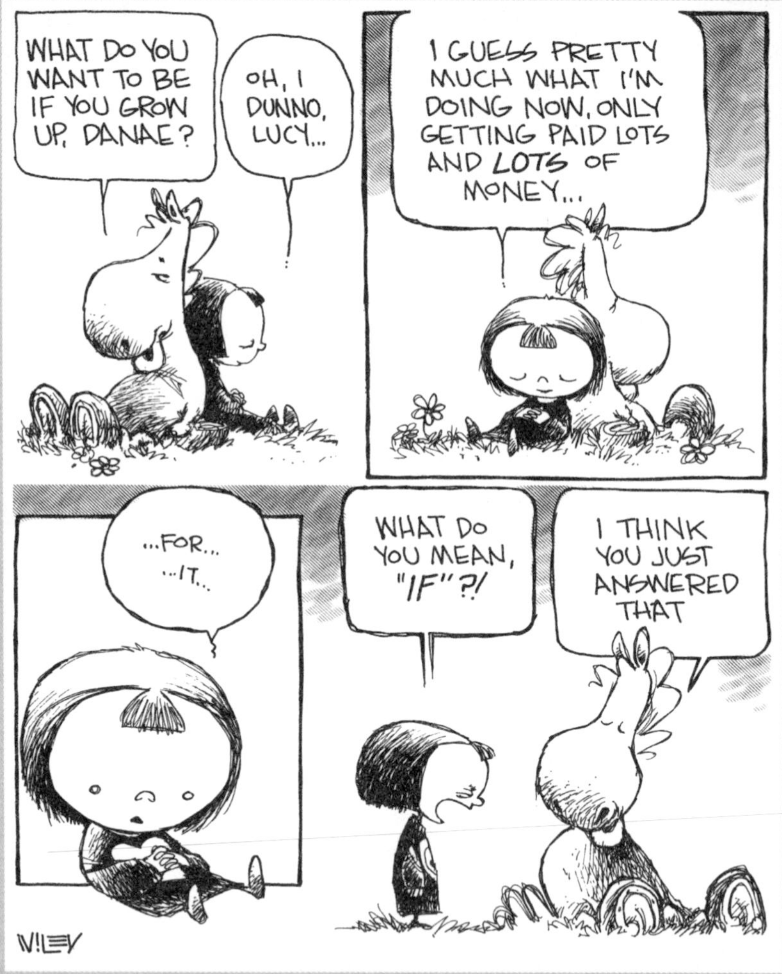
WHAT DO YOU WANT TO BE IF YOU GROW UP, DANAE?
OH, I DUNNO, LUCY...
I GUESS PRETTY MUCH WHAT I'M DOING NOW, ONLY GETTING PAID LOTS AND LOTS OF MONEY...
...FOR... ...IT...
WHAT DO YOU MEAN, "IF"?!
I THINK YOU JUST ANSWERED THAT
W!LEY

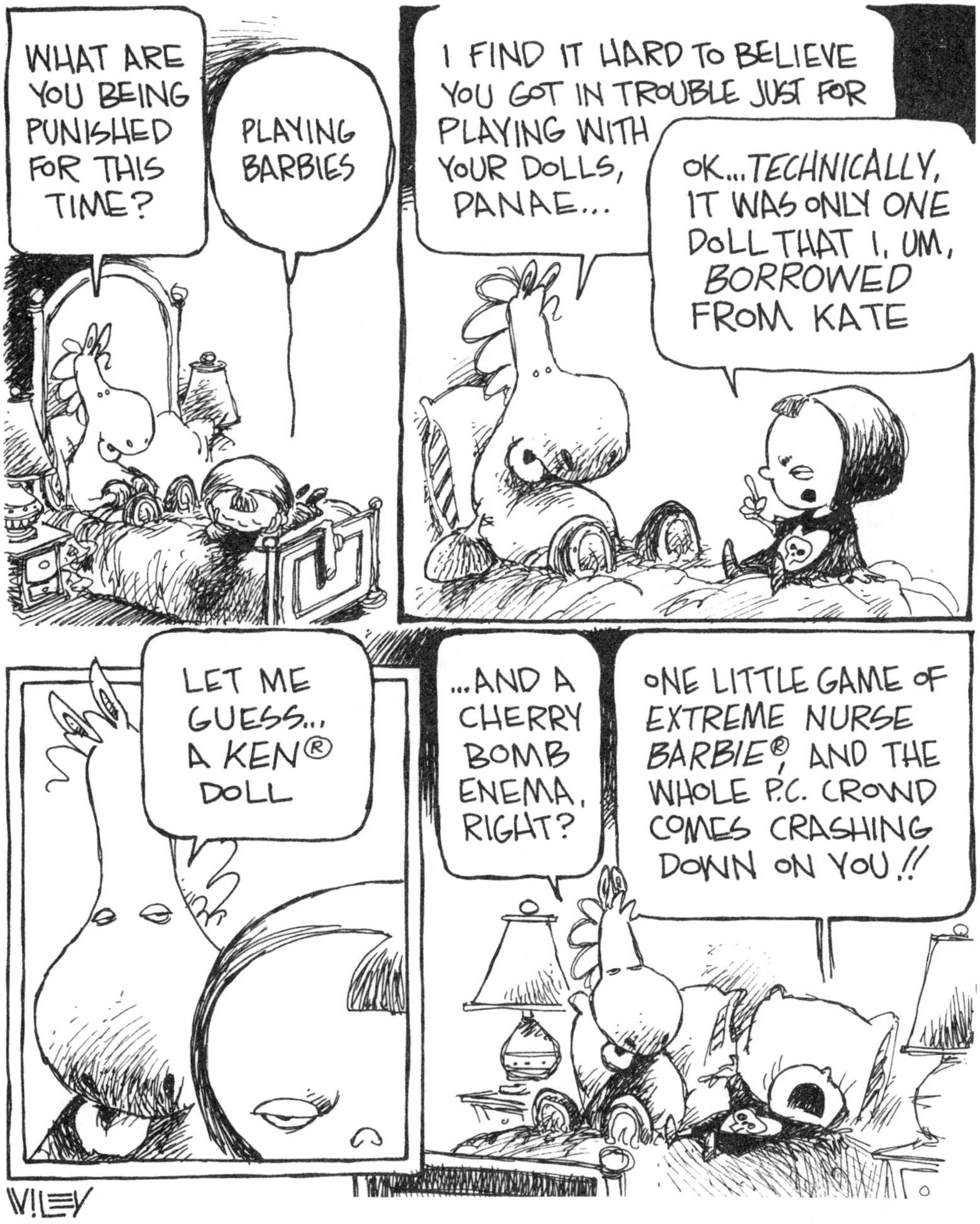
WHAT ARE YOU BEING PUNISHED FOR THIS TIME?
PLAYING BARBIES
I FIND IT HARD TO BELIEVE YOU GOT IN TROUBLE JUST FOR PLAYING WITH YOUR DOLLS, PANAE...
OK...*TECHNICALLY,* IT WAS ONLY ONE DOLL THAT I, UM, *BORROWED* FROM KATE
LET ME GUESS... A *KEN®* DOLL
...AND A CHERRY BOMB ENEMA, RIGHT?
ONE LITTLE GAME OF *EXTREME NURSE BARBIE®,* AND THE WHOLE P.C. CROWD COMES CRASHING DOWN ON YOU!!
WILEY

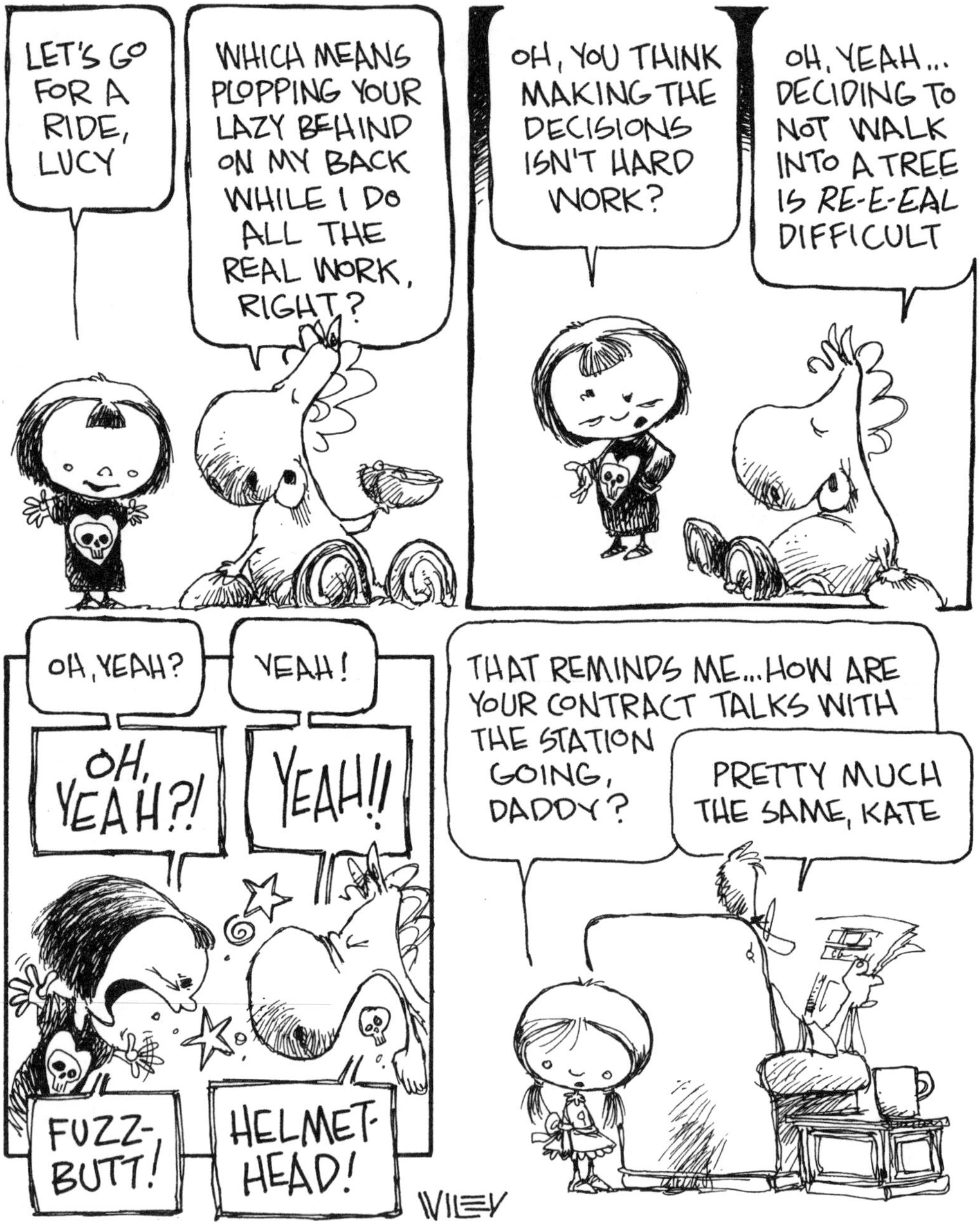
LET'S GO FOR A RIDE, LUCY
WHICH MEANS PLOPPING YOUR LAZY BEHIND ON MY BACK WHILE I DO ALL THE REAL WORK, RIGHT?
OH, YOU THINK MAKING THE DECISIONS ISN'T HARD WORK?
OH, YEAH... DECIDING TO NOT WALK INTO A TREE IS *RE-E-EAL* DIFFICULT
OH, YEAH?
YEAH!
OH, YEAH?!
YEAH!!
FUZZ-BUTT!
HELMET-HEAD!
WILEY
THAT REMINDS ME...HOW ARE YOUR CONTRACT TALKS WITH THE STATION GOING, DADDY?
PRETTY MUCH THE SAME, KATE

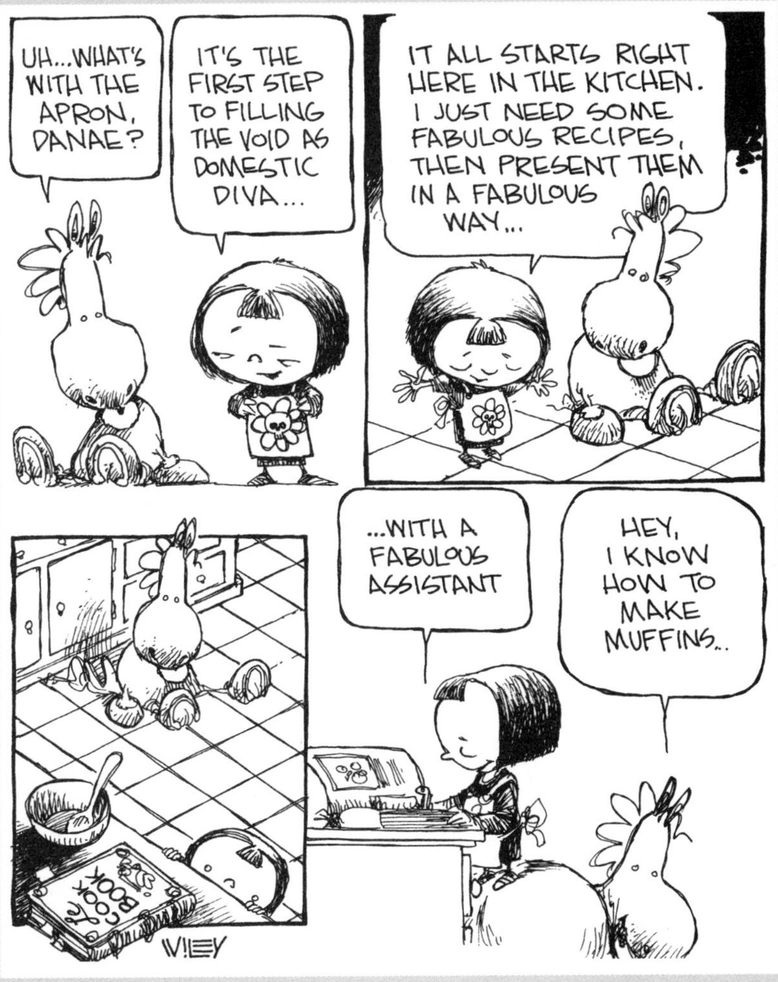
UH...WHAT'S WITH THE APRON, DANAE?
IT'S THE FIRST STEP TO FILLING THE VOID AS DOMESTIC DIVA...
IT ALL STARTS RIGHT HERE IN THE KITCHEN. I JUST NEED SOME FABULOUS RECIPES, THEN PRESENT THEM IN A FABULOUS WAY...
...WITH A FABULOUS ASSISTANT
HEY, I KNOW HOW TO MAKE MUFFINS..
COOK BOOK
WILEY

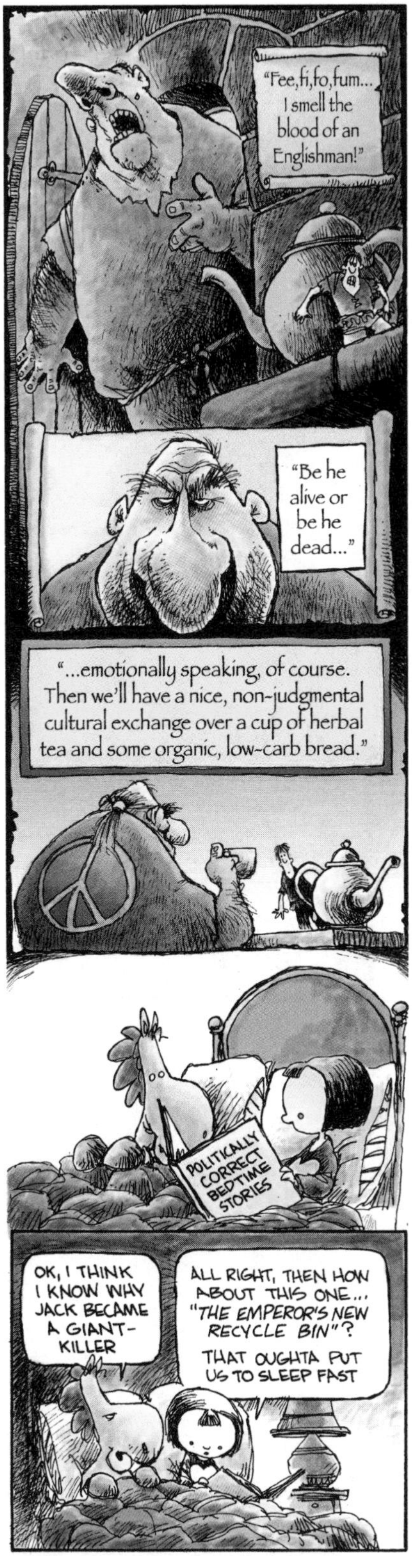
"Fee, fi, fo, fum... I smell the blood of an Englishman!"
"Be he alive or be he dead..."
"...emotionally speaking, of course. Then we'll have a nice, non-judgmental cultural exchange over a cup of herbal tea and some organic, low-carb bread."
POLITICALLY CORRECT BEDTIME STORIES
OK, I THINK I KNOW WHY JACK BECAME A GIANT-KILLER
ALL RIGHT, THEN HOW ABOUT THIS ONE... "THE EMPEROR'S NEW RECYCLE BIN"? THAT OUGHTA PUT US TO SLEEP FAST
WILEY

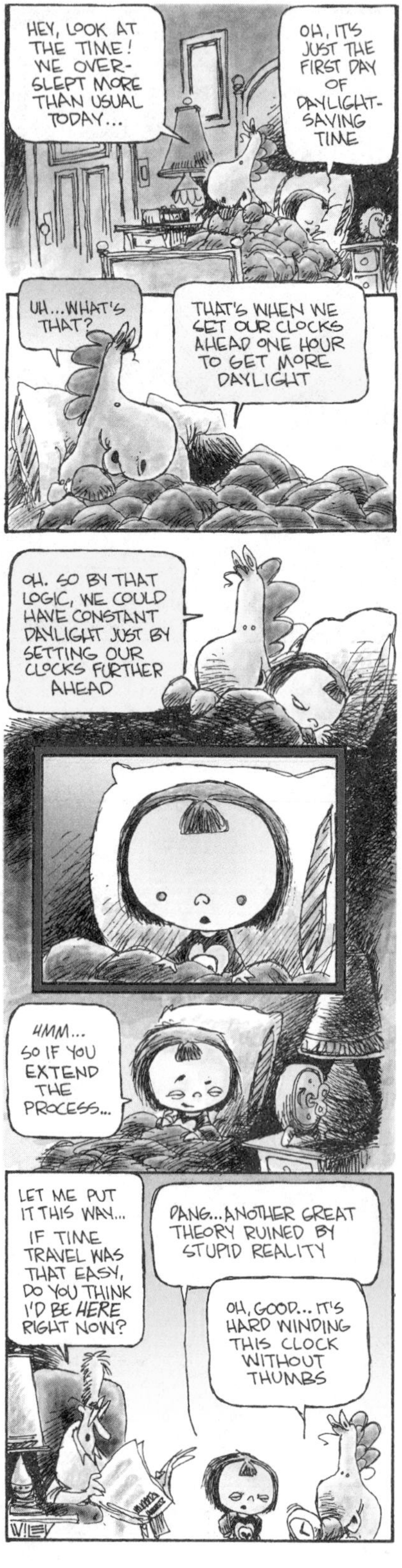
HEY, LOOK AT THE TIME! WE OVER-SLEPT MORE THAN USUAL TODAY...
OH, IT'S JUST THE FIRST DAY OF DAYLIGHT-SAVING TIME
UH...WHAT'S THAT?
THAT'S WHEN WE SET OUR CLOCKS AHEAD ONE HOUR TO GET MORE DAYLIGHT
OH. SO BY THAT LOGIC, WE COULD HAVE CONSTANT DAYLIGHT JUST BY SETTING OUR CLOCKS FURTHER AHEAD
HMM... SO IF YOU EXTEND THE PROCESS...
LET ME PUT IT THIS WAY... IF TIME TRAVEL WAS THAT EASY, DO YOU THINK I'D BE HERE RIGHT NOW?
DANG...ANOTHER GREAT THEORY RUINED BY STUPID REALITY
OH, GOOD... IT'S HARD WINDING THIS CLOCK WITHOUT THUMBS
WILEY

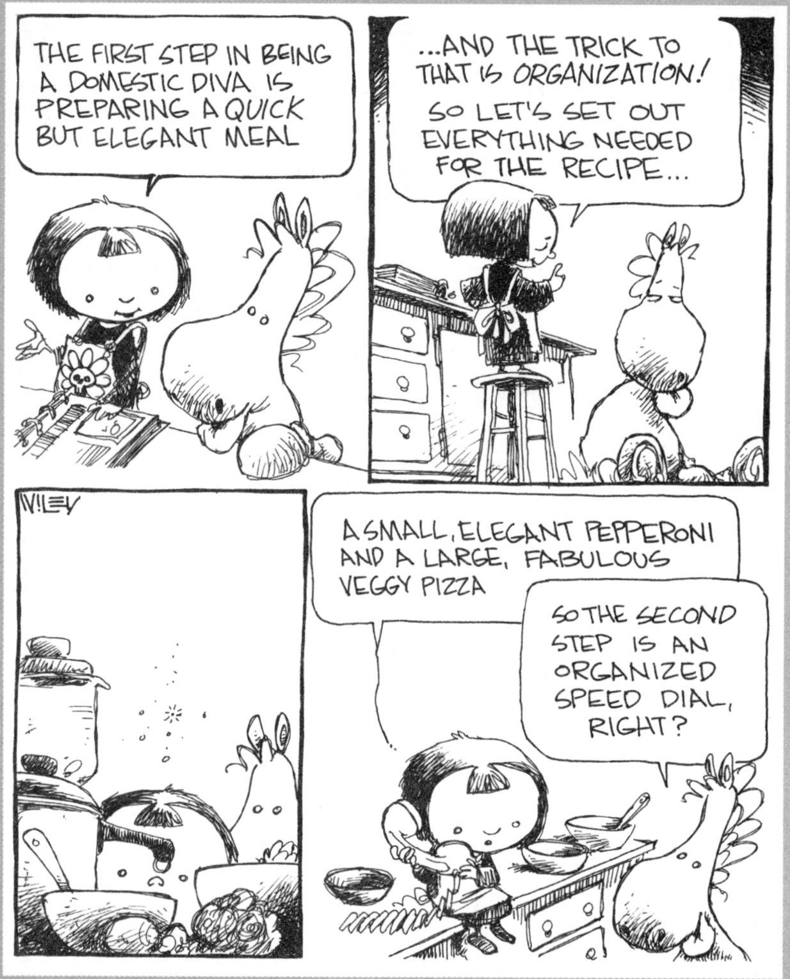
THE FIRST STEP IN BEING A DOMESTIC DIVA IS PREPARING A QUICK BUT ELEGANT MEAL
...AND THE TRICK TO THAT IS ORGANIZATION!
SO LET'S SET OUT EVERYTHING NEEDED FOR THE RECIPE...
WILEY
A SMALL, ELEGANT PEPPERONI AND A LARGE, FABULOUS VEGGY PIZZA
SO THE SECOND STEP IS AN ORGANIZED SPEED DIAL, RIGHT?

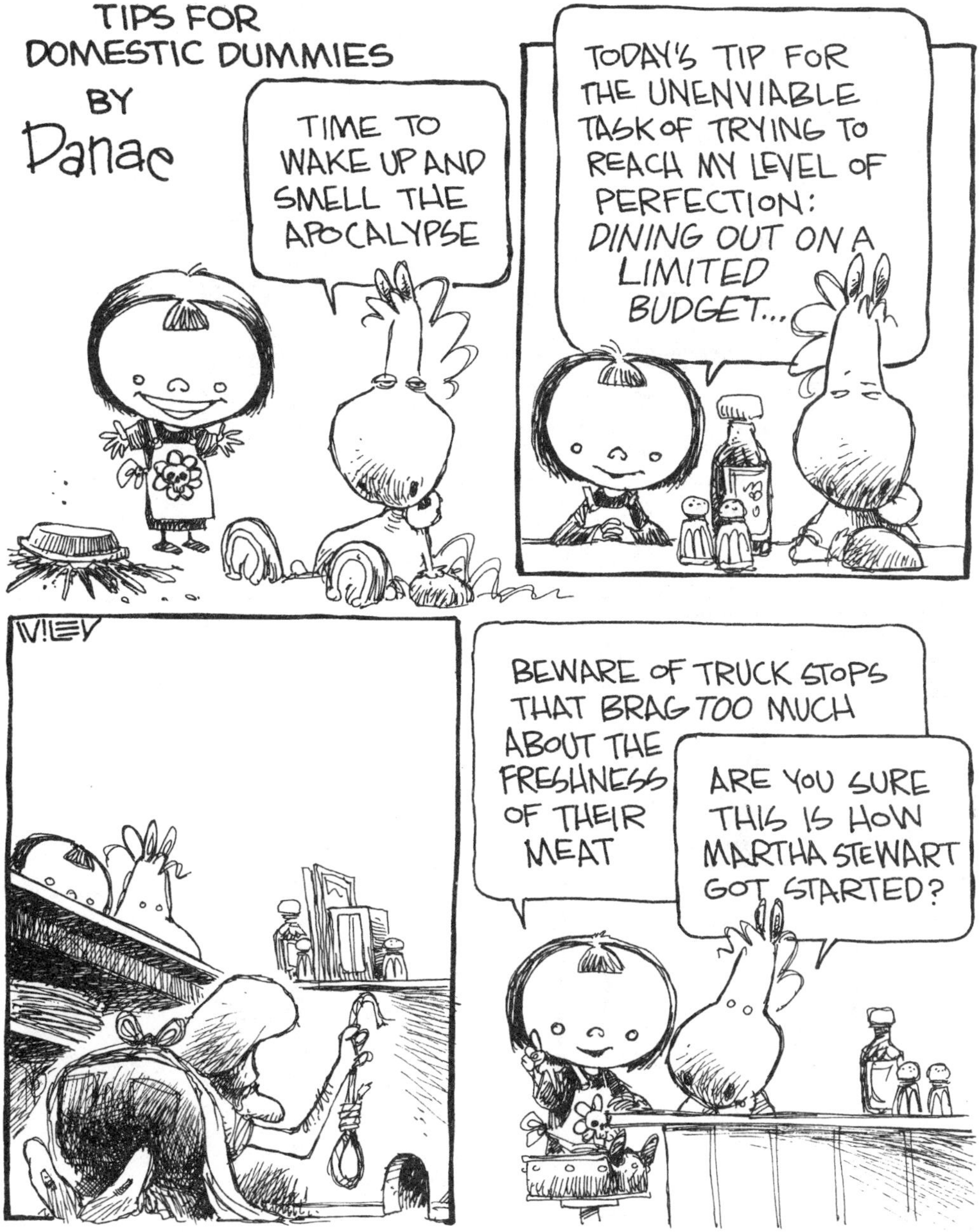
TIPS FOR DOMESTIC DUMMIES BY Danae
TIME TO WAKE UP AND SMELL THE APOCALYPSE
TODAY'S TIP FOR THE UNENVIABLE TASK OF TRYING TO REACH MY LEVEL OF PERFECTION: DINING OUT ON A LIMITED BUDGET...
WILEY
BEWARE OF TRUCK STOPS THAT BRAG TOO MUCH ABOUT THE FRESHNESS OF THEIR MEAT
ARE YOU SURE THIS IS HOW MARTHA STEWART GOT STARTED?

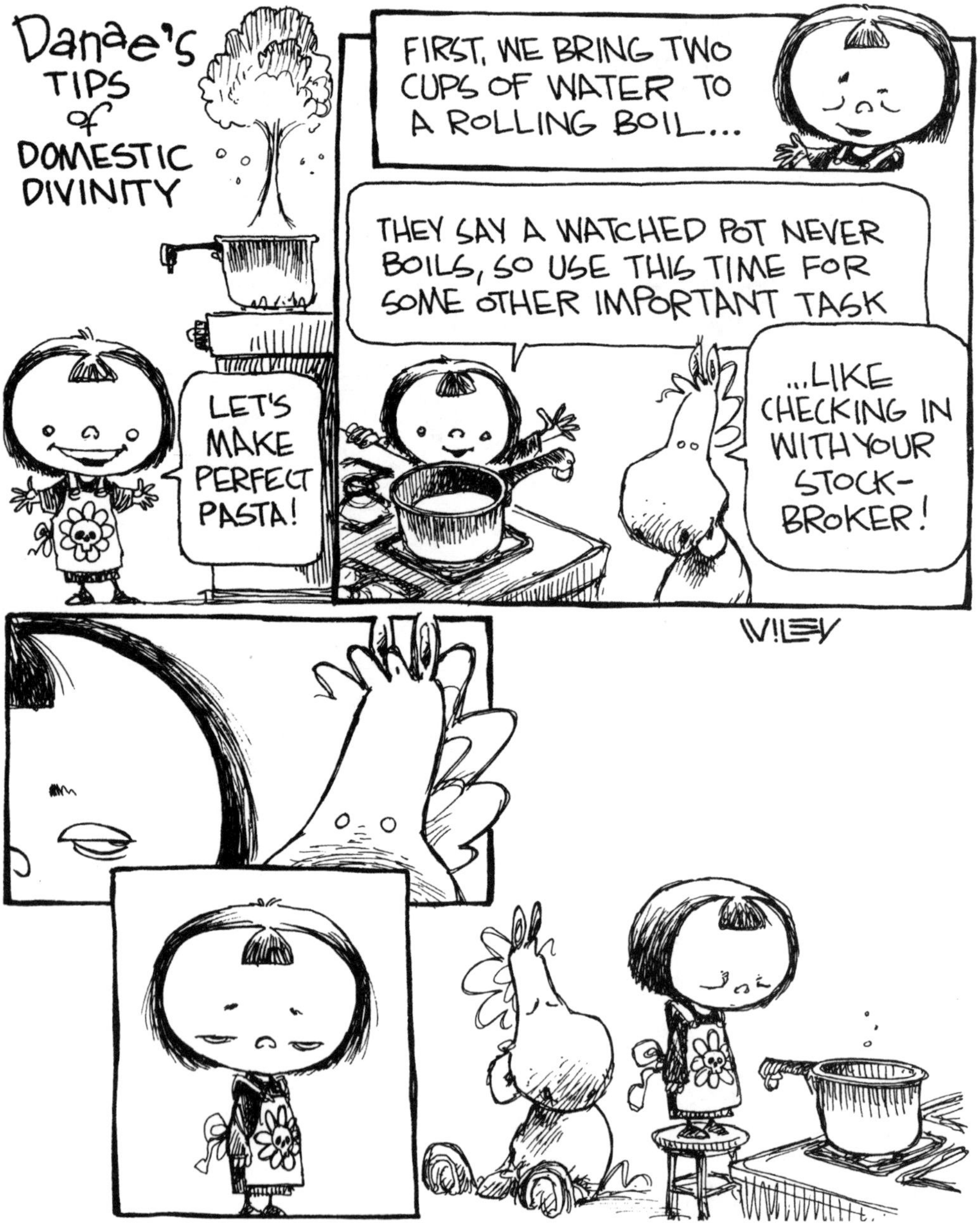
Danae's TIPS of DOMESTIC DIVINITY
LET'S MAKE PERFECT PASTA!
FIRST, WE BRING TWO CUPS OF WATER TO A ROLLING BOIL...
THEY SAY A WATCHED POT NEVER BOILS, SO USE THIS TIME FOR SOME OTHER IMPORTANT TASK
...LIKE CHECKING IN WITH YOUR STOCK-BROKER!
WILEY

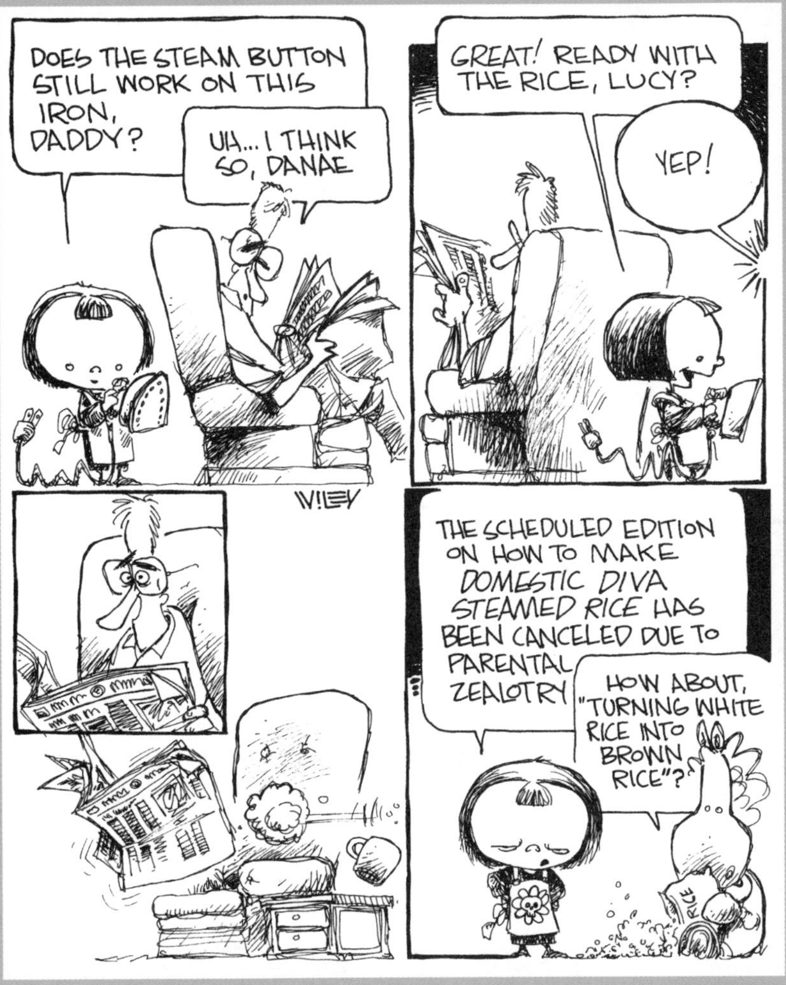
DOES THE STEAM BUTTON STILL WORK ON THIS IRON, DADDY?
UH... I THINK SO, DANAE
GREAT! READY WITH THE RICE, LUCY?
YEP!
WILEY
THE SCHEDULED EDITION ON HOW TO MAKE DOMESTIC DIVA STEAMED RICE HAS BEEN CANCELED DUE TO PARENTAL ZEALOTRY
HOW ABOUT, "TURNING WHITE RICE INTO BROWN RICE"?
RICE

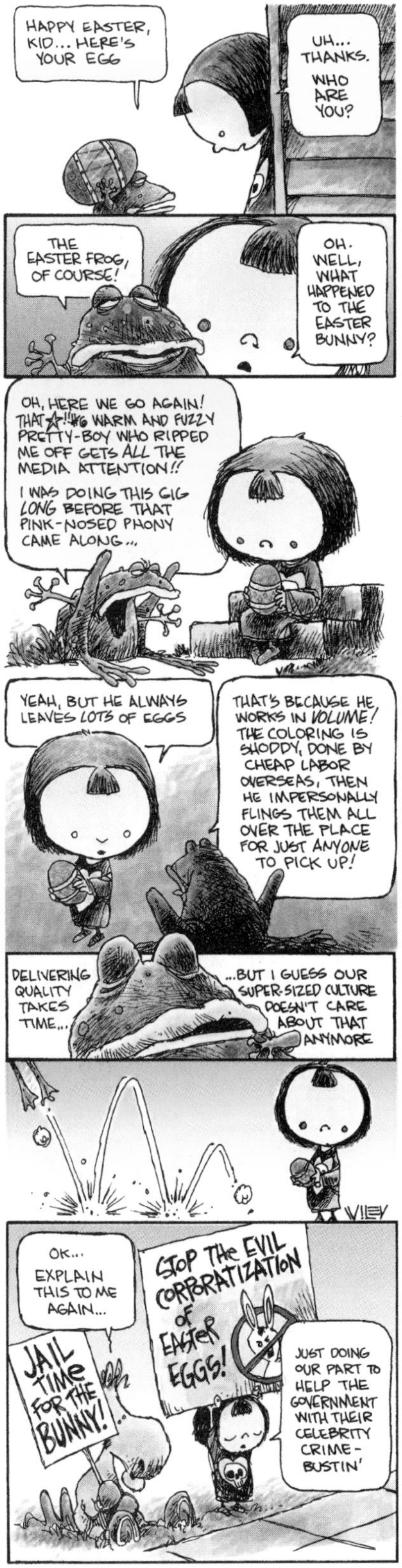
HAPPY EASTER, KID... HERE'S YOUR EGG
UH... THANKS. WHO ARE YOU?
THE EASTER FROG, OF COURSE!
OH. WELL, WHAT HAPPENED TO THE EASTER BUNNY?
OH, HERE WE GO AGAIN! THAT ☆!!#@ WARM AND FUZZY PRETTY-BOY WHO RIPPED ME OFF GETS ALL THE MEDIA ATTENTION!!
I WAS DOING THIS GIG LONG BEFORE THAT PINK-NOSED PHONY CAME ALONG...
YEAH, BUT HE ALWAYS LEAVES LOTS OF EGGS
THAT'S BECAUSE HE WORKS IN VOLUME! THE COLORING IS SHODDY, DONE BY CHEAP LABOR OVERSEAS, THEN HE IMPERSONALLY FLINGS THEM ALL OVER THE PLACE FOR JUST ANYONE TO PICK UP!
DELIVERING QUALITY TAKES TIME...
...BUT I GUESS OUR SUPER-SIZED CULTURE DOESN'T CARE ABOUT THAT ANYMORE
WILEY
OK... EXPLAIN THIS TO ME AGAIN...
STOP THE EVIL CORPORATIZATION of EASTER EGGS!
JAIL TIME FOR THE BUNNY!
JUST DOING OUR PART TO HELP THE GOVERNMENT WITH THEIR CELEBRITY CRIME-BUSTIN'

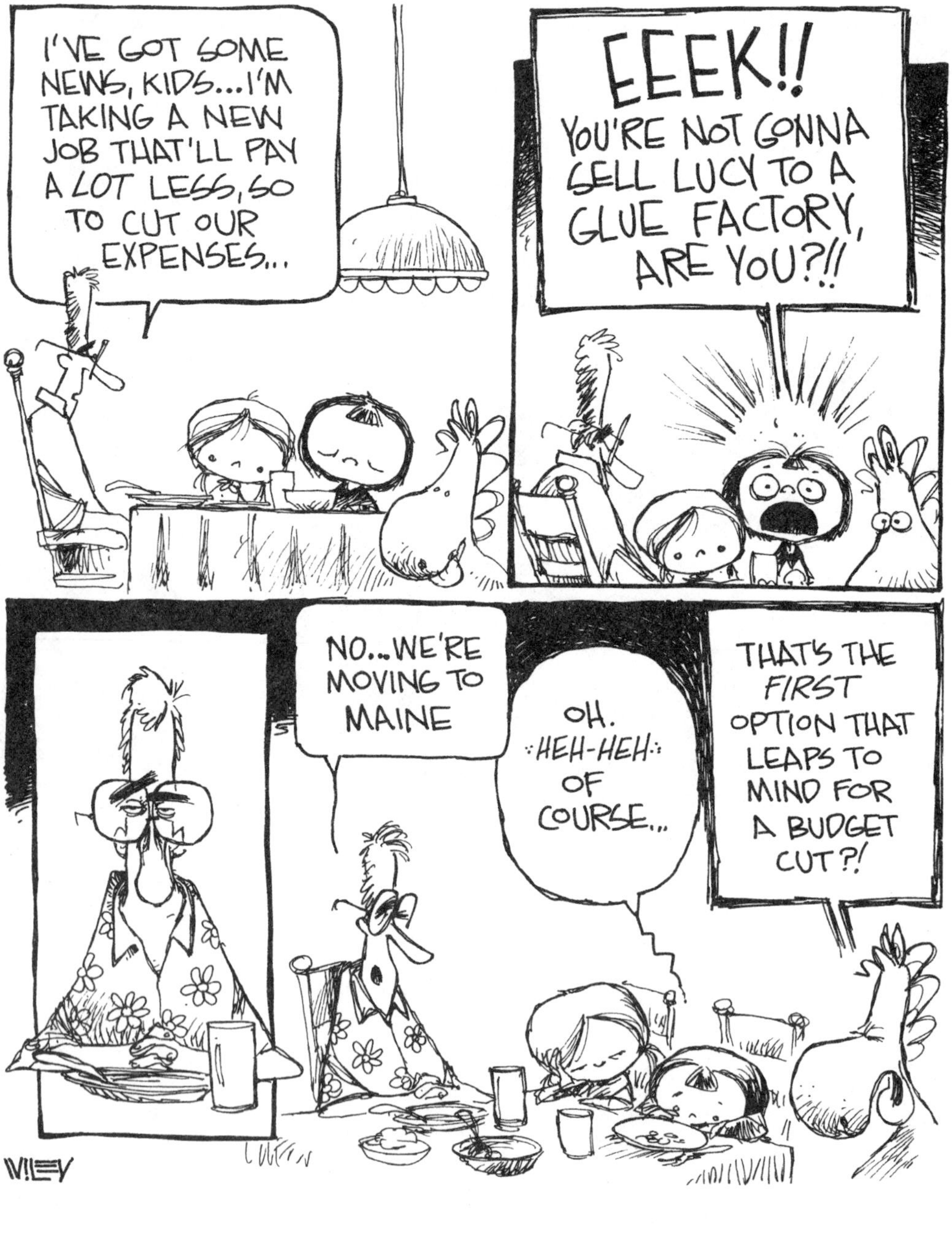
I'VE GOT SOME NEWS, KIDS...I'M TAKING A NEW JOB THAT'LL PAY A LOT LESS, SO TO CUT OUR EXPENSES...
EEEK!!
YOU'RE NOT GONNA SELL LUCY TO A GLUE FACTORY, ARE YOU?!!
NO...WE'RE MOVING TO MAINE
OH. ·HEH-HEH· OF COURSE...
THAT'S THE *FIRST* OPTION THAT LEAPS TO MIND FOR A BUDGET CUT?!
WILEY

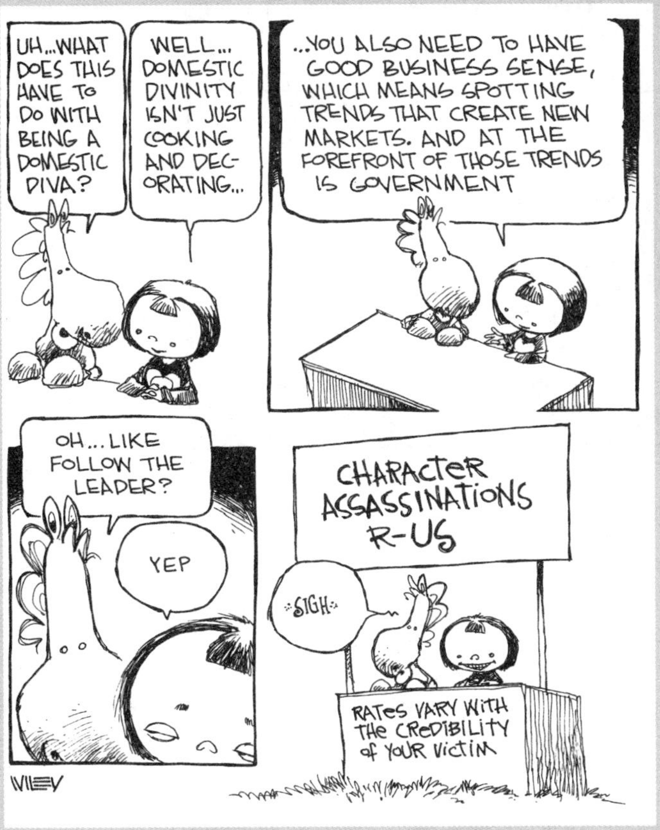
UH...WHAT DOES THIS HAVE TO DO WITH BEING A DOMESTIC DIVA?
WELL... DOMESTIC DIVINITY ISN'T JUST COOKING AND DEC-ORATING...
..YOU ALSO NEED TO HAVE GOOD BUSINESS SENSE, WHICH MEANS SPOTTING TRENDS THAT CREATE NEW MARKETS. AND AT THE FOREFRONT OF THOSE TRENDS IS GOVERNMENT
OH... LIKE FOLLOW THE LEADER?
YEP
CHARACTER ASSASSINATIONS R-US
SIGH
RATES VARY WITH THE CREDIBILITY OF YOUR VICTIM
WILEY

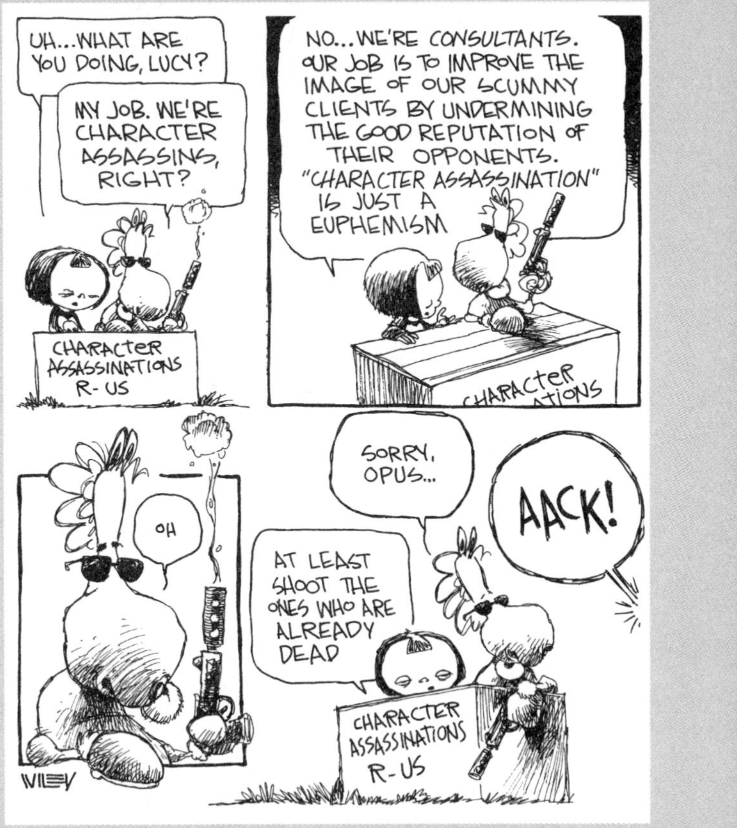
UH...WHAT ARE YOU DOING, LUCY?
MY JOB. WE'RE CHARACTER ASSASSINS, RIGHT?
CHARACTER ASSASSINATIONS R-US
NO... WE'RE CONSULTANTS. OUR JOB IS TO IMPROVE THE IMAGE OF OUR SCUMMY CLIENTS BY UNDERMINING THE GOOD REPUTATION OF THEIR OPPONENTS. "CHARACTER ASSASSINATION" IS JUST A EUPHEMISM
OH
SORRY, OPUS...
AT LEAST SHOOT THE ONES WHO ARE ALREADY DEAD
AACK!
CHARACTER ASSASSINATIONS R-US
WILEY

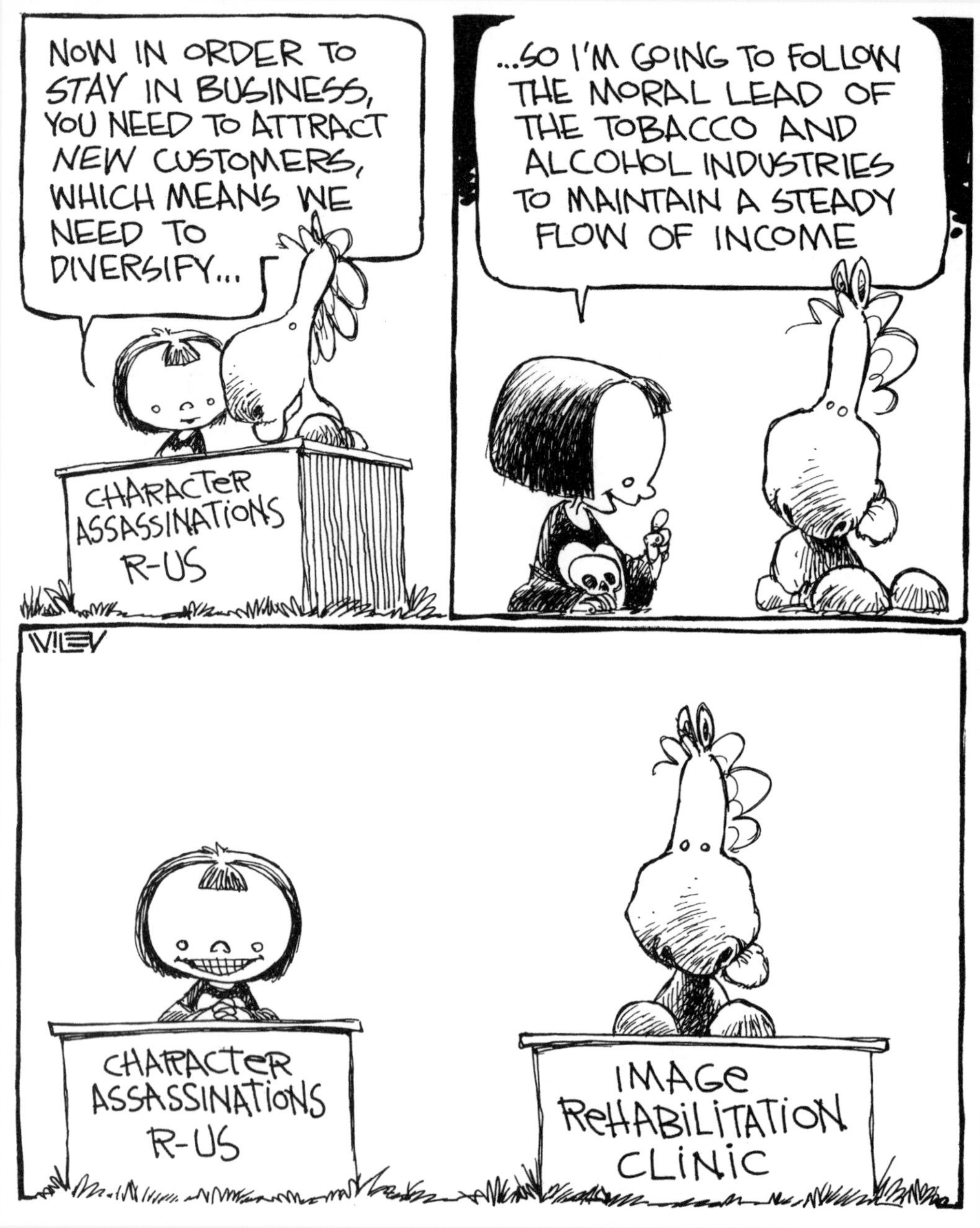
NOW IN ORDER TO STAY IN BUSINESS, YOU NEED TO ATTRACT NEW CUSTOMERS, WHICH MEANS WE NEED TO DIVERSIFY...
CHARACTER ASSASSINATIONS R-US
...SO I'M GOING TO FOLLOW THE MORAL LEAD OF THE TOBACCO AND ALCOHOL INDUSTRIES TO MAINTAIN A STEADY FLOW OF INCOME
WILEY
CHARACTER ASSASSINATIONS R-US
IMAGE REHABILITATION CLINIC

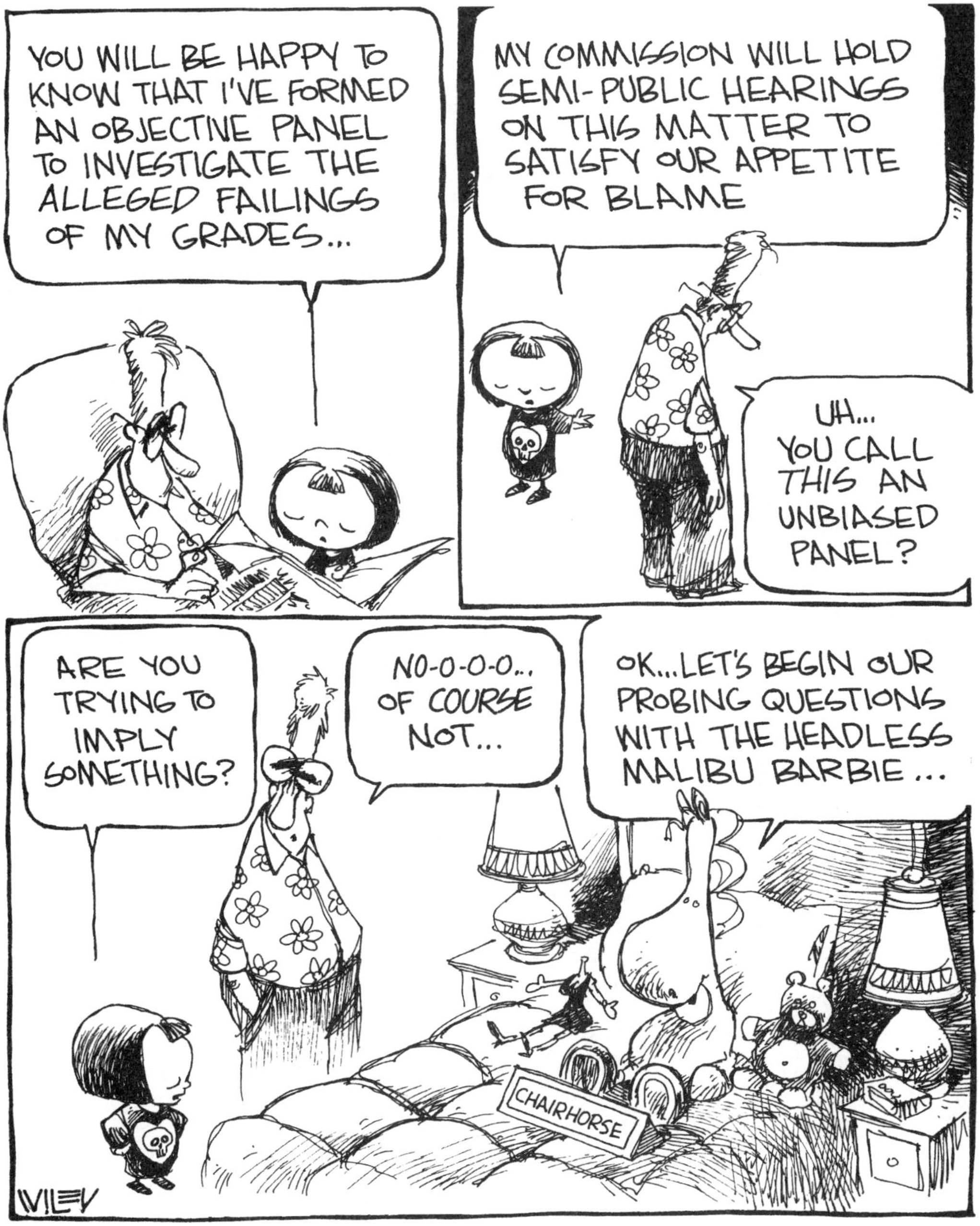
YOU WILL BE HAPPY TO KNOW THAT I'VE FORMED AN OBJECTIVE PANEL TO INVESTIGATE THE ALLEGED FAILINGS OF MY GRADES...
MY COMMISSION WILL HOLD SEMI-PUBLIC HEARINGS ON THIS MATTER TO SATISFY OUR APPETITE FOR BLAME
UH... YOU CALL THIS AN UNBIASED PANEL?
ARE YOU TRYING TO IMPLY SOMETHING?
NO-O-O-O... OF COURSE NOT...
OK...LET'S BEGIN OUR PROBING QUESTIONS WITH THE HEADLESS MALIBU BARBIE...
CHAIRHORSE
WILEY

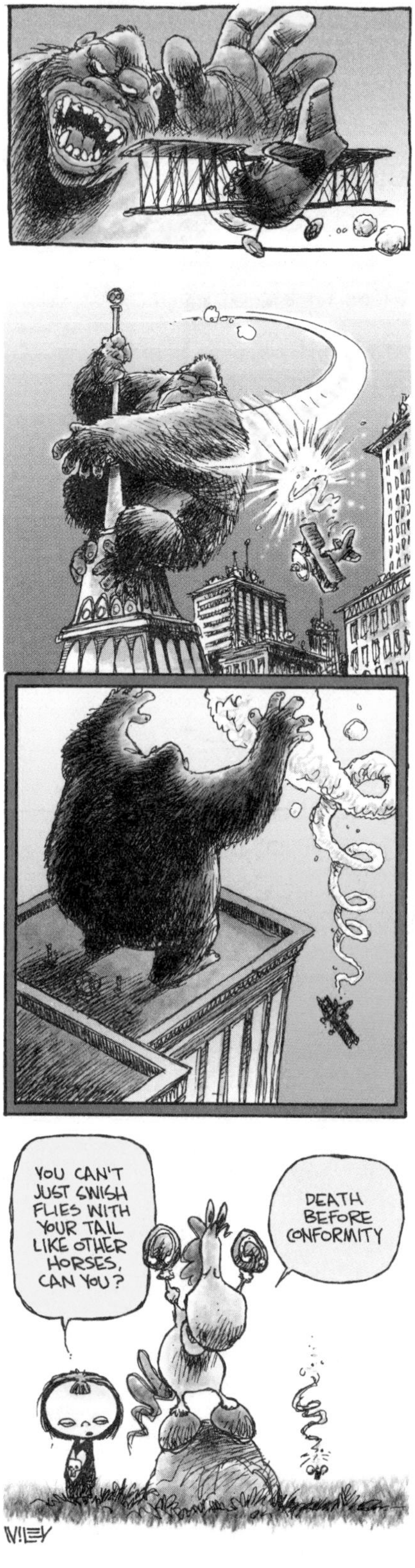
YOU CAN'T JUST SWISH FLIES WITH YOUR TAIL LIKE OTHER HORSES, CAN YOU?
DEATH BEFORE CONFORMITY
WILEY

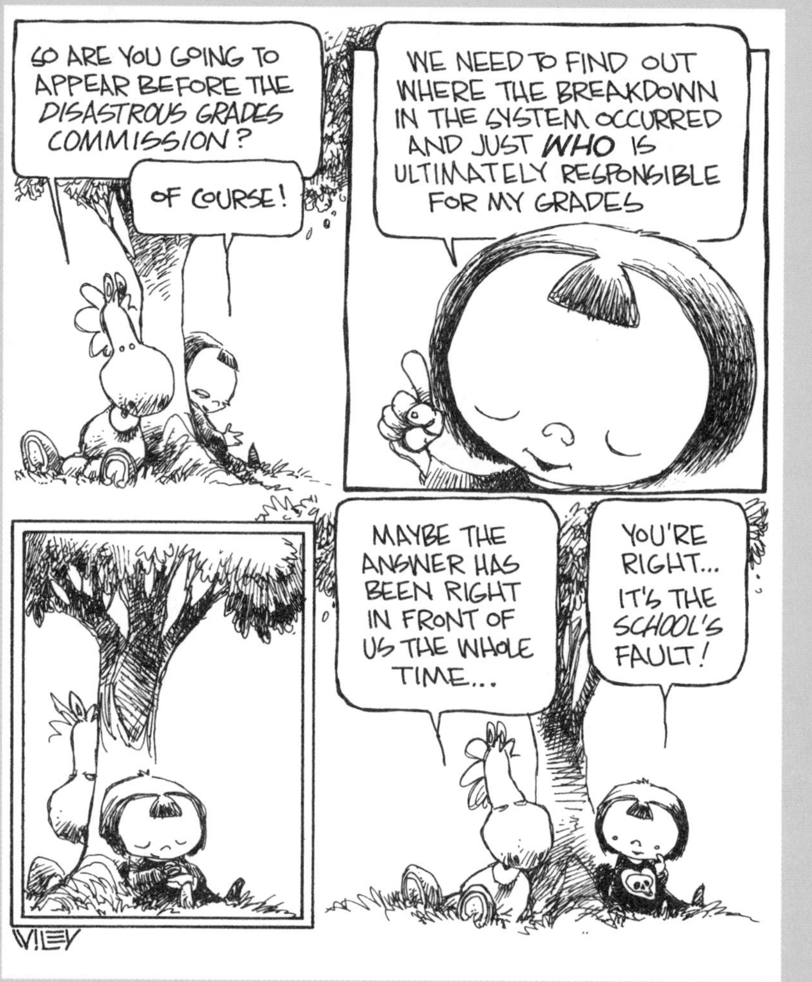
SO ARE YOU GOING TO APPEAR BEFORE THE *DISASTROUS GRADES* COMMISSION?
OF COURSE!
WE NEED TO FIND OUT WHERE THE BREAKDOWN IN THE SYSTEM OCCURRED AND JUST **WHO** IS ULTIMATELY RESPONSIBLE FOR MY GRADES
MAYBE THE ANSWER HAS BEEN RIGHT IN FRONT OF US THE WHOLE TIME...
YOU'RE RIGHT... IT'S THE SCHOOL'S FAULT!
WILEY

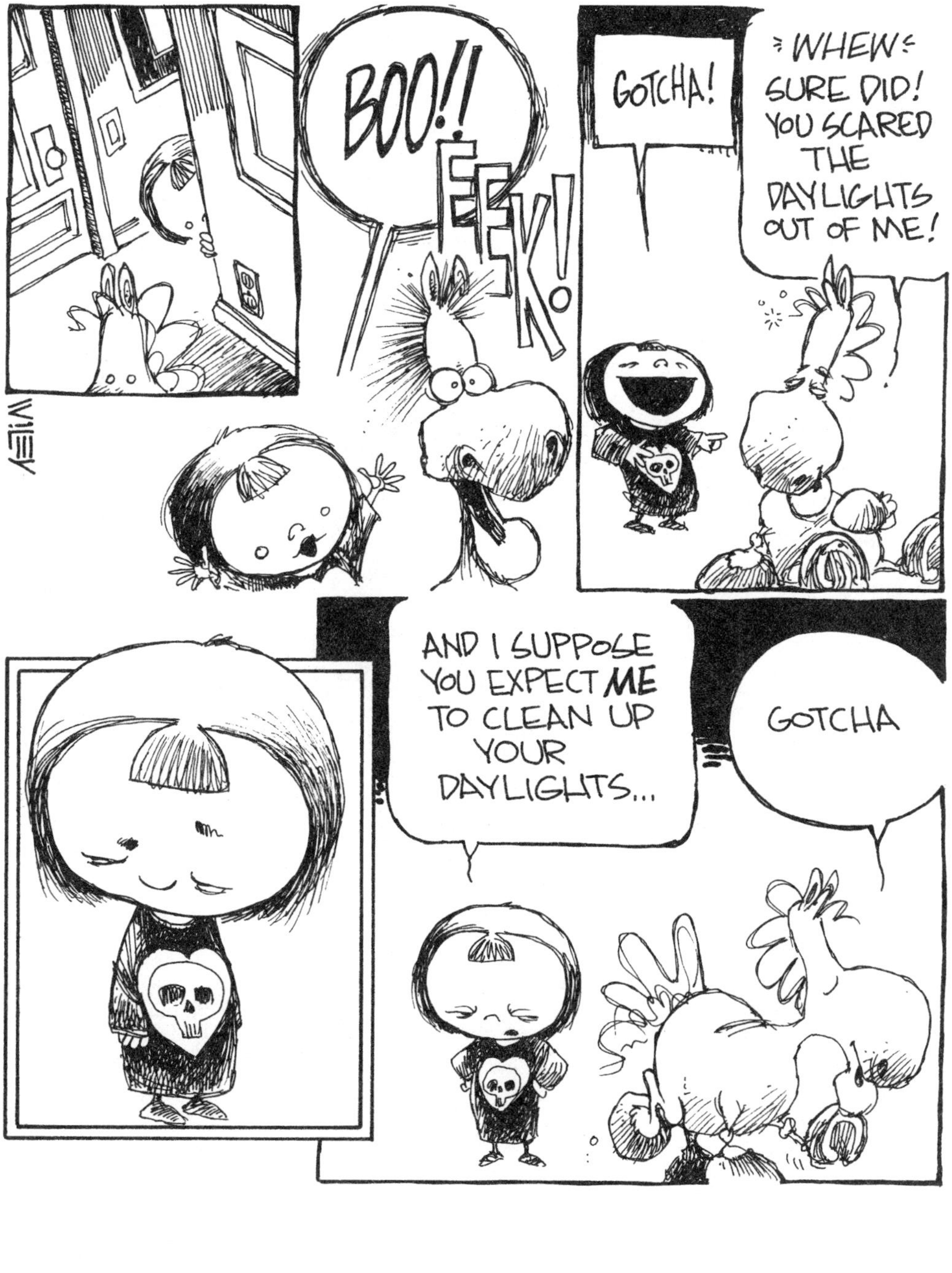
BOO!!
EEEK!
GOTCHA!
WHEW
SURE DID! YOU SCARED THE DAYLIGHTS OUT OF ME!
AND I SUPPOSE YOU EXPECT **ME** TO CLEAN UP YOUR DAYLIGHTS...
GOTCHA

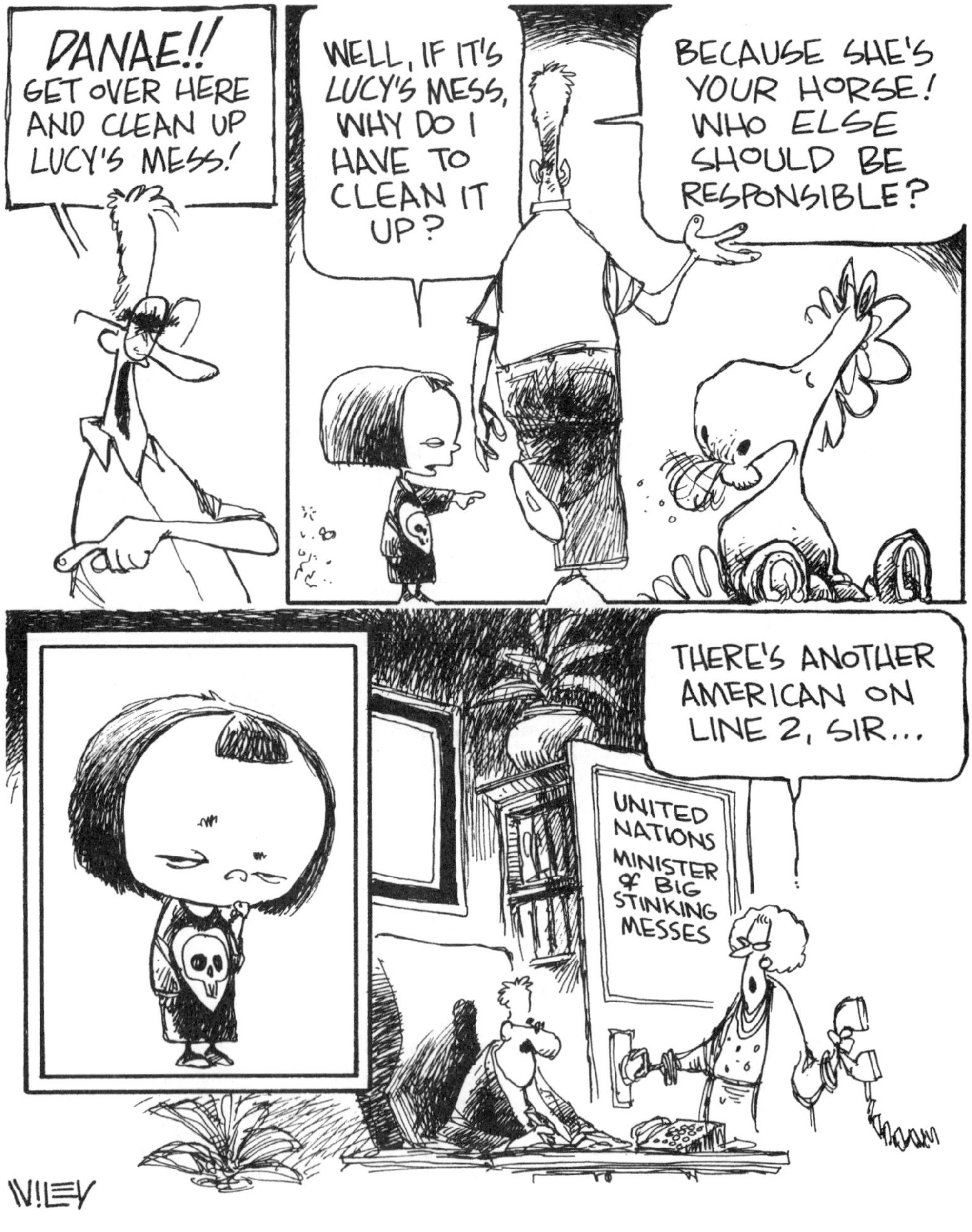
DANAE!! GET OVER HERE AND CLEAN UP LUCY'S MESS!
WELL, IF IT'S LUCY'S MESS, WHY DO I HAVE TO CLEAN IT UP?
BECAUSE SHE'S YOUR HORSE! WHO ELSE SHOULD BE RESPONSIBLE?
THERE'S ANOTHER AMERICAN ON LINE 2, SIR...
UNITED NATIONS MINISTER of BIG STINKING MESSES
WILEY

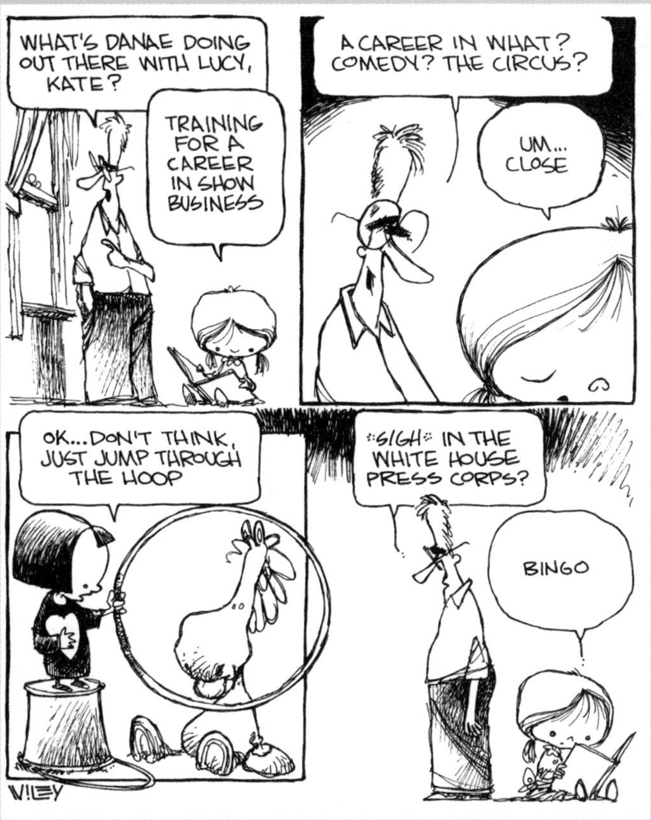
WHAT'S DANAE DOING OUT THERE WITH LUCY, KATE?
TRAINING FOR A CAREER IN SHOW BUSINESS
A CAREER IN WHAT? COMEDY? THE CIRCUS?
UM... CLOSE
OK... DON'T THINK, JUST JUMP THROUGH THE HOOP
SIGH IN THE WHITE HOUSE PRESS CORPS?
BINGO
WILEY

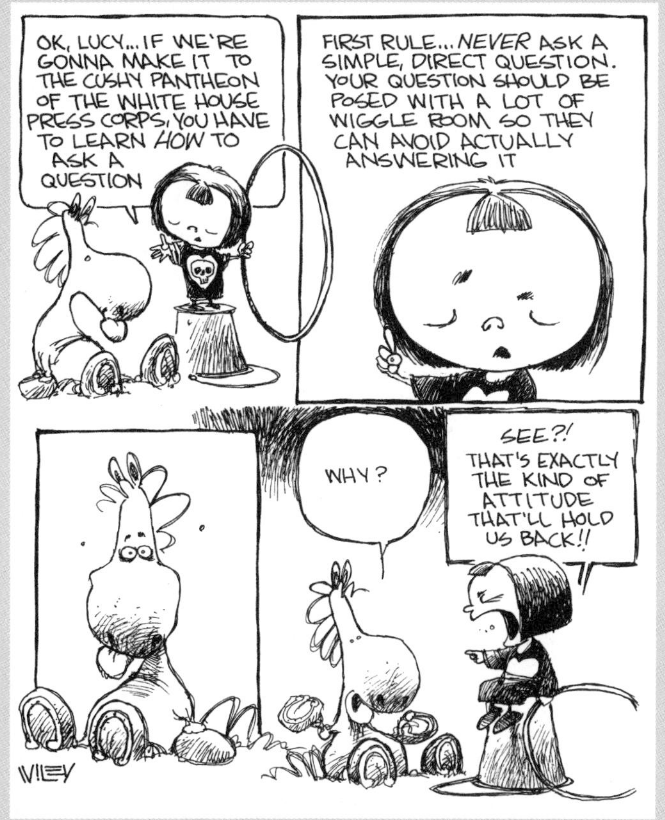
OK, LUCY... IF WE'RE GONNA MAKE IT TO THE CUSHY PANTHEON OF THE WHITE HOUSE PRESS CORPS, YOU HAVE TO LEARN HOW TO ASK A QUESTION
FIRST RULE... NEVER ASK A SIMPLE, DIRECT QUESTION. YOUR QUESTION SHOULD BE POSED WITH A LOT OF WIGGLE ROOM SO THEY CAN AVOID ACTUALLY ANSWERING IT
WHY?
SEE?! THAT'S EXACTLY THE KIND OF ATTITUDE THAT'LL HOLD US BACK!!
WILEY

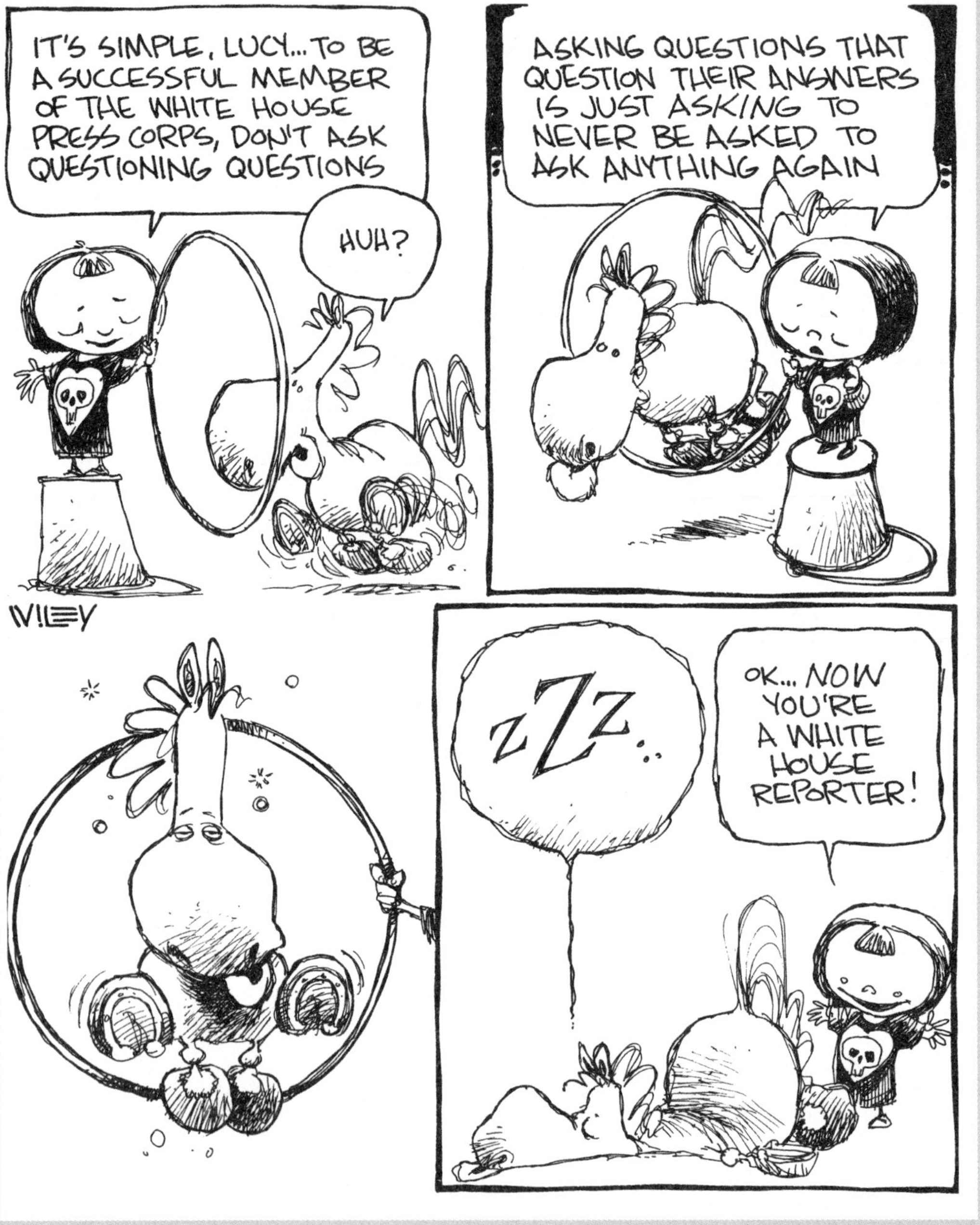
IT'S SIMPLE, LUCY... TO BE A SUCCESSFUL MEMBER OF THE WHITE HOUSE PRESS CORPS, DON'T ASK QUESTIONING QUESTIONS
HUH?
ASKING QUESTIONS THAT QUESTION THEIR ANSWERS IS JUST ASKING TO NEVER BE ASKED TO ASK ANYTHING AGAIN
WILEY
zZz..
OK... NOW YOU'RE A WHITE HOUSE REPORTER!

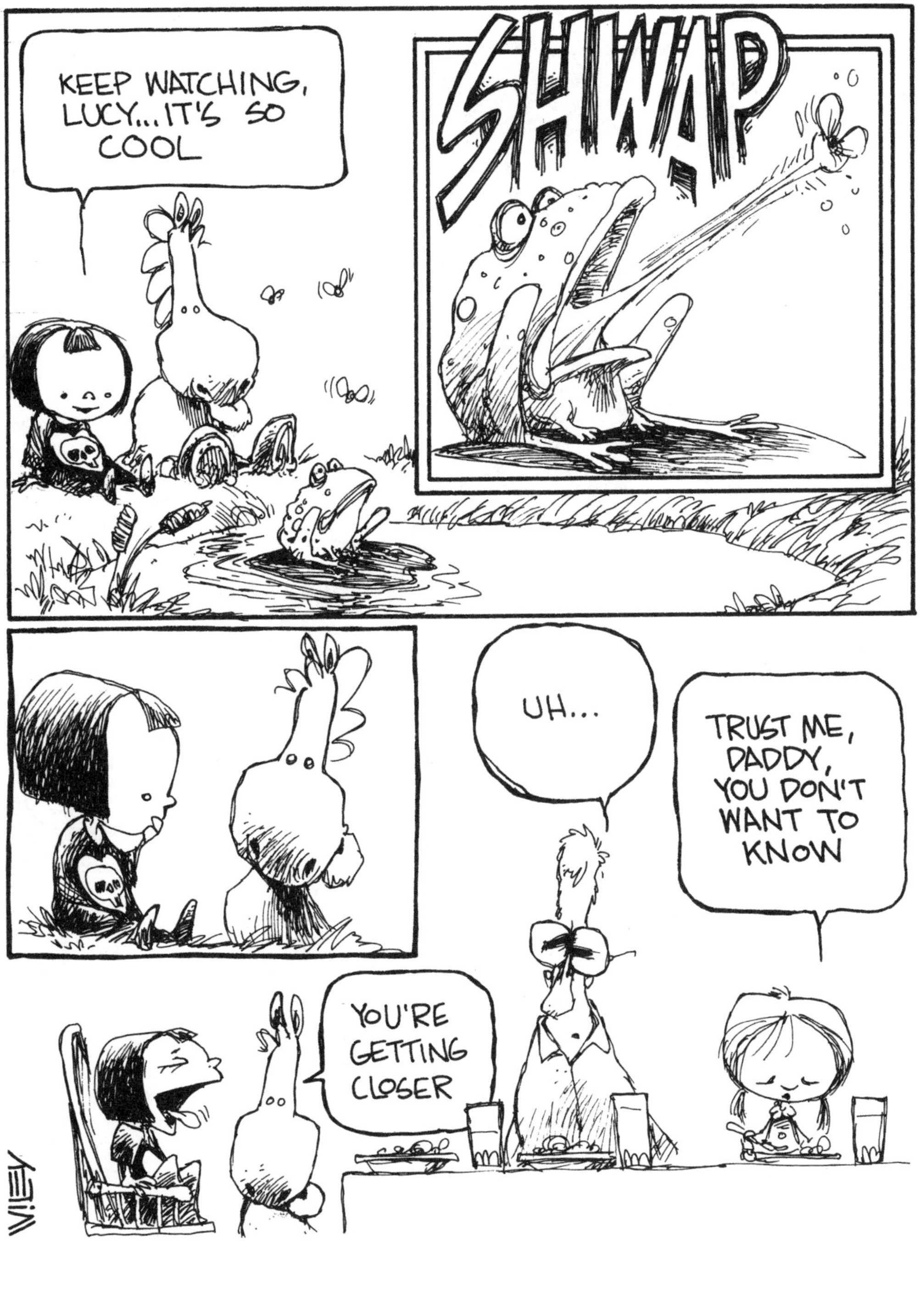
KEEP WATCHING, LUCY... IT'S SO COOL
SHWAP
UH...
TRUST ME, DADDY, YOU DON'T WANT TO KNOW
YOU'RE GETTING CLOSER
WILEY

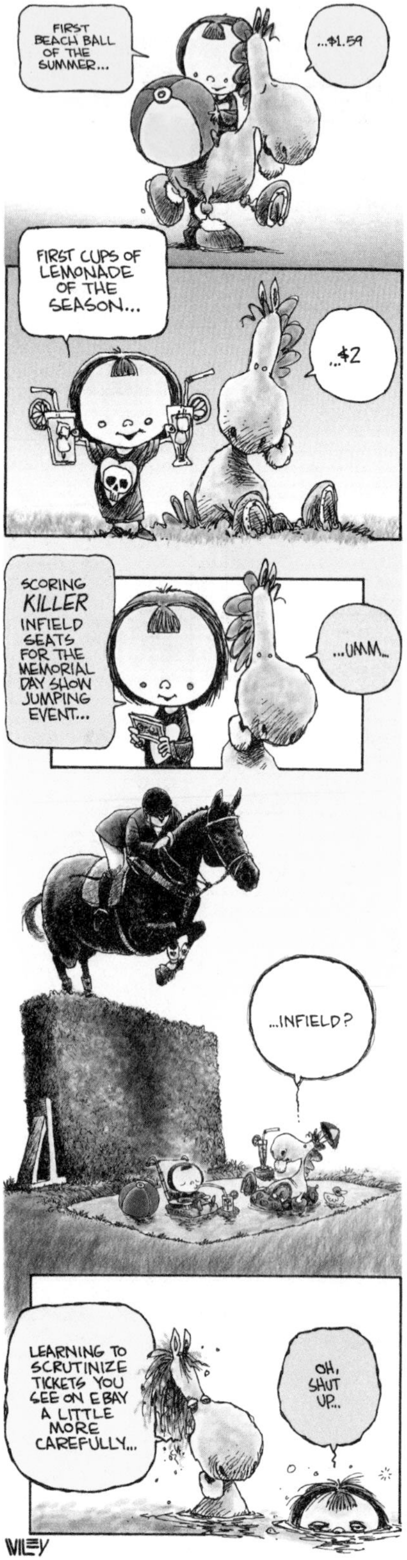
FIRST BEACH BALL OF THE SUMMER...
...$1.59
FIRST CUPS OF LEMONADE OF THE SEASON...
...$2
SCORING KILLER INFIELD SEATS FOR THE MEMORIAL DAY SHOW JUMPING EVENT...
...UMM...
...INFIELD?
LEARNING TO SCRUTINIZE TICKETS YOU SEE ON EBAY A LITTLE MORE CAREFULLY...
OH, SHUT UP...
WILEY

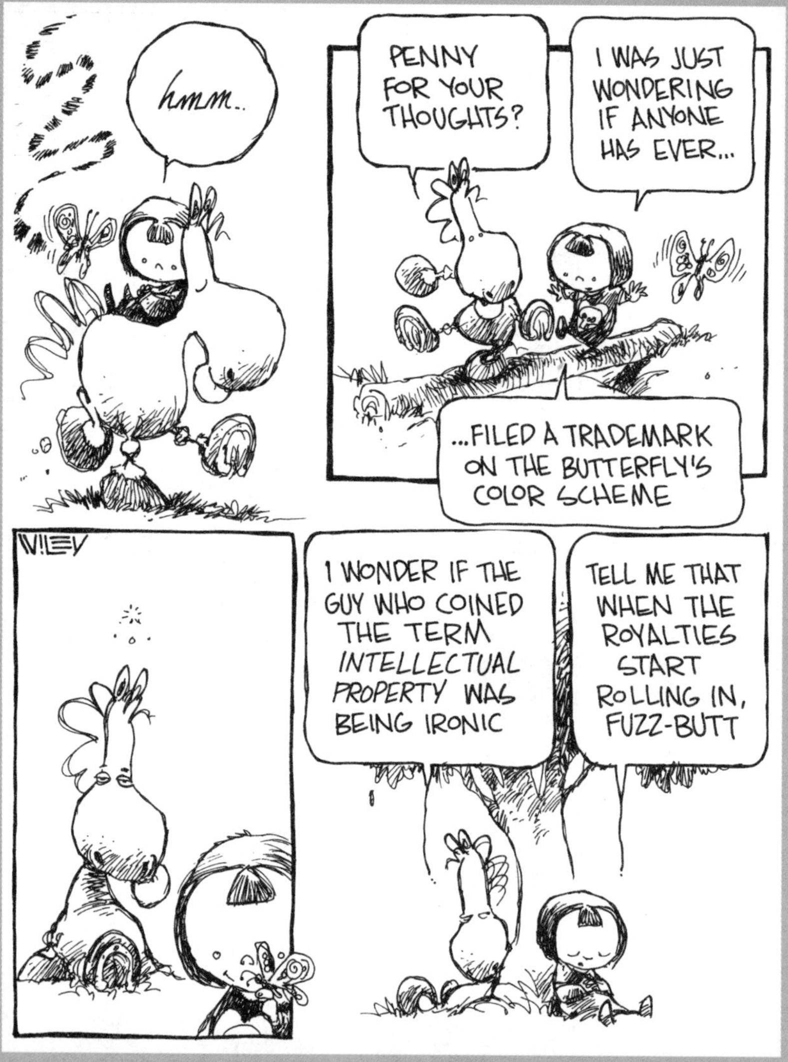
hmm..
PENNY FOR YOUR THOUGHTS?
I WAS JUST WONDERING IF ANYONE HAS EVER...
...FILED A TRADEMARK ON THE BUTTERFLY'S COLOR SCHEME
WILEY
I WONDER IF THE GUY WHO COINED THE TERM INTELLECTUAL PROPERTY WAS BEING IRONIC
TELL ME THAT WHEN THE ROYALTIES START ROLLING IN, FUZZ-BUTT

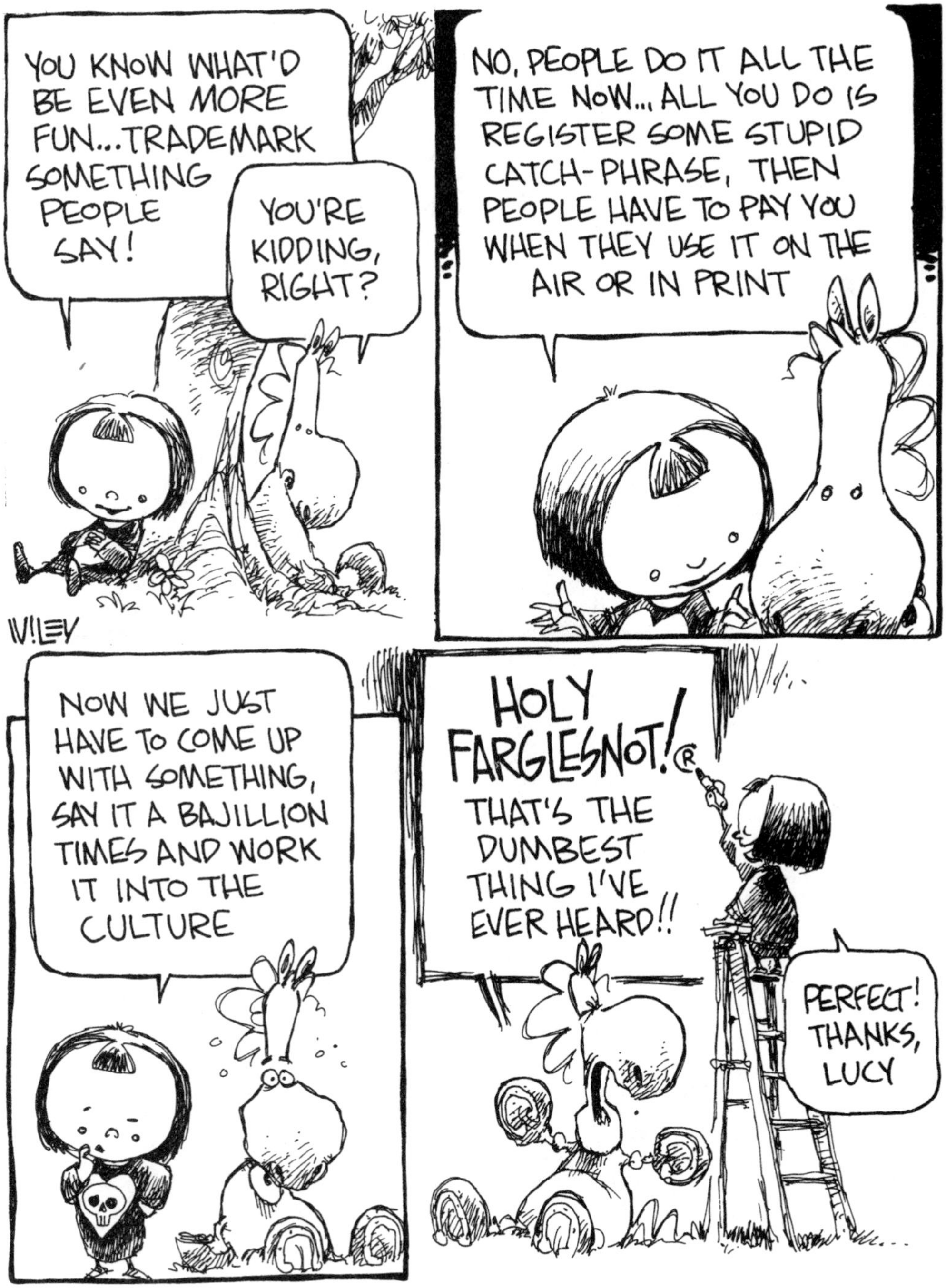
YOU KNOW WHAT'D BE EVEN MORE FUN...TRADEMARK SOMETHING PEOPLE SAY!
YOU'RE KIDDING, RIGHT?
WILEY
NO, PEOPLE DO IT ALL THE TIME NOW... ALL YOU DO IS REGISTER SOME STUPID CATCH-PHRASE, THEN PEOPLE HAVE TO PAY YOU WHEN THEY USE IT ON THE AIR OR IN PRINT
NOW WE JUST HAVE TO COME UP WITH SOMETHING, SAY IT A BAJILLION TIMES AND WORK IT INTO THE CULTURE
HOLY FARGLESNOT!®
THAT'S THE DUMBEST THING I'VE EVER HEARD!!
PERFECT! THANKS, LUCY

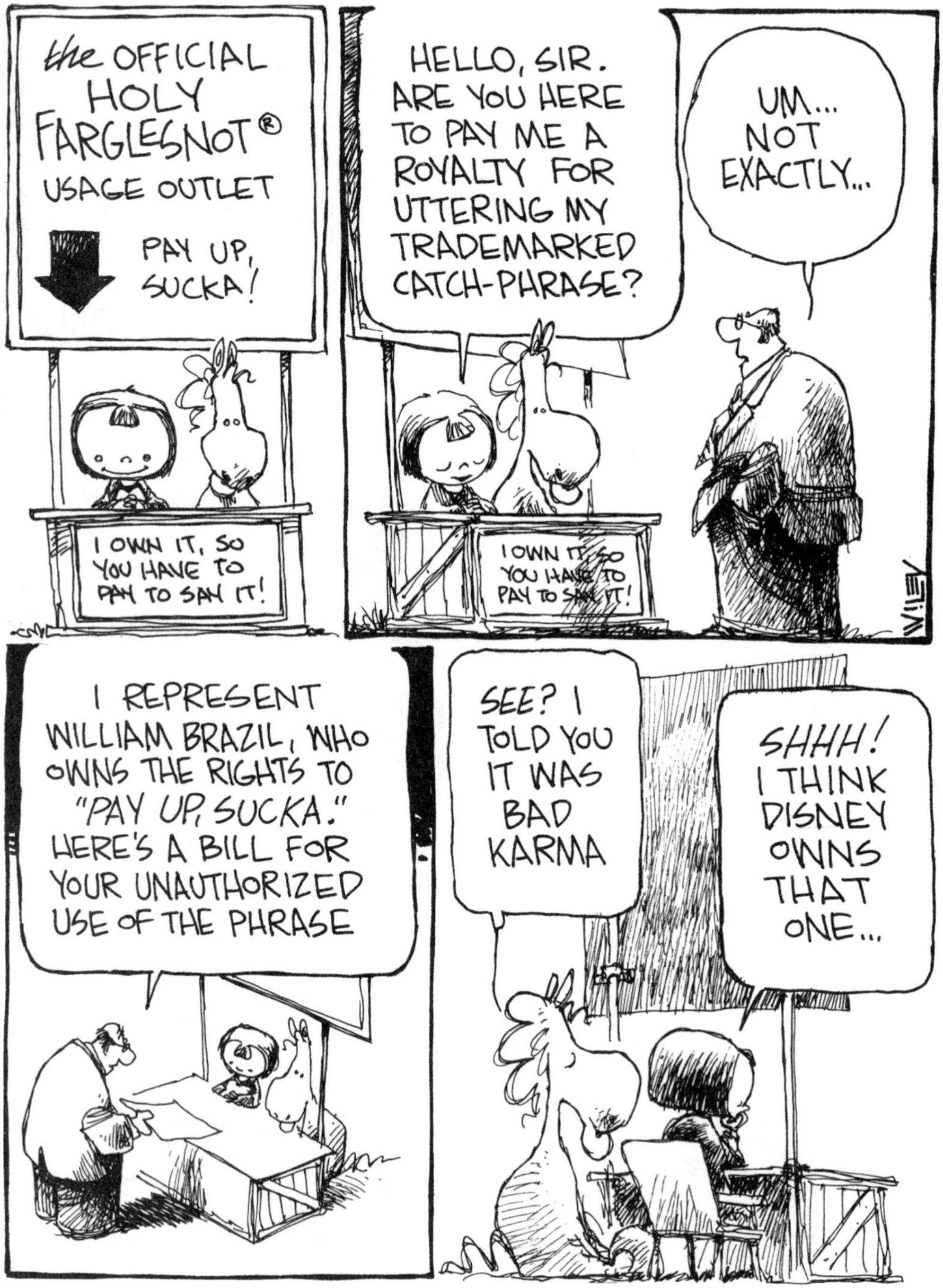

the OFFICIAL HOLY FARGLESNOT® USAGE OUTLET
PAY UP, SUCKA!
I OWN IT, SO YOU HAVE TO PAY TO SAY IT!
HELLO, SIR. ARE YOU HERE TO PAY ME A ROYALTY FOR UTTERING MY TRADEMARKED CATCH-PHRASE?
UM... NOT EXACTLY...
I OWN IT, SO YOU HAVE TO PAY TO SAY IT!
WILEY
I REPRESENT WILLIAM BRAZIL, WHO OWNS THE RIGHTS TO "PAY UP, SUCKA." HERE'S A BILL FOR YOUR UNAUTHORIZED USE OF THE PHRASE
SEE? I TOLD YOU IT WAS BAD KARMA
SHHH! I THINK DISNEY OWNS THAT ONE...

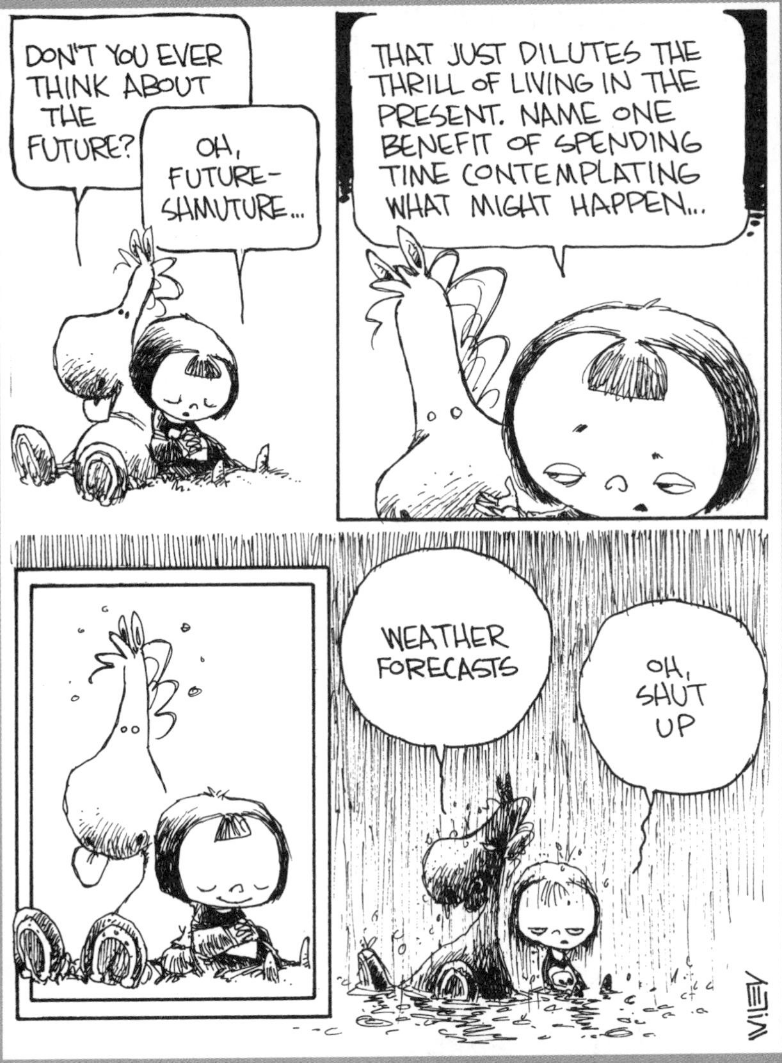
DON'T YOU EVER THINK ABOUT THE FUTURE?
OH, FUTURE-SHMUTURE...
THAT JUST DILUTES THE THRILL OF LIVING IN THE PRESENT. NAME ONE BENEFIT OF SPENDING TIME CONTEMPLATING WHAT MIGHT HAPPEN...
WEATHER FORECASTS
OH, SHUT UP
WILEY

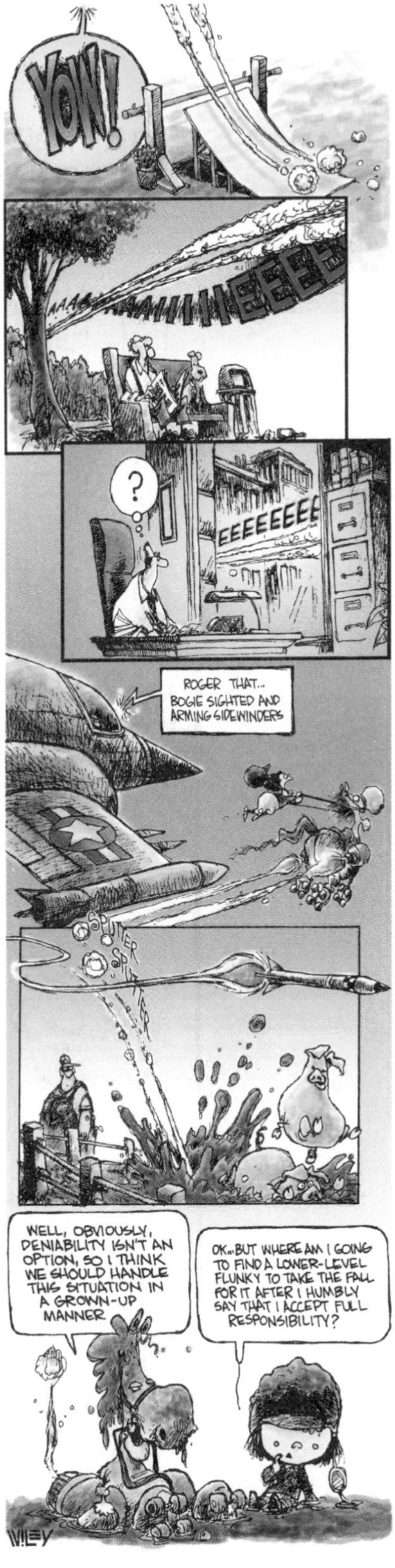
YOW!
AAAAAAAAIIIIIEEEEE
?
EEEEEEEE
ROGER THAT... BOGIE SIGHTED AND ARMING SIDEWINDERS
SPUTTER SPUTTER
WELL, OBVIOUSLY, DENIABILITY ISN'T AN OPTION, SO I THINK WE SHOULD HANDLE THIS SITUATION IN A GROWN-UP MANNER
OK...BUT WHERE AM I GOING TO FIND A LOWER-LEVEL FLUNKY TO TAKE THE FALL FOR IT AFTER I HUMBLY SAY THAT I ACCEPT FULL RESPONSIBILITY?
WILEY

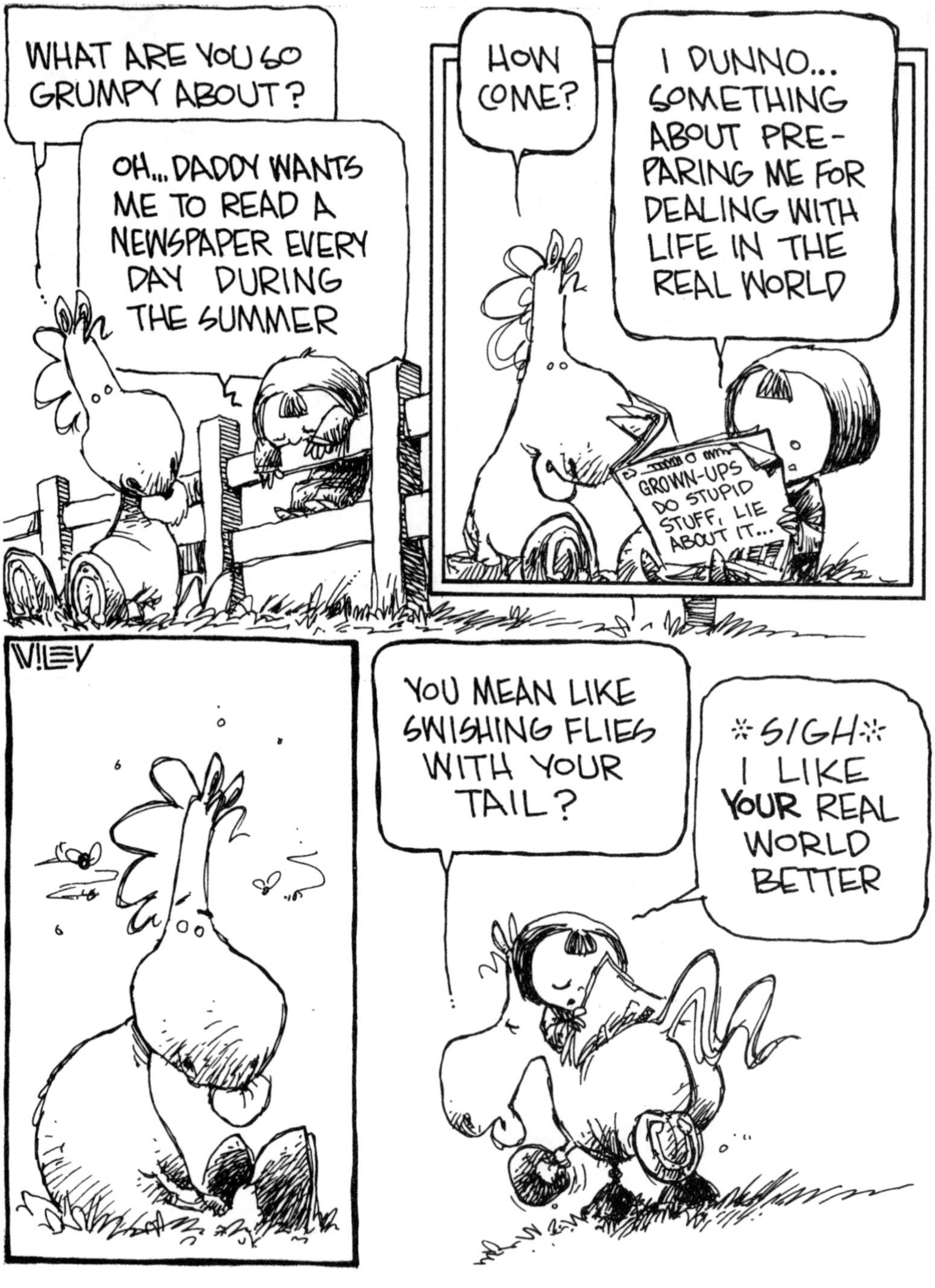
WHAT ARE YOU SO GRUMPY ABOUT?
OH... DADDY WANTS ME TO READ A NEWSPAPER EVERY DAY DURING THE SUMMER
HOW COME?
I DUNNO... SOMETHING ABOUT PRE-PARING ME FOR DEALING WITH LIFE IN THE REAL WORLD
GROWN-UPS DO STUPID STUFF, LIE ABOUT IT...
WILEY
YOU MEAN LIKE SWISHING FLIES WITH YOUR TAIL?
SIGH I LIKE **YOUR** REAL WORLD BETTER

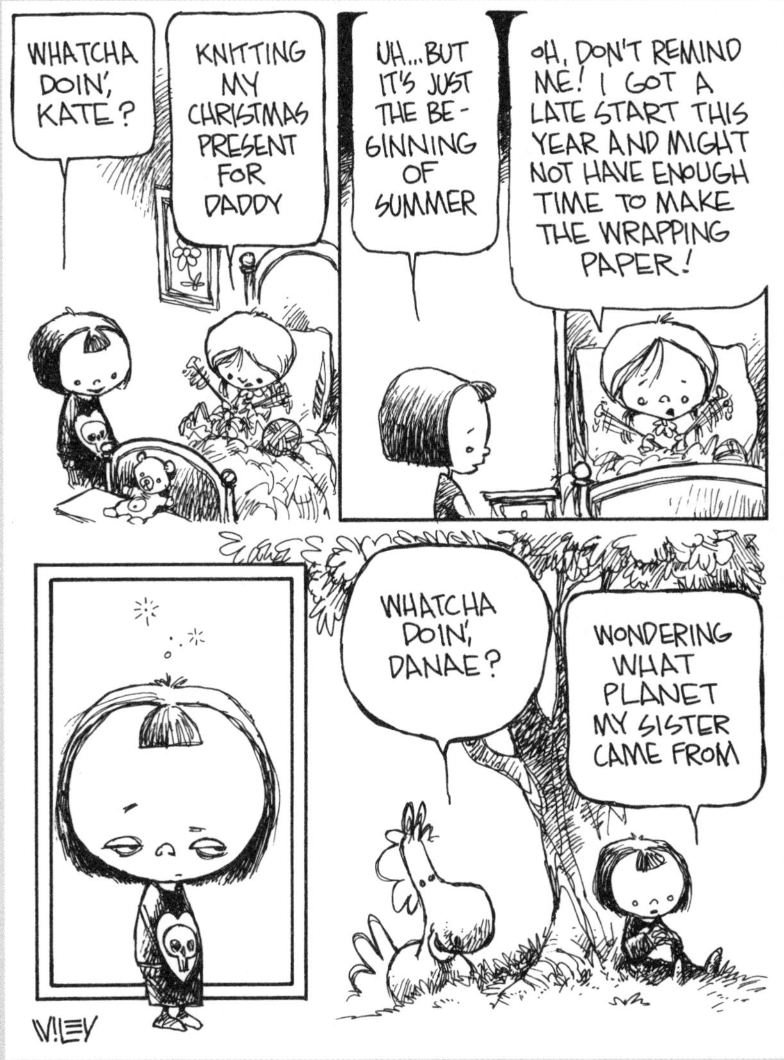
WHATCHA DOIN', KATE?
KNITTING MY CHRISTMAS PRESENT FOR DADDY
UH...BUT IT'S JUST THE BE-GINNING OF SUMMER
OH, DON'T REMIND ME! I GOT A LATE START THIS YEAR AND MIGHT NOT HAVE ENOUGH TIME TO MAKE THE WRAPPING PAPER!
WHATCHA DOIN', DANAE?
WONDERING WHAT PLANET MY SISTER CAME FROM
W!LEY

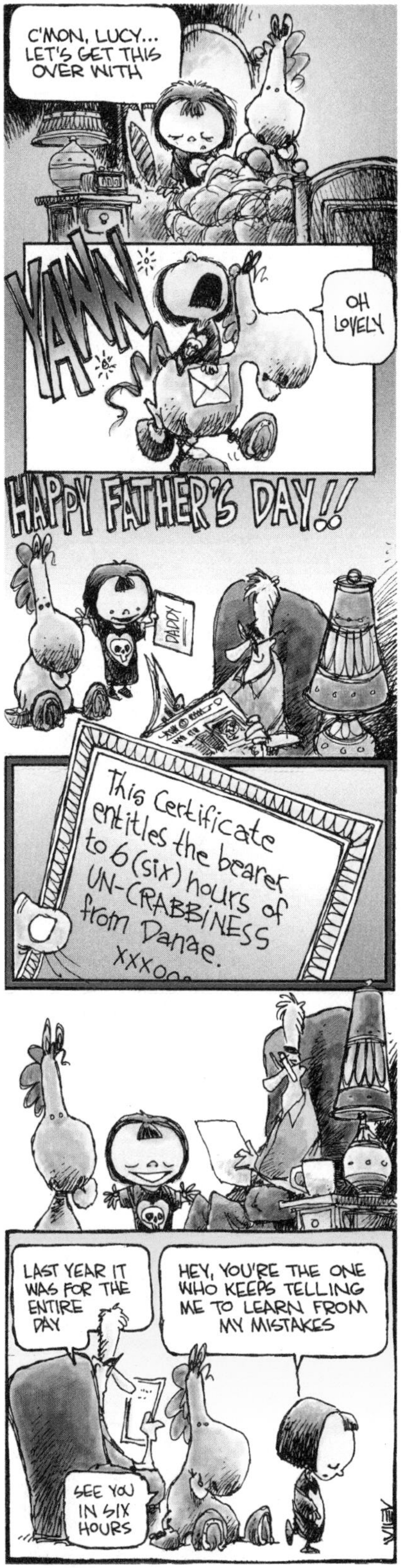
C'MON, LUCY... LET'S GET THIS OVER WITH
YAWN
OH LOVELY
HAPPY FATHER'S DAY!!
DADDY
This Certificate entitles the bearer to 6 (six) hours of UN-CRABBINESS from Danae.
LAST YEAR IT WAS FOR THE ENTIRE DAY
HEY, YOU'RE THE ONE WHO KEEPS TELLING ME TO LEARN FROM MY MISTAKES
SEE YOU IN SIX HOURS
W!LEY

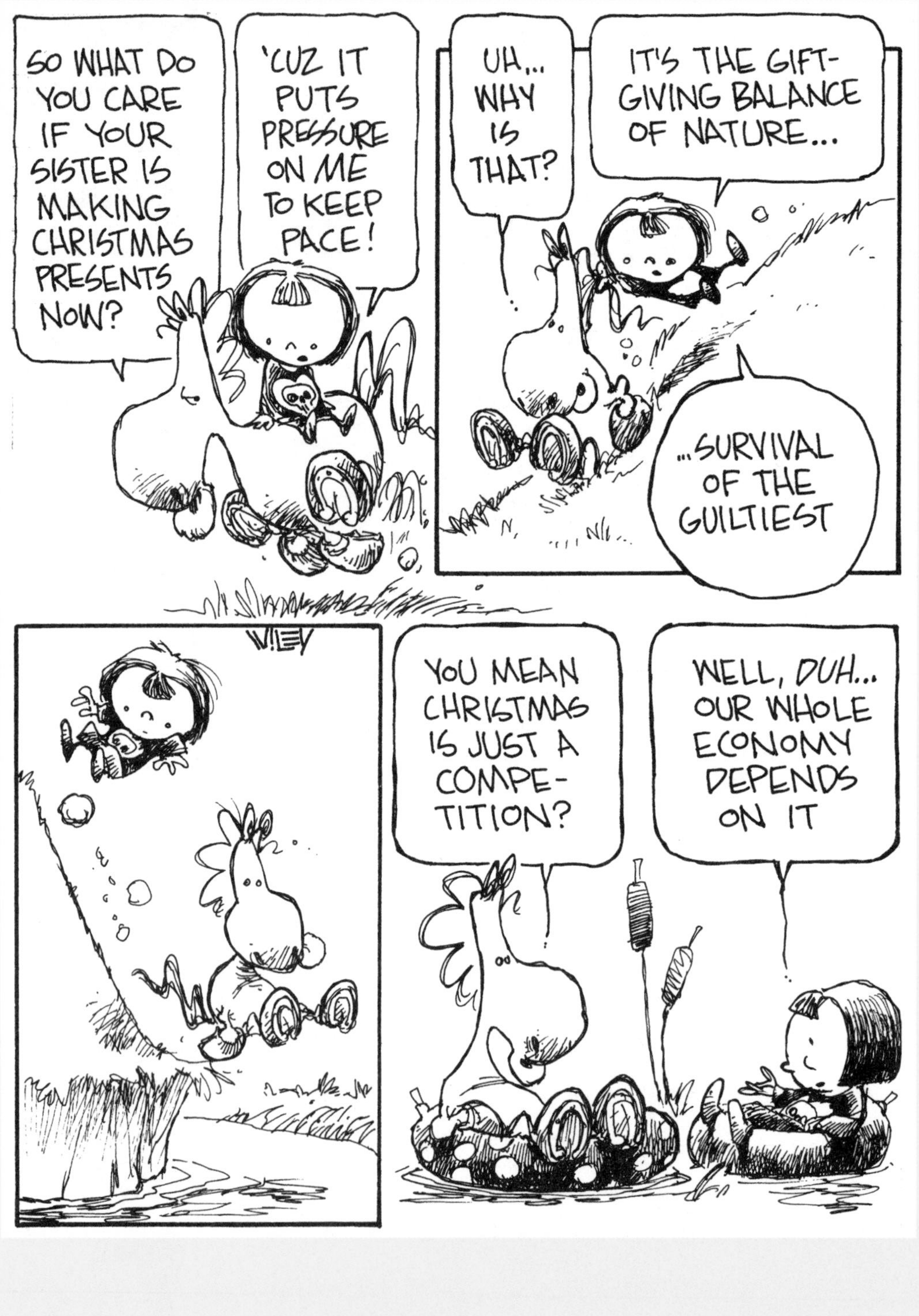
SO WHAT DO YOU CARE IF YOUR SISTER IS MAKING CHRISTMAS PRESENTS NOW?
'CUZ IT PUTS PRESSURE ON ME TO KEEP PACE!
UH... WHY IS THAT?
IT'S THE GIFT-GIVING BALANCE OF NATURE...
...SURVIVAL OF THE GUILTIEST
WILEY
YOU MEAN CHRISTMAS IS JUST A COMPE-TITION?
WELL, DUH... OUR WHOLE ECONOMY DEPENDS ON IT

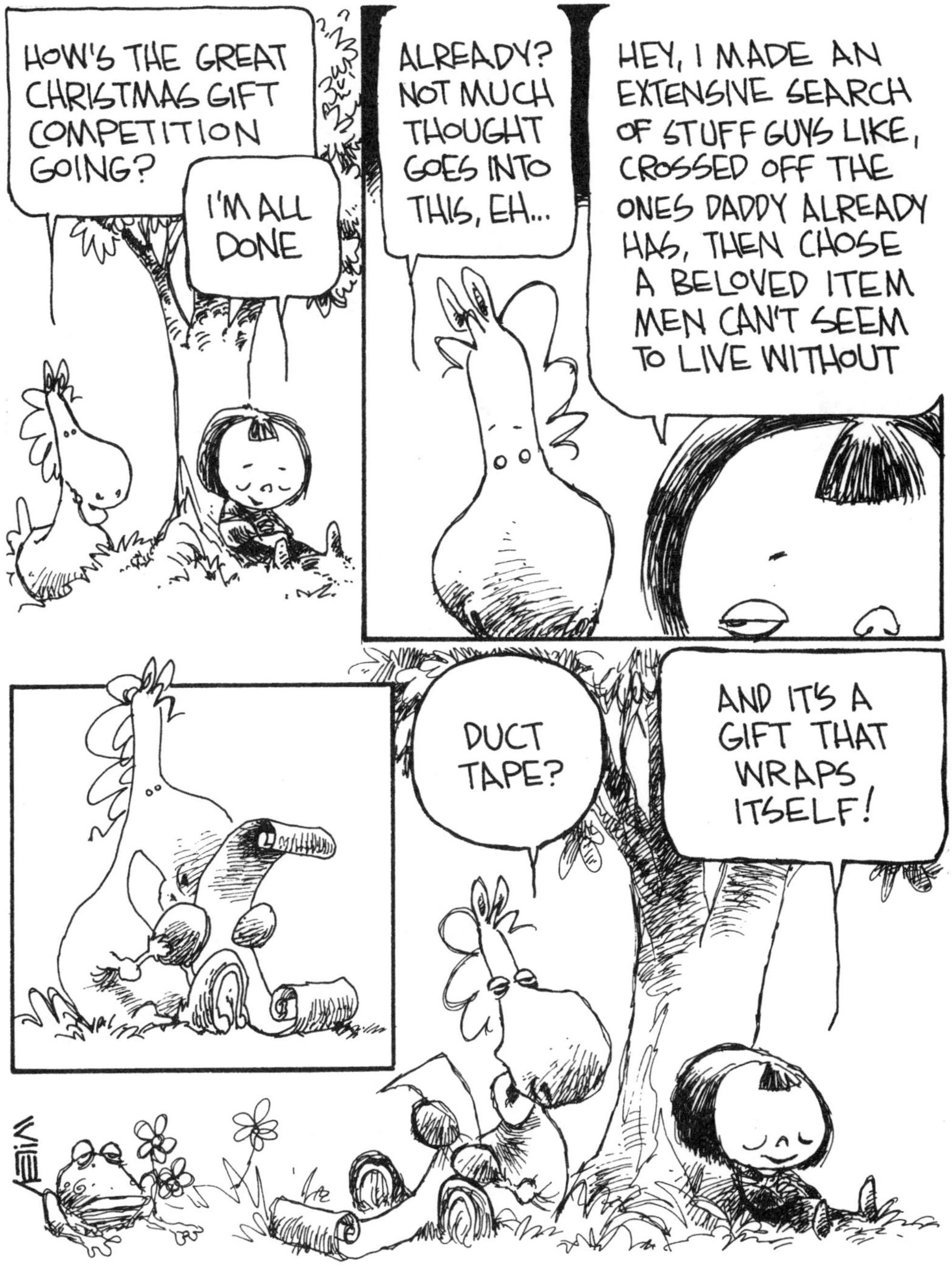
HOW'S THE GREAT CHRISTMAS GIFT COMPETITION GOING?
I'M ALL DONE
ALREADY? NOT MUCH THOUGHT GOES INTO THIS, EH...
HEY, I MADE AN EXTENSIVE SEARCH OF STUFF GUYS LIKE, CROSSED OFF THE ONES DADDY ALREADY HAS, THEN CHOSE A BELOVED ITEM MEN CAN'T SEEM TO LIVE WITHOUT
DUCT TAPE?
AND IT'S A GIFT THAT WRAPS ITSELF!

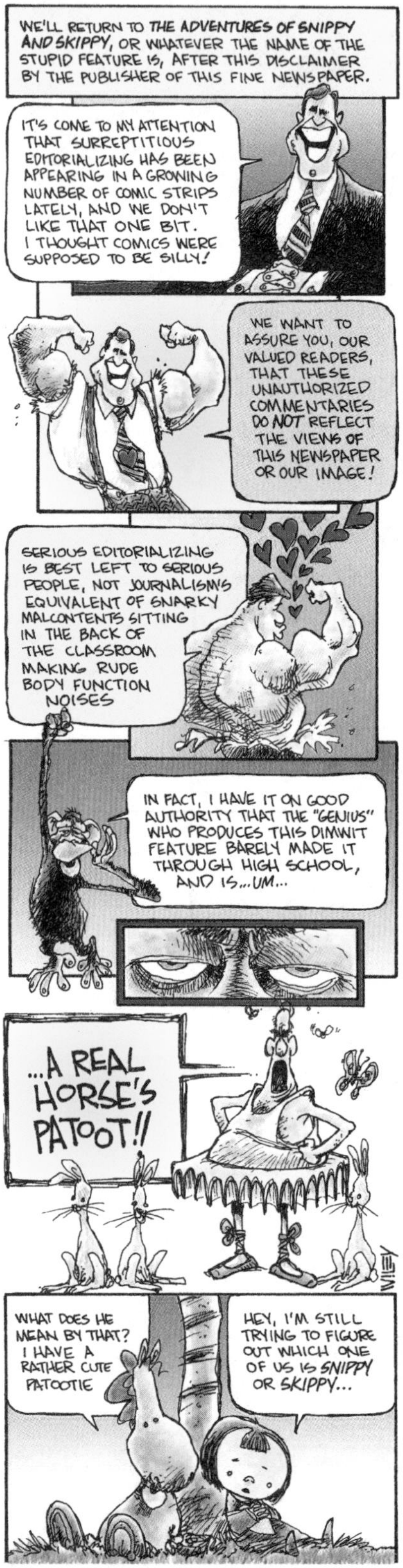
WE'LL RETURN TO THE ADVENTURES OF SNIPPY AND SKIPPY, OR WHATEVER THE NAME OF THE STUPID FEATURE IS, AFTER THIS DISCLAIMER BY THE PUBLISHER OF THIS FINE NEWSPAPER.
IT'S COME TO MY ATTENTION THAT SURREPTITIOUS EDITORIALIZING HAS BEEN APPEARING IN A GROWING NUMBER OF COMIC STRIPS LATELY, AND WE DON'T LIKE THAT ONE BIT. I THOUGHT COMICS WERE SUPPOSED TO BE SILLY!
WE WANT TO ASSURE YOU, OUR VALUED READERS, THAT THESE UNAUTHORIZED COMMENTARIES DO NOT REFLECT THE VIEWS OF THIS NEWSPAPER OR OUR IMAGE!
SERIOUS EDITORIALIZING IS BEST LEFT TO SERIOUS PEOPLE, NOT JOURNALISM'S EQUIVALENT OF SNARKY MALCONTENTS SITTING IN THE BACK OF THE CLASSROOM MAKING RUDE BODY FUNCTION NOISES
IN FACT, I HAVE IT ON GOOD AUTHORITY THAT THE "GENIUS" WHO PRODUCES THIS DIMWIT FEATURE BARELY MADE IT THROUGH HIGH SCHOOL, AND IS...UM...
...A REAL HORSE'S PATOOT!!
WILEY
WHAT DOES HE MEAN BY THAT? I HAVE A RATHER CUTE PATOOTIE
HEY, I'M STILL TRYING TO FIGURE OUT WHICH ONE OF US IS SNIPPY OR SKIPPY...

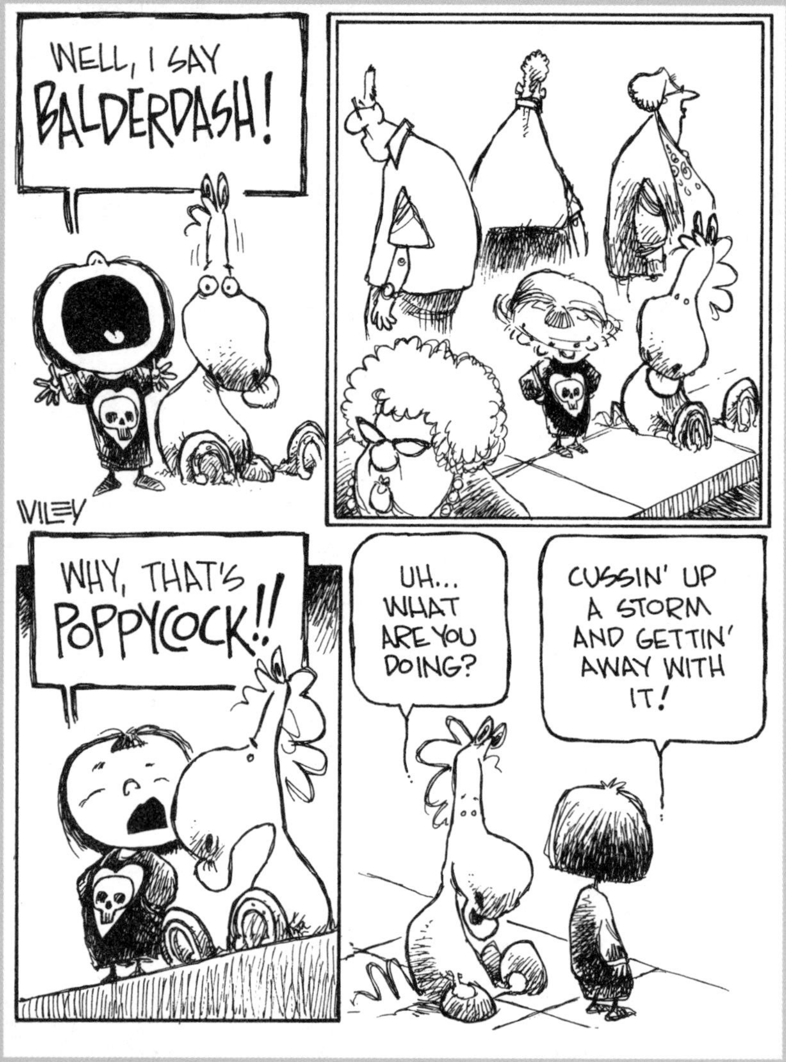
WELL, I SAY BALDERDASH!
WILEY
WHY, THAT'S POPPYCOCK!!
UH... WHAT ARE YOU DOING?
CUSSIN' UP A STORM AND GETTIN' AWAY WITH IT!

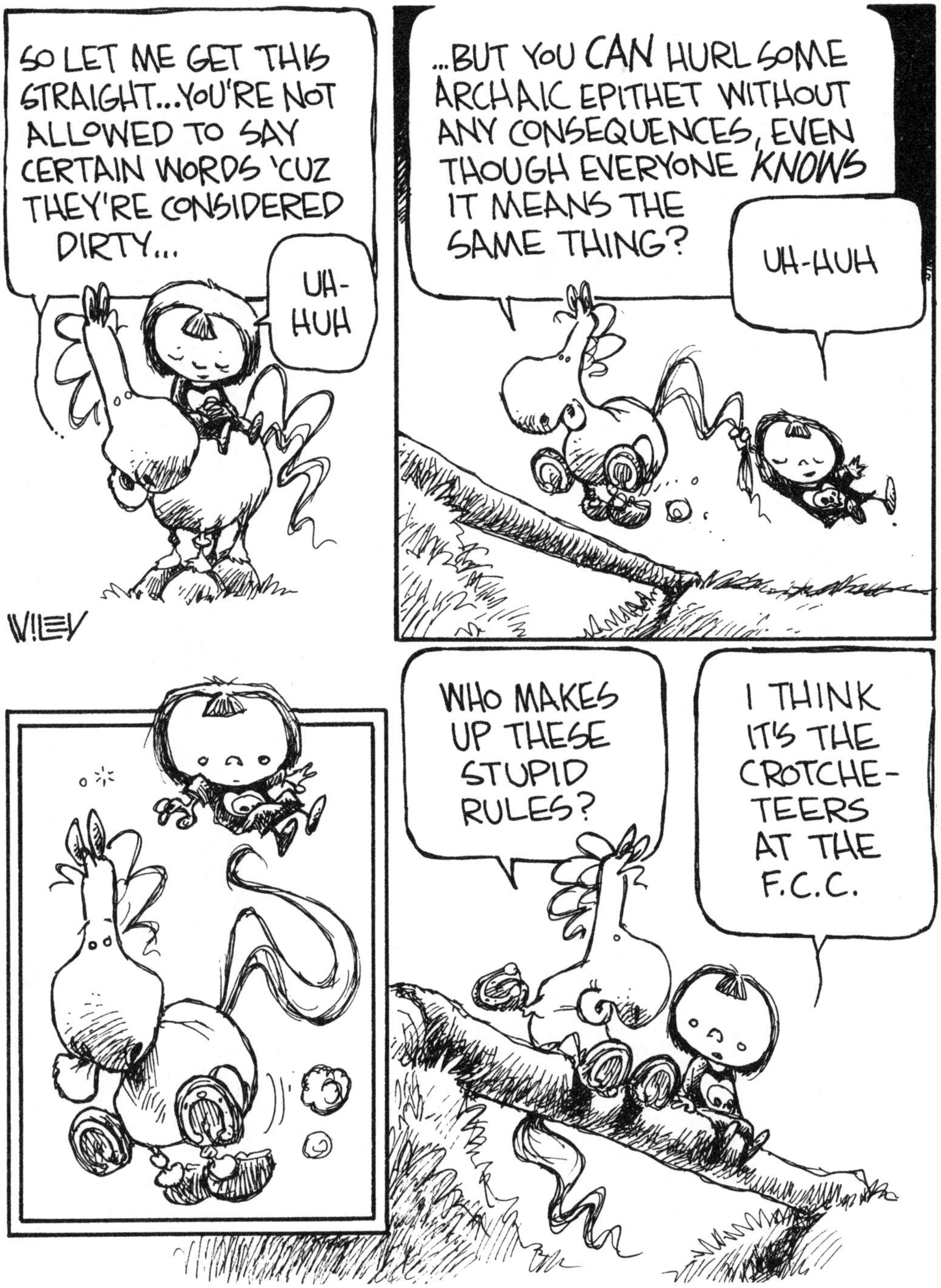

SO LET ME GET THIS STRAIGHT...YOU'RE NOT ALLOWED TO SAY CERTAIN WORDS 'CUZ THEY'RE CONSIDERED DIRTY...
UH-HUH
...BUT YOU CAN HURL SOME ARCHAIC EPITHET WITHOUT ANY CONSEQUENCES, EVEN THOUGH EVERYONE KNOWS IT MEANS THE SAME THING?
UH-HUH
WHO MAKES UP THESE STUPID RULES?
I THINK IT'S THE CROTCHE-TEERS AT THE F.C.C.
WILEY

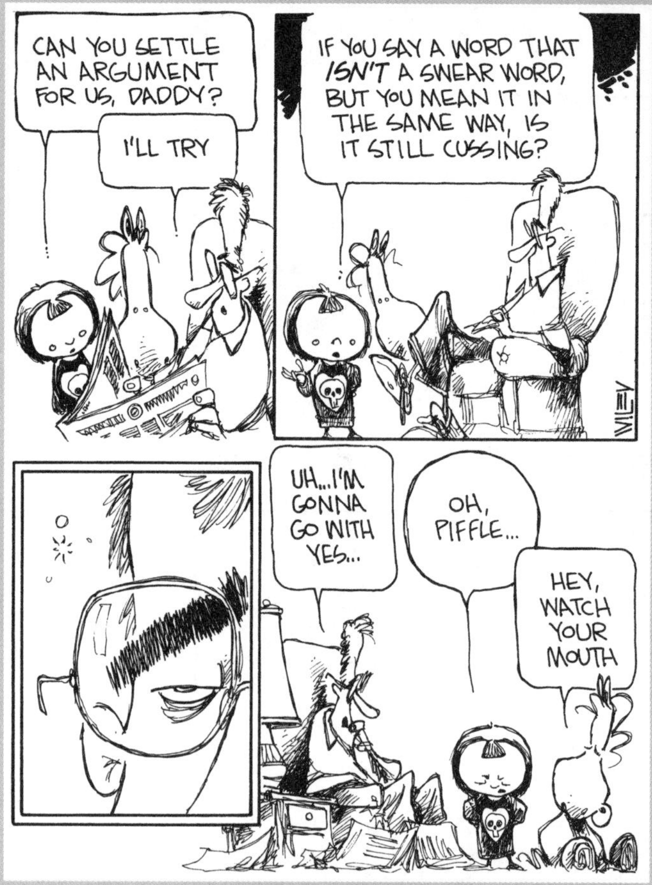
CAN YOU SETTLE AN ARGUMENT FOR US, DADDY?
I'LL TRY
IF YOU SAY A WORD THAT *ISN'T* A SWEAR WORD, BUT YOU MEAN IT IN THE SAME WAY, IS IT STILL CUSSING?
UH...I'M GONNA GO WITH YES...
OH, PIFFLE...
HEY, WATCH YOUR MOUTH

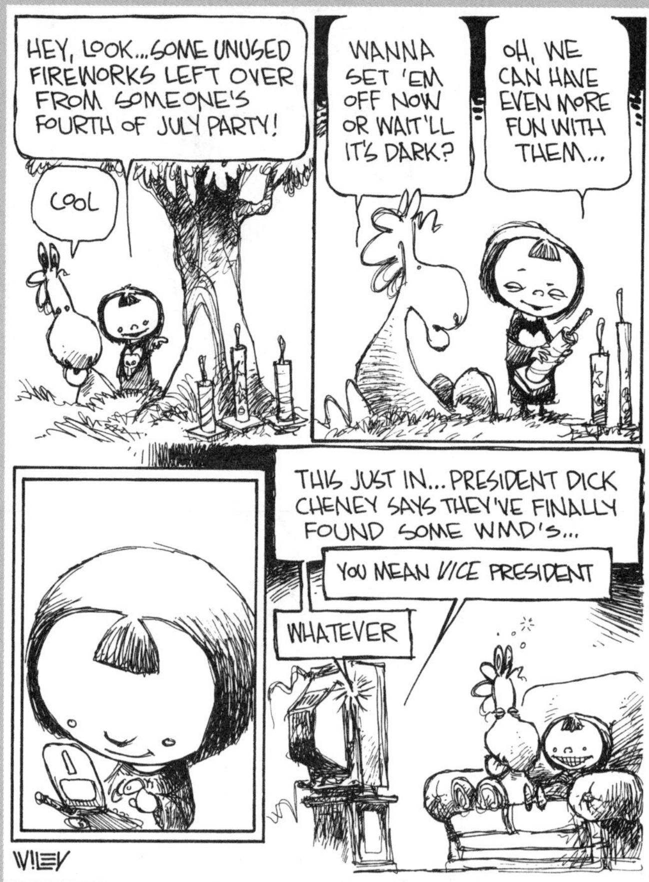
HEY, LOOK...SOME UNUSED FIREWORKS LEFT OVER FROM SOMEONE'S FOURTH OF JULY PARTY!
COOL
WANNA SET 'EM OFF NOW OR WAIT'LL IT'S DARK?
OH, WE CAN HAVE EVEN MORE FUN WITH THEM...
THIS JUST IN... PRESIDENT DICK CHENEY SAYS THEY'VE FINALLY FOUND SOME WMD'S...
YOU MEAN *VICE* PRESIDENT
WHATEVER

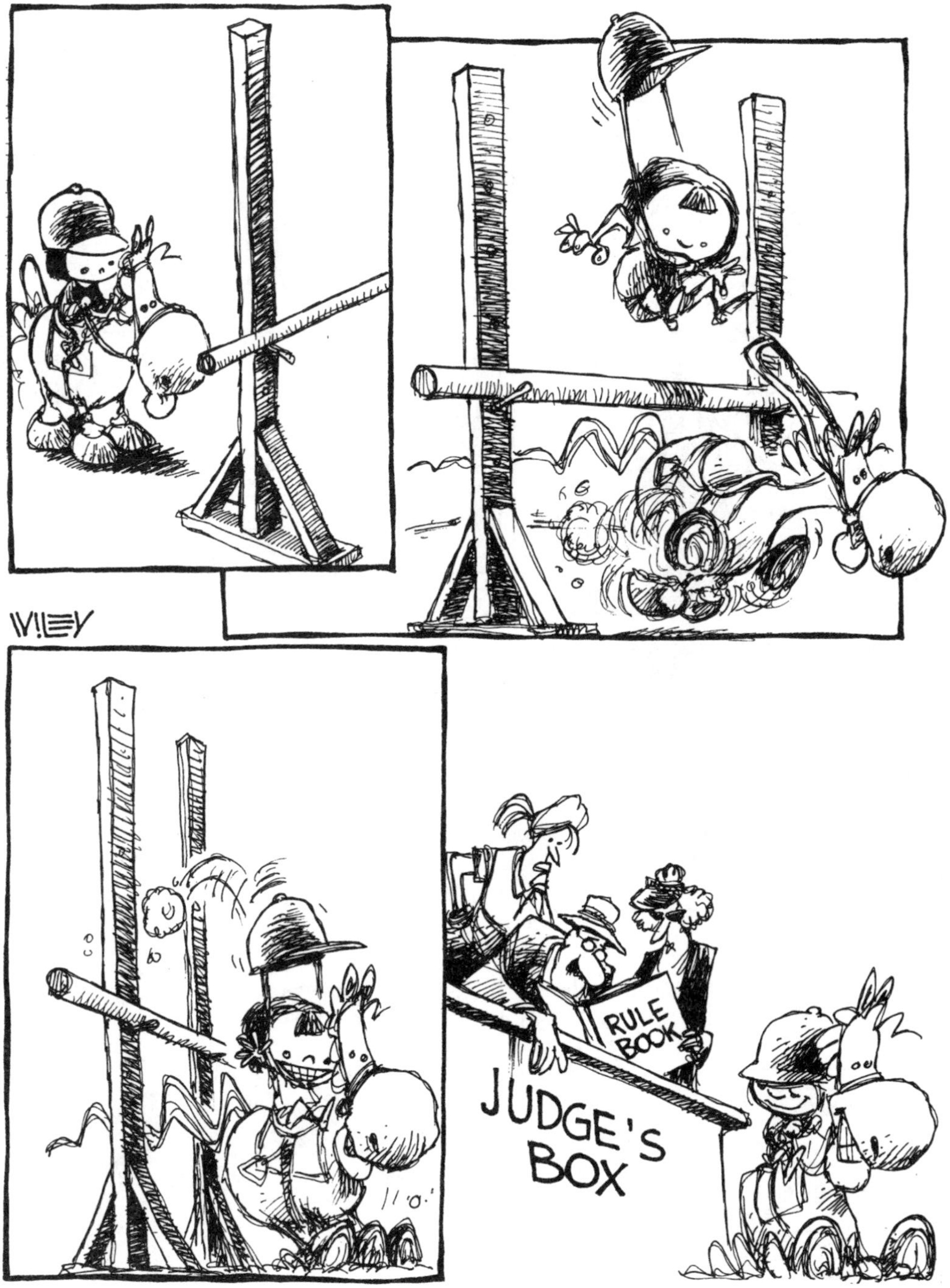
WILEY
RULE BOOK
JUDGE'S BOX

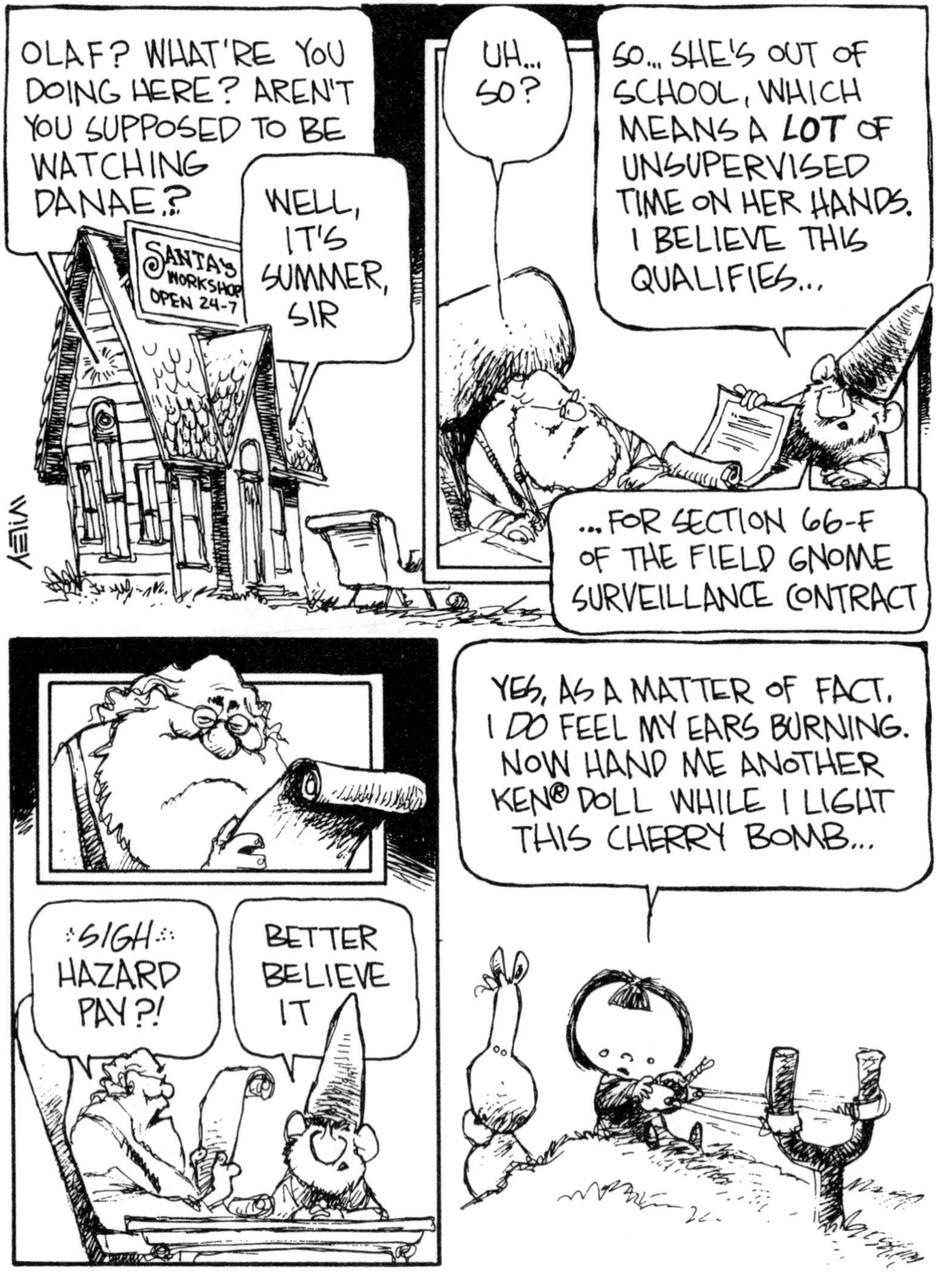
OLAF? WHAT'RE YOU DOING HERE? AREN'T YOU SUPPOSED TO BE WATCHING DANAE?!
SANTA'S WORKSHOP OPEN 24-7
WELL, IT'S SUMMER, SIR
UH... SO?
SO... SHE'S OUT OF SCHOOL, WHICH MEANS A **LOT** OF UNSUPERVISED TIME ON HER HANDS. I BELIEVE THIS QUALIFIES...
...FOR SECTION 66-F OF THE FIELD GNOME SURVEILLANCE CONTRACT
WILEY
:SIGH: HAZARD PAY?!
BETTER BELIEVE IT
YES, AS A MATTER OF FACT, I *DO* FEEL MY EARS BURNING. NOW HAND ME ANOTHER KEN® DOLL WHILE I LIGHT THIS CHERRY BOMB...

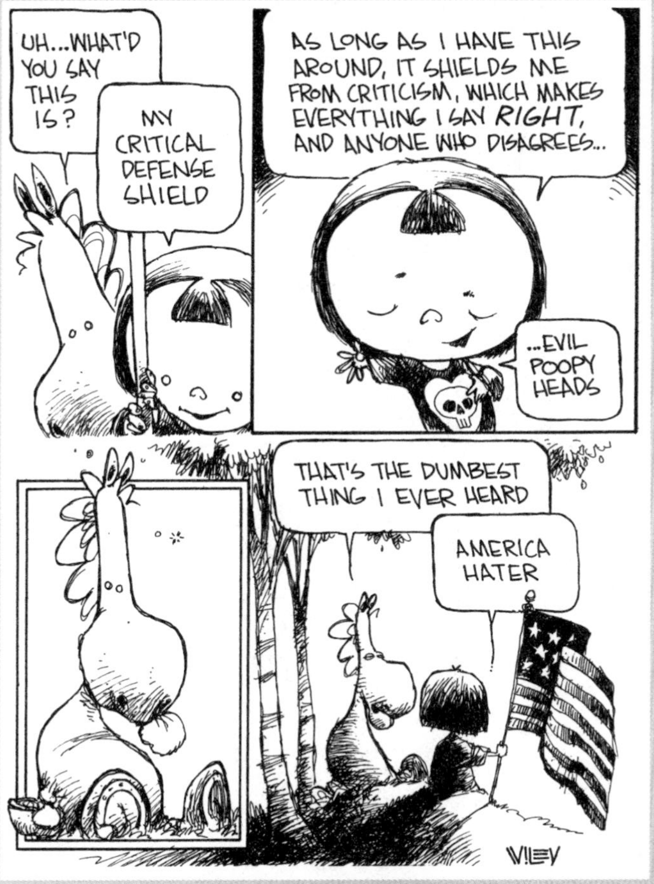
UH...WHAT'D YOU SAY THIS IS?
MY CRITICAL DEFENSE SHIELD
AS LONG AS I HAVE THIS AROUND, IT SHIELDS ME FROM CRITICISM, WHICH MAKES EVERYTHING I SAY RIGHT, AND ANYONE WHO DISAGREES...
...EVIL POOPY HEADS
THAT'S THE DUMBEST THING I EVER HEARD
AMERICA HATER
WILEY

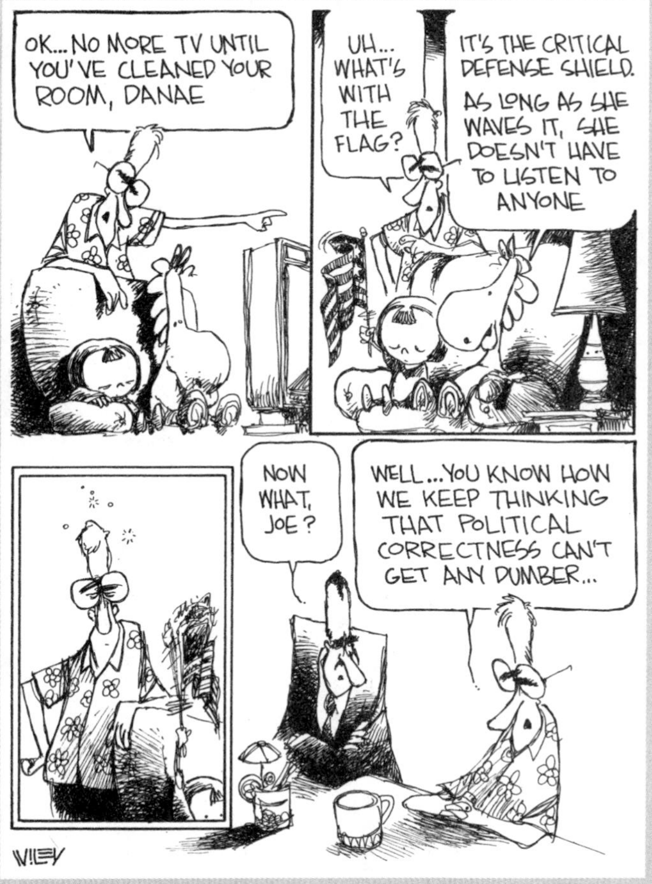
OK...NO MORE TV UNTIL YOU'VE CLEANED YOUR ROOM, DANAE
UH... WHAT'S WITH THE FLAG?
IT'S THE CRITICAL DEFENSE SHIELD.
AS LONG AS SHE WAVES IT, SHE DOESN'T HAVE TO LISTEN TO ANYONE
NOW WHAT, JOE?
WELL...YOU KNOW HOW WE KEEP THINKING THAT POLITICAL CORRECTNESS CAN'T GET ANY DUMBER...
WILEY

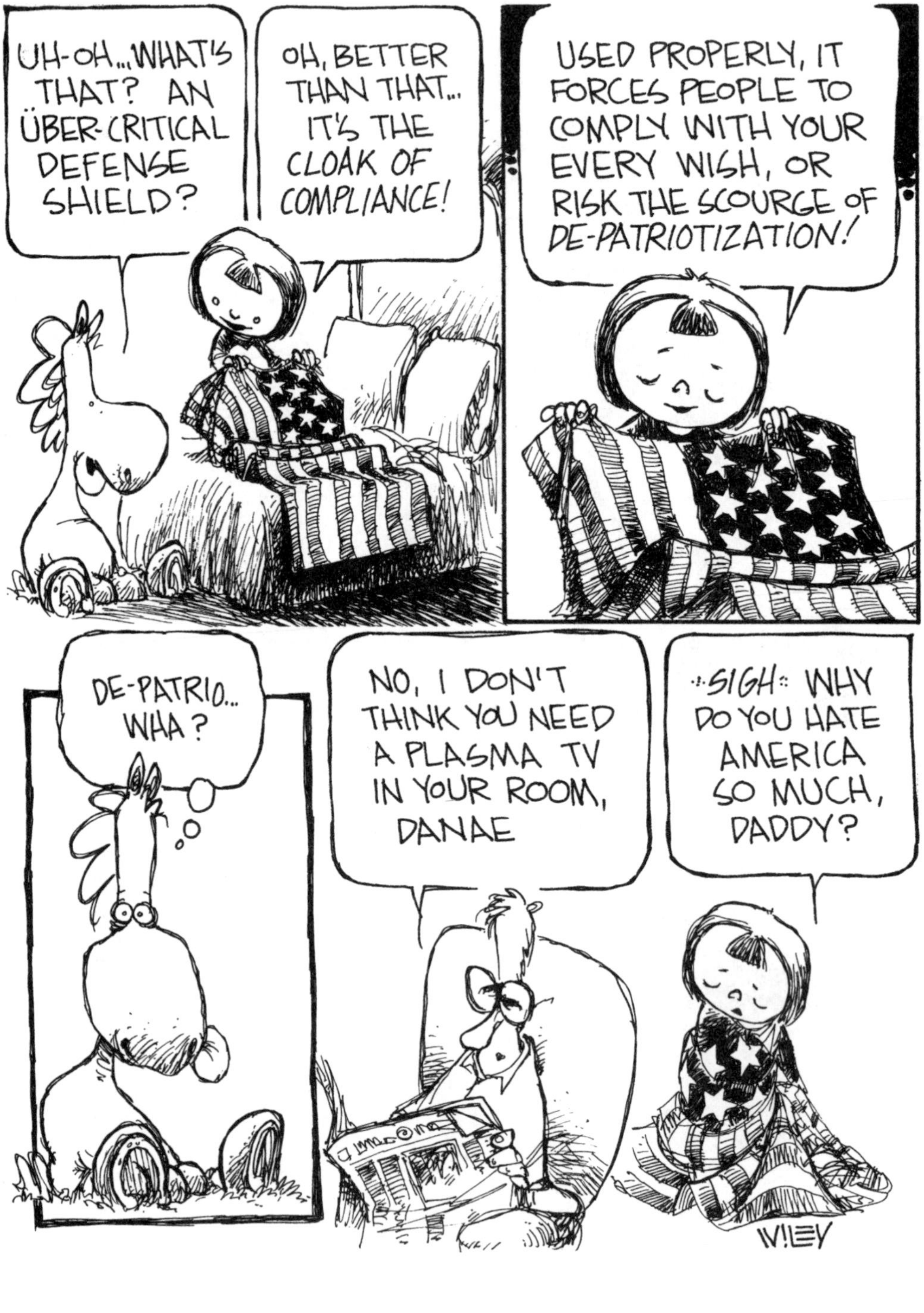
UH-OH... WHAT'S THAT? AN ÜBER-CRITICAL DEFENSE SHIELD?
OH, BETTER THAN THAT... IT'S THE CLOAK OF COMPLIANCE!
USED PROPERLY, IT FORCES PEOPLE TO COMPLY WITH YOUR EVERY WISH, OR RISK THE SCOURGE OF DE-PATRIOTIZATION!
DE-PATRIO... WHA?
NO, I DON'T THINK YOU NEED A PLASMA TV IN YOUR ROOM, DANAE
SIGH WHY DO YOU HATE AMERICA SO MUCH, DADDY?
WILEY

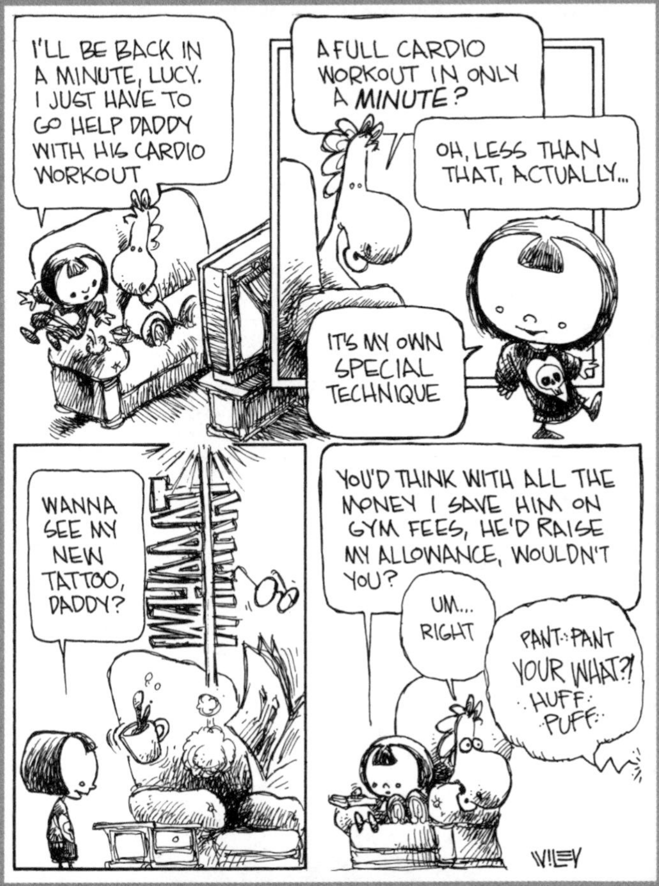
I'LL BE BACK IN A MINUTE, LUCY. I JUST HAVE TO GO HELP DADDY WITH HIS CARDIO WORKOUT
A FULL CARDIO WORKOUT IN ONLY A MINUTE?
OH, LESS THAN THAT, ACTUALLY...
IT'S MY OWN SPECIAL TECHNIQUE
WANNA SEE MY NEW TATTOO, DADDY?
YOU'D THINK WITH ALL THE MONEY I SAVE HIM ON GYM FEES, HE'D RAISE MY ALLOWANCE, WOULDN'T YOU?
UM... RIGHT
PANT PANT YOUR WHAT?! HUFF PUFF
WILEY

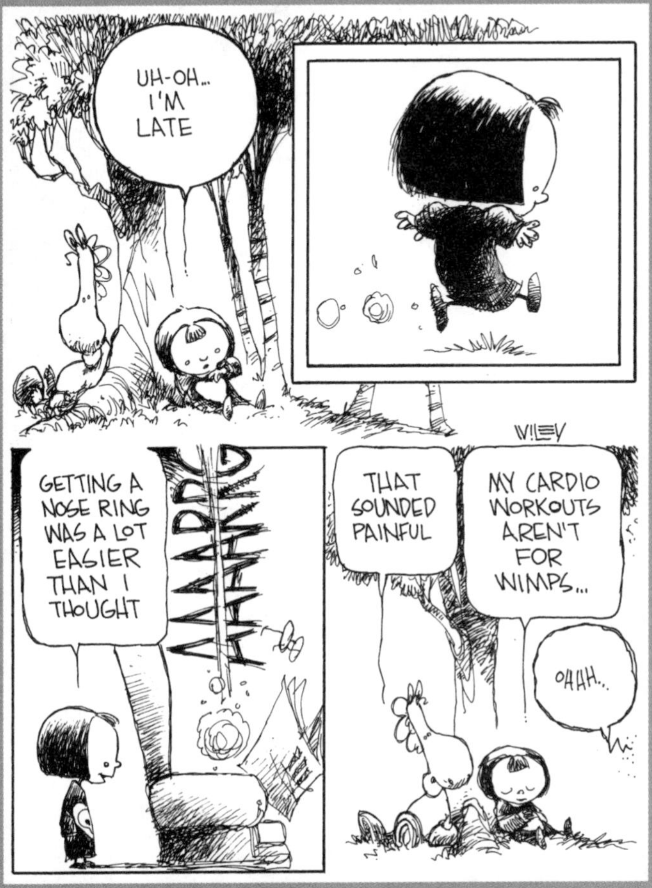
UH-OH.. I'M LATE
WILEY
GETTING A NOSE RING WAS A LOT EASIER THAN I THOUGHT
AAAARRG
THAT SOUNDED PAINFUL
MY CARDIO WORKOUTS AREN'T FOR WIMPS...
OHHH...

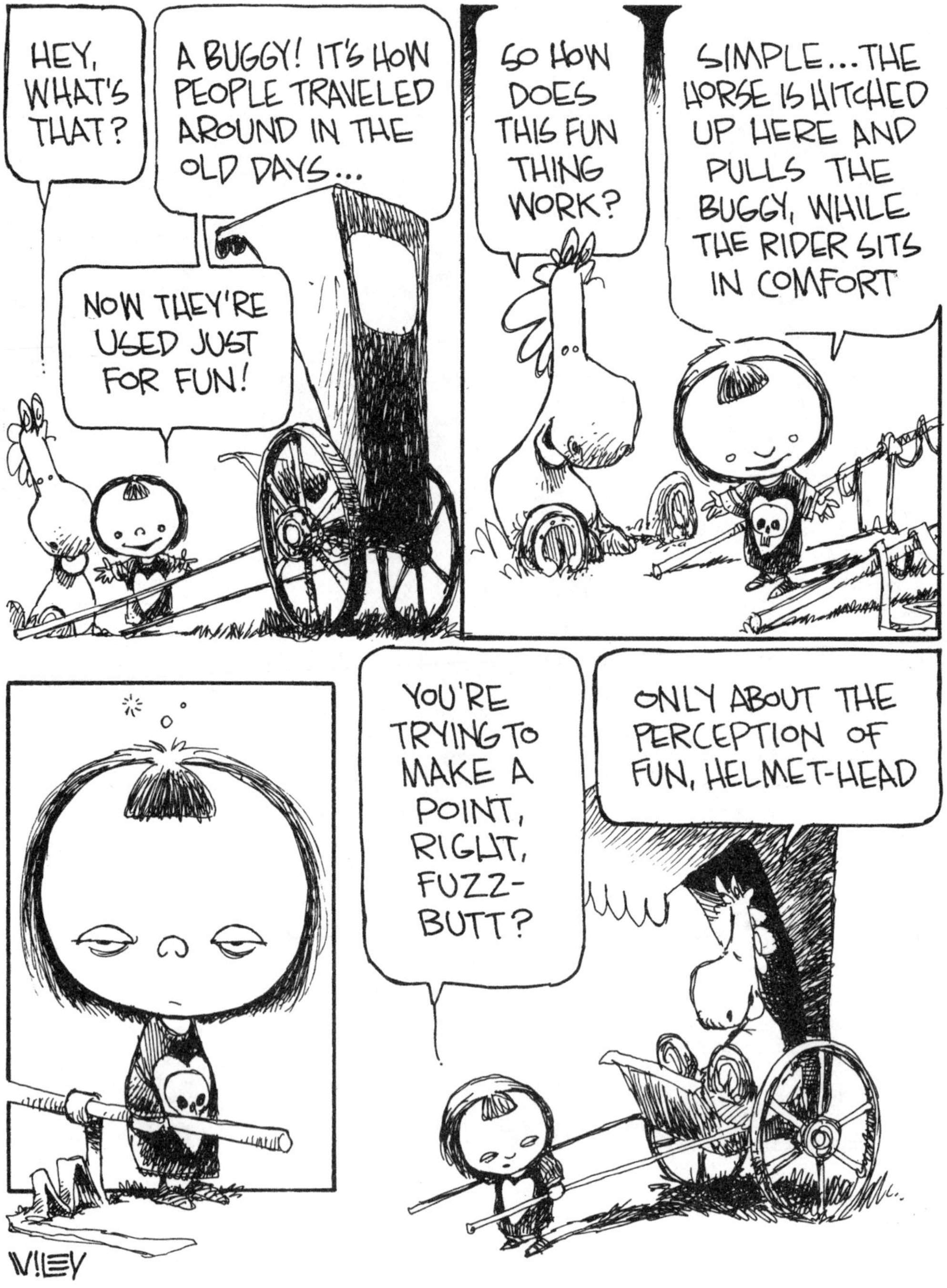
HEY, WHAT'S THAT?
A BUGGY! IT'S HOW PEOPLE TRAVELED AROUND IN THE OLD DAYS...
NOW THEY'RE USED JUST FOR FUN!
SO HOW DOES THIS FUN THING WORK?
SIMPLE...THE HORSE IS HITCHED UP HERE AND PULLS THE BUGGY, WHILE THE RIDER SITS IN COMFORT
YOU'RE TRYING TO MAKE A POINT, RIGHT, FUZZ-BUTT?
ONLY ABOUT THE PERCEPTION OF FUN, HELMET-HEAD
WILEY

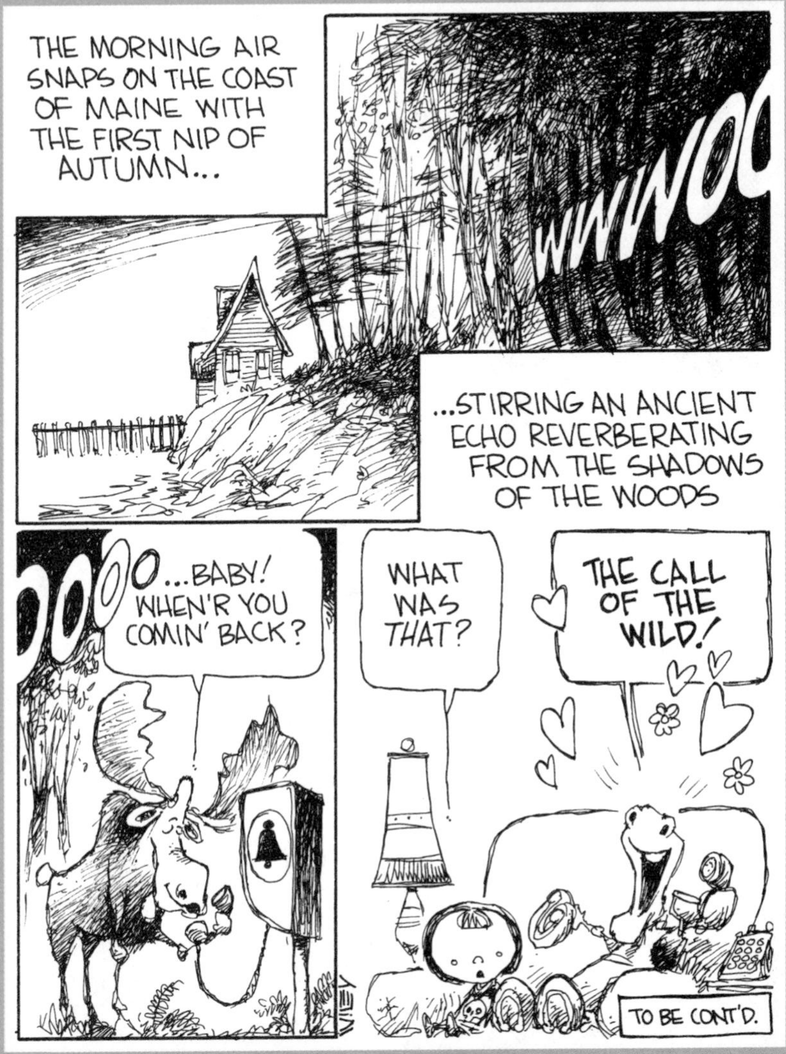
THE MORNING AIR SNAPS ON THE COAST OF MAINE WITH THE FIRST NIP OF AUTUMN...
WWWOO
...STIRRING AN ANCIENT ECHO REVERBERATING FROM THE SHADOWS OF THE WOODS
OOOO...BABY! WHEN'R YOU COMIN' BACK?
WHAT WAS THAT?
THE CALL OF THE WILD!
TO BE CONT'D.

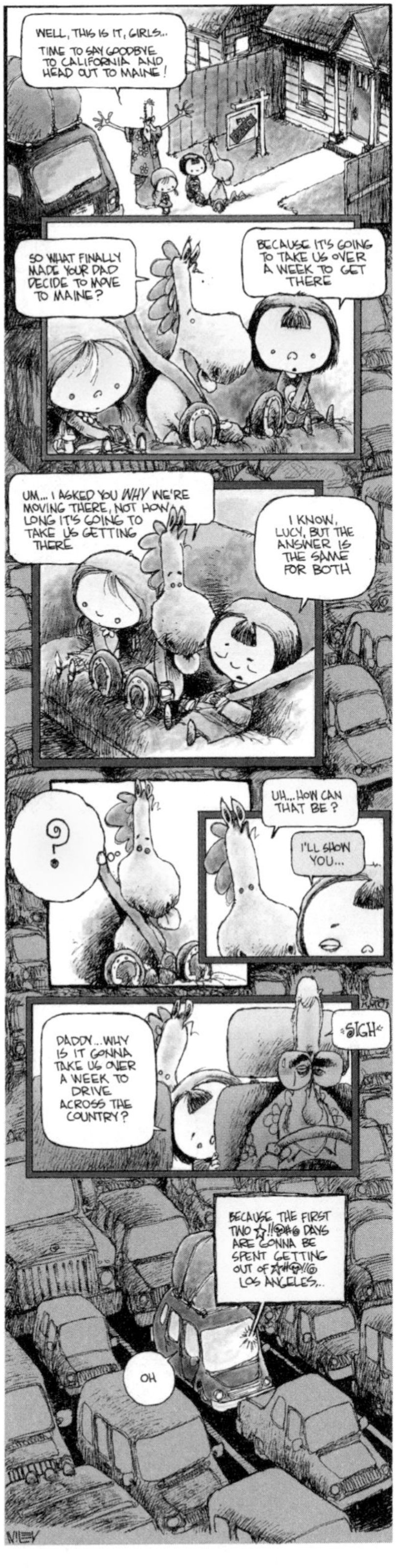
WELL, THIS IS IT, GIRLS... TIME TO SAY GOODBYE TO CALIFORNIA AND HEAD OUT TO MAINE!
SO WHAT FINALLY MADE YOUR DAD DECIDE TO MOVE TO MAINE?
BECAUSE IT'S GOING TO TAKE US OVER A WEEK TO GET THERE
UM... I ASKED YOU WHY WE'RE MOVING THERE, NOT HOW LONG IT'S GOING TO TAKE US GETTING THERE
I KNOW, LUCY, BUT THE ANSWER IS THE SAME FOR BOTH
?
UH... HOW CAN THAT BE?
I'LL SHOW YOU...
DADDY... WHY IS IT GONNA TAKE US OVER A WEEK TO DRIVE ACROSS THE COUNTRY?
SIGH
BECAUSE THE FIRST TWO ☆!!@#@ DAYS ARE GONNA BE SPENT GETTING OUT OF ☆#@!@ LOS ANGELES...
OH

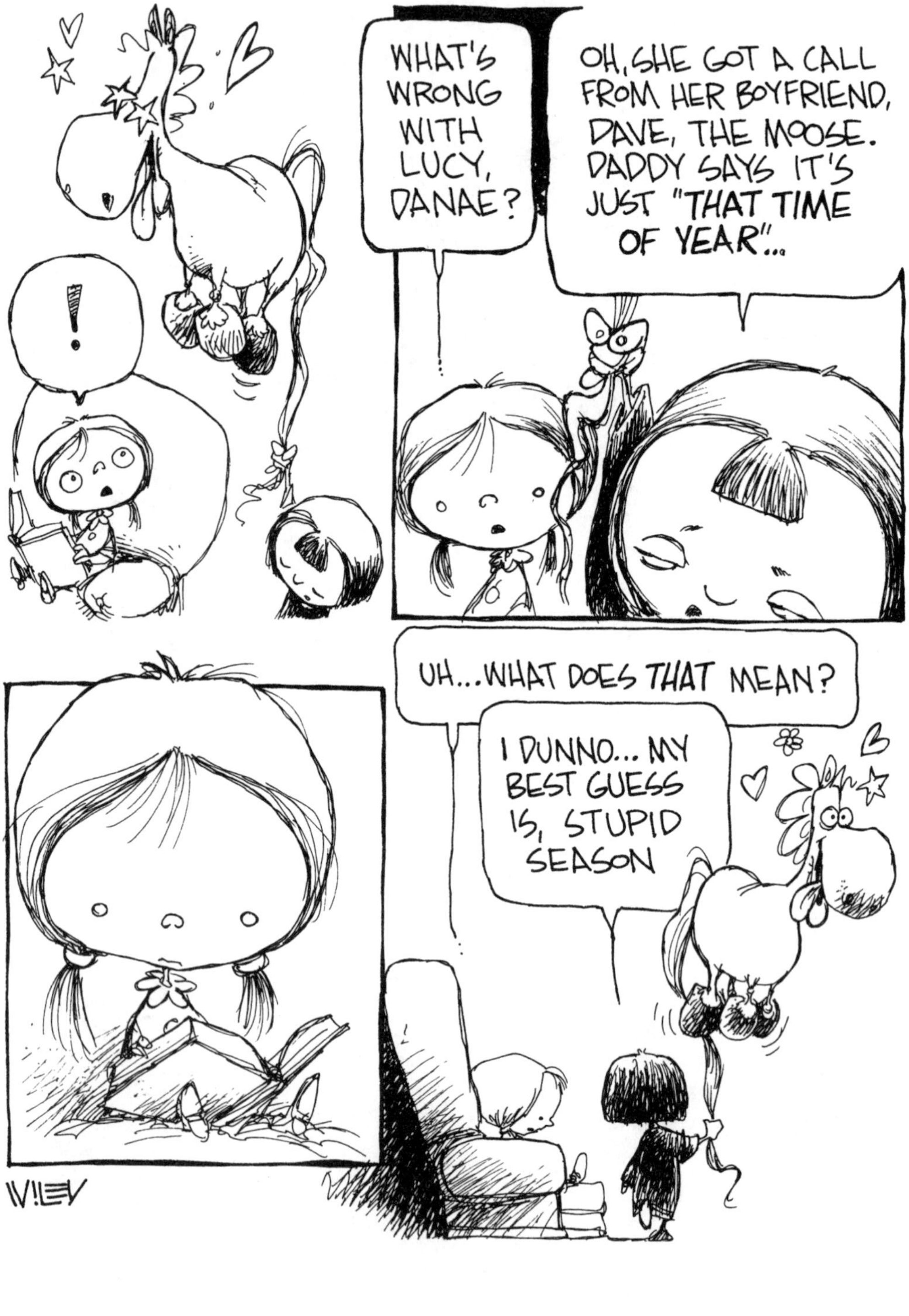
!
WHAT'S WRONG WITH LUCY, DANAE?
OH, SHE GOT A CALL FROM HER BOYFRIEND, DAVE, THE MOOSE. DADDY SAYS IT'S JUST "THAT TIME OF YEAR"...
UH... WHAT DOES THAT MEAN?
I DUNNO... MY BEST GUESS IS, STUPID SEASON
WILEY

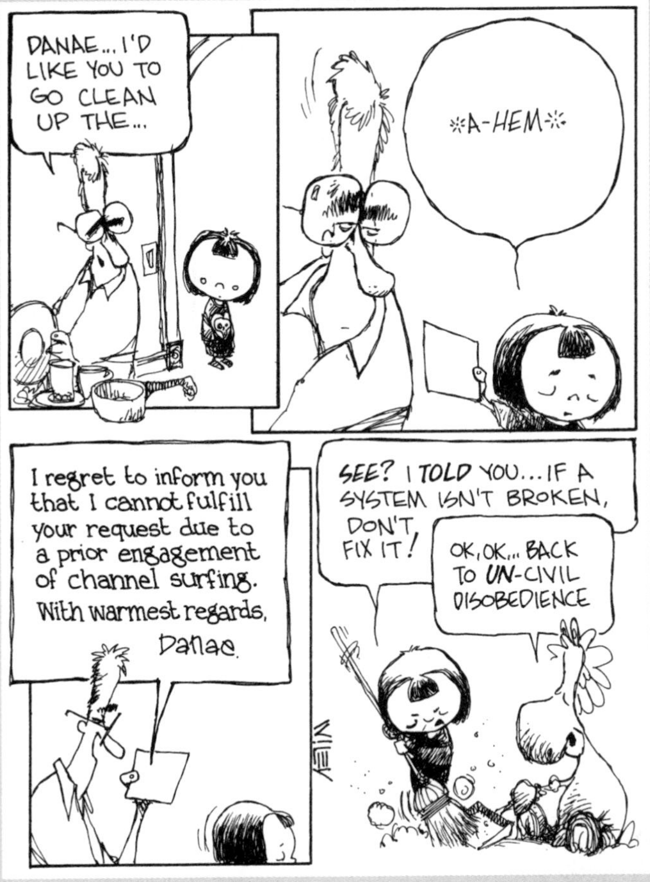
DANAE... I'D LIKE YOU TO GO CLEAN UP THE...
A-HEM
I regret to inform you that I cannot fulfill your request due to a prior engagement of channel surfing. With warmest regards, Danae
SEE? I TOLD YOU... IF A SYSTEM ISN'T BROKEN, DON'T FIX IT!
OK, OK... BACK TO UN-CIVIL DISOBEDIENCE
WILEY

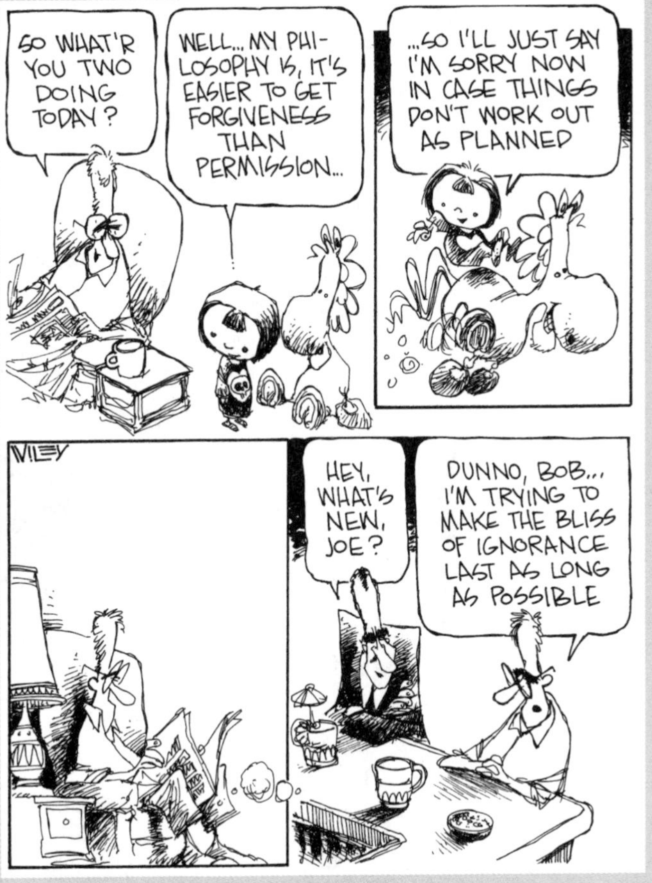
SO WHAT'R YOU TWO DOING TODAY?
WELL... MY PHILOSOPHY IS, IT'S EASIER TO GET FORGIVENESS THAN PERMISSION...
...SO I'LL JUST SAY I'M SORRY NOW IN CASE THINGS DON'T WORK OUT AS PLANNED
WILEY
HEY, WHAT'S NEW, JOE?
DUNNO, BOB... I'M TRYING TO MAKE THE BLISS OF IGNORANCE LAST AS LONG AS POSSIBLE

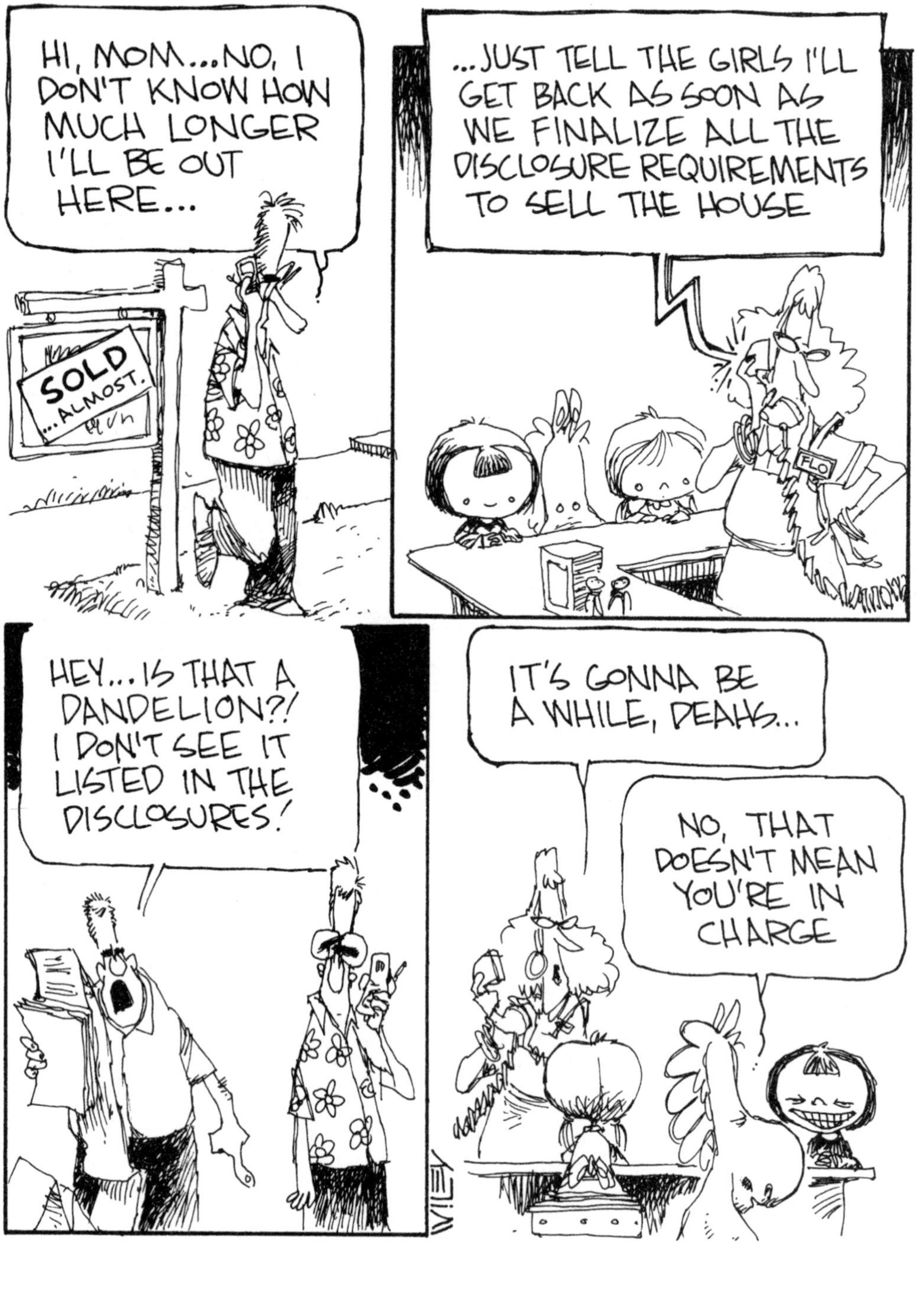
HI, MOM...NO, I DON'T KNOW HOW MUCH LONGER I'LL BE OUT HERE...
SOLD ...ALMOST.
...JUST TELL THE GIRLS I'LL GET BACK AS SOON AS WE FINALIZE ALL THE DISCLOSURE REQUIREMENTS TO SELL THE HOUSE
FLO
HEY...IS THAT A DANDELION?! I DON'T SEE IT LISTED IN THE DISCLOSURES!
IT'S GONNA BE A WHILE, DEAHS...
NO, THAT DOESN'T MEAN YOU'RE IN CHARGE

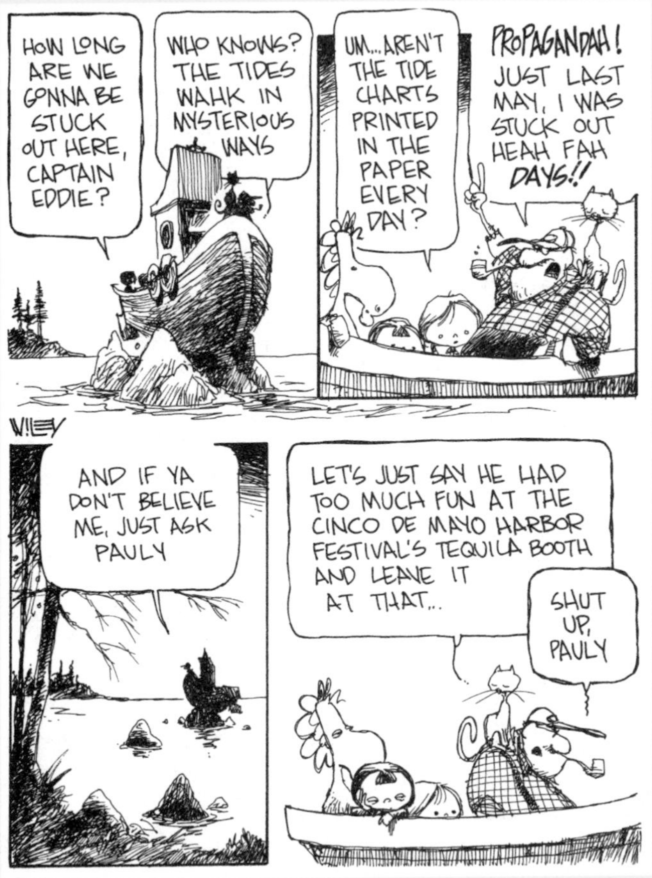
HOW LONG ARE WE GONNA BE STUCK OUT HERE, CAPTAIN EDDIE?
WHO KNOWS? THE TIDES WAHK IN MYSTERIOUS WAYS
UM... AREN'T THE TIDE CHARTS PRINTED IN THE PAPER EVERY DAY?
PROPAGANDAH! JUST LAST MAY, I WAS STUCK OUT HEAH FAH DAYS!!
WILEY
AND IF YA DON'T BELIEVE ME, JUST ASK PAULY
LET'S JUST SAY HE HAD TOO MUCH FUN AT THE CINCO DE MAYO HARBOR FESTIVAL'S TEQUILA BOOTH AND LEAVE IT AT THAT...
SHUT UP, PAULY

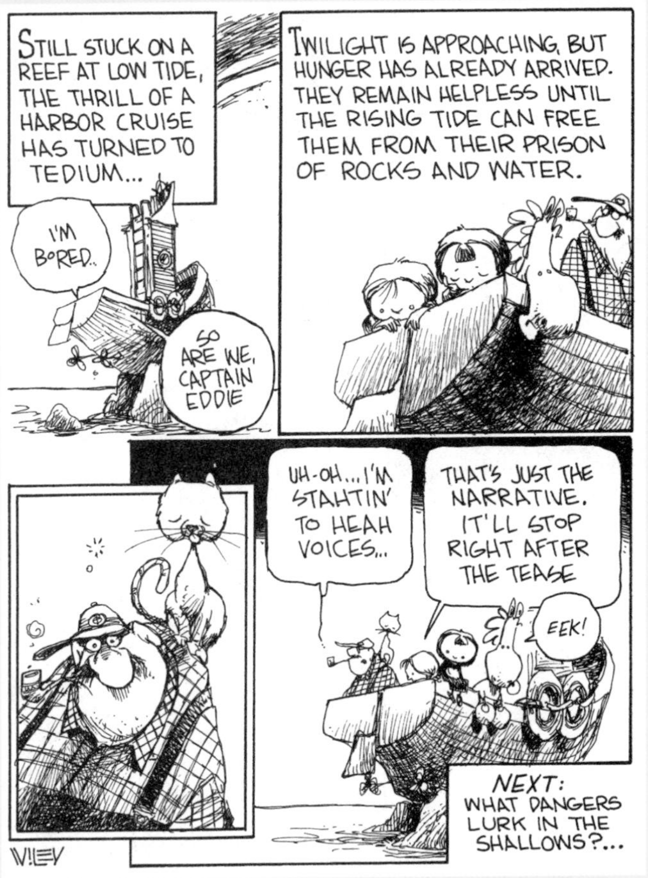
STILL STUCK ON A REEF AT LOW TIDE, THE THRILL OF A HARBOR CRUISE HAS TURNED TO TEDIUM...
I'M BORED..
SO ARE WE, CAPTAIN EDDIE
TWILIGHT IS APPROACHING, BUT HUNGER HAS ALREADY ARRIVED. THEY REMAIN HELPLESS UNTIL THE RISING TIDE CAN FREE THEM FROM THEIR PRISON OF ROCKS AND WATER.
UH-OH... I'M STAHTIN' TO HEAH VOICES...
THAT'S JUST THE NARRATIVE. IT'LL STOP RIGHT AFTER THE TEASE
EEK!
NEXT: WHAT DANGERS LURK IN THE SHALLOWS?...
WILEY

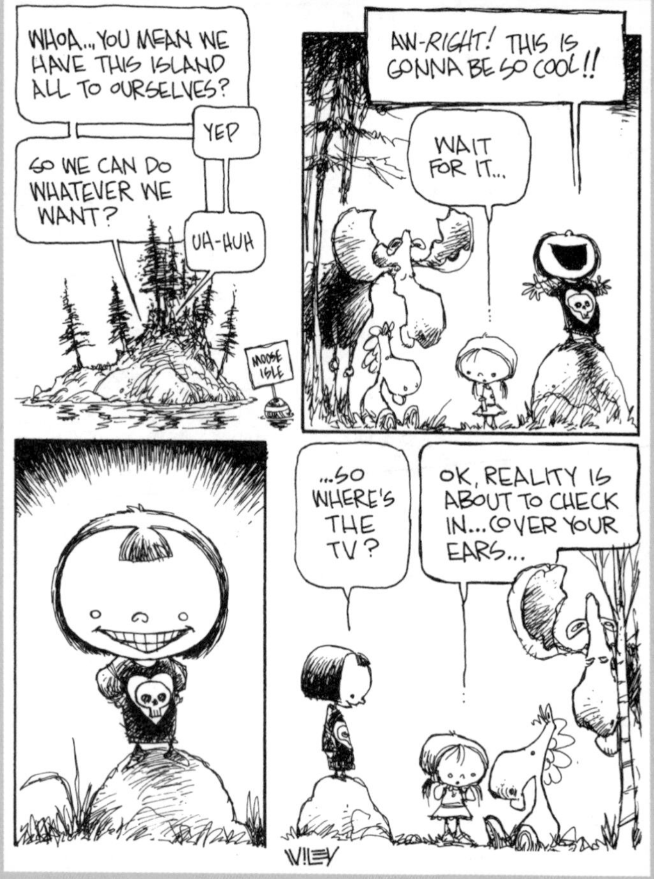
WHOA... YOU MEAN WE HAVE THIS ISLAND ALL TO OURSELVES?
YEP
SO WE CAN DO WHATEVER WE WANT?
UH-HUH
MOOSE ISLE
AW-RIGHT! THIS IS GONNA BE SO COOL!!
WAIT FOR IT...
...SO WHERE'S THE TV?
OK, REALITY IS ABOUT TO CHECK IN... COVER YOUR EARS...
WILEY

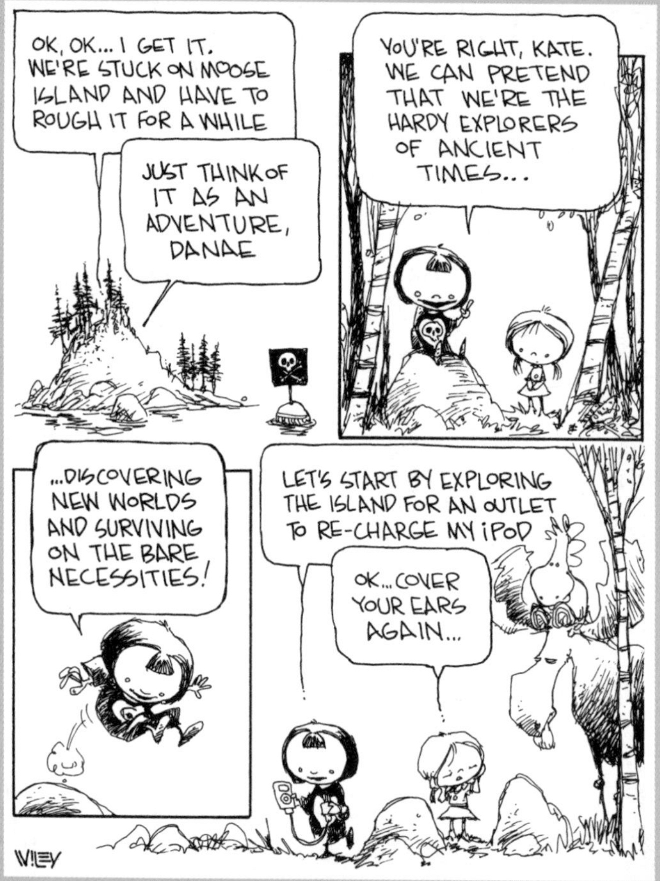
OK, OK... I GET IT. WE'RE STUCK ON MOOSE ISLAND AND HAVE TO ROUGH IT FOR A WHILE
JUST THINK OF IT AS AN ADVENTURE, DANAE
YOU'RE RIGHT, KATE. WE CAN PRETEND THAT WE'RE THE HARDY EXPLORERS OF ANCIENT TIMES...
...DISCOVERING NEW WORLDS AND SURVIVING ON THE BARE NECESSITIES!
LET'S START BY EXPLORING THE ISLAND FOR AN OUTLET TO RE-CHARGE MY iPOD
OK... COVER YOUR EARS AGAIN...
WILEY

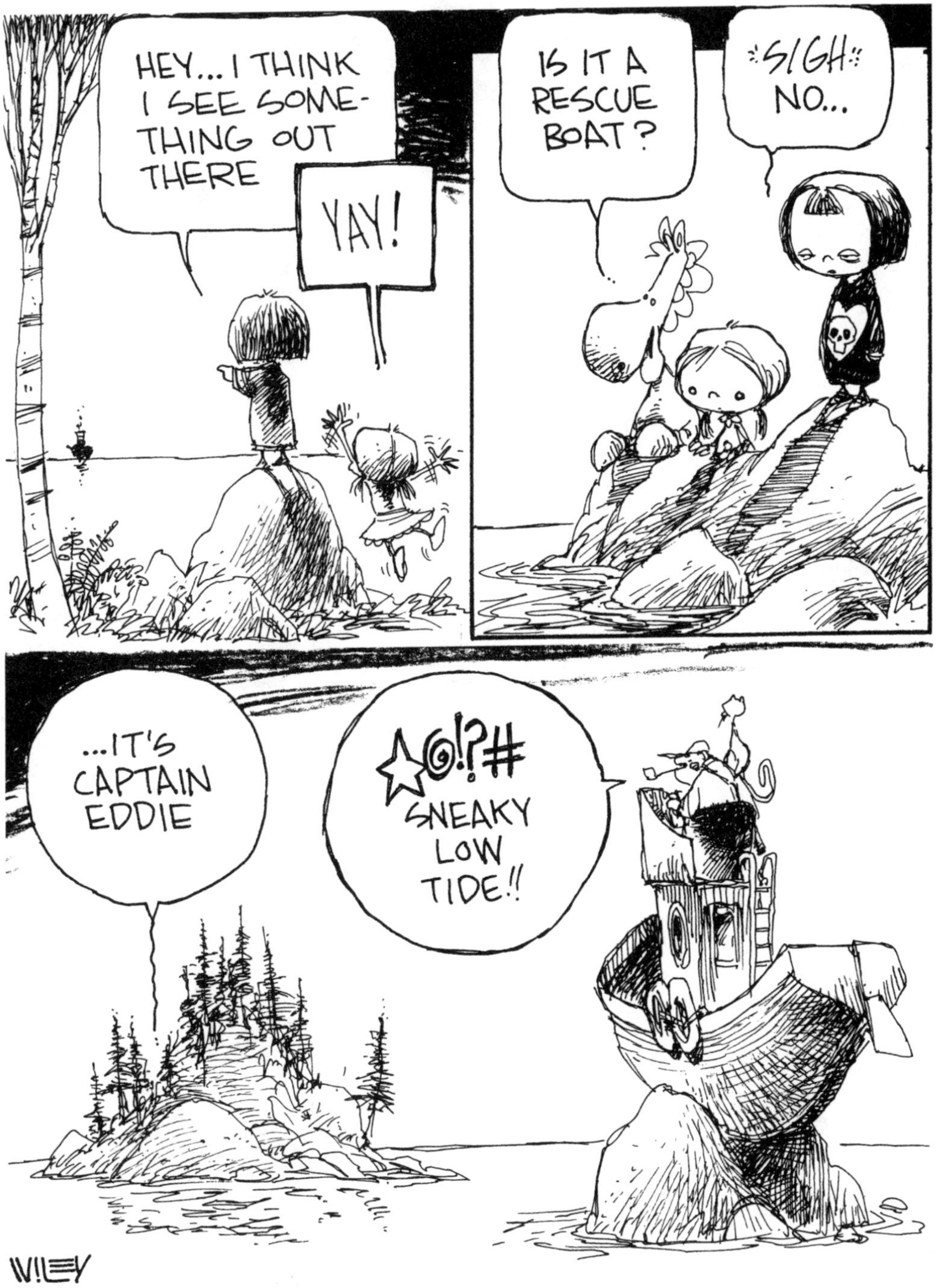
HEY... I THINK I SEE SOME-THING OUT THERE
YAY!
IS IT A RESCUE BOAT?
SIGH NO...
...IT'S CAPTAIN EDDIE
SNEAKY LOW TIDE!!
WILEY

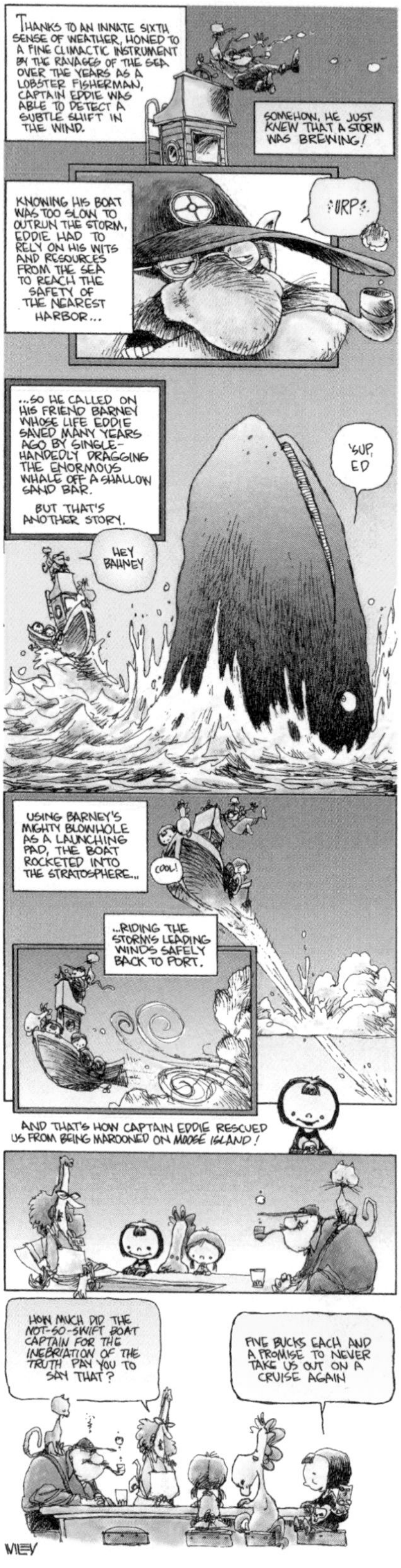
THANKS TO AN INNATE SIXTH SENSE OF WEATHER, HONED TO A FINE CLIMACTIC INSTRUMENT BY THE RAVAGES OF THE SEA OVER THE YEARS AS A LOBSTER FISHERMAN, CAPTAIN EDDIE WAS ABLE TO DETECT A SUBTLE SHIFT IN THE WIND.
SOMEHOW, HE JUST KNEW THAT A STORM WAS BREWING!
KNOWING HIS BOAT WAS TOO SLOW TO OUTRUN THE STORM, EDDIE HAD TO RELY ON HIS WITS AND RESOURCES FROM THE SEA TO REACH THE SAFETY OF THE NEAREST HARBOR...
URP
...SO HE CALLED ON HIS FRIEND BARNEY WHOSE LIFE EDDIE SAVED MANY YEARS AGO BY SINGLE-HANDEDLY DRAGGING THE ENORMOUS WHALE OFF A SHALLOW SAND BAR.
BUT THAT'S ANOTHER STORY.
HEY BAHNEY
'SUP, ED
USING BARNEY'S MIGHTY BLOWHOLE AS A LAUNCHING PAD, THE BOAT ROCKETED INTO THE STRATOSPHERE...
COOL!
...RIDING THE STORM'S LEADING WINDS SAFELY BACK TO PORT.
AND THAT'S HOW CAPTAIN EDDIE RESCUED US FROM BEING MAROONED ON MOOSE ISLAND!
HOW MUCH DID THE NOT-SO-SWIFT BOAT CAPTAIN FOR THE INEBRIATION OF THE TRUTH PAY YOU TO SAY THAT?
FIVE BUCKS EACH AND A PROMISE TO NEVER TAKE US OUT ON A CRUISE AGAIN
WILEY

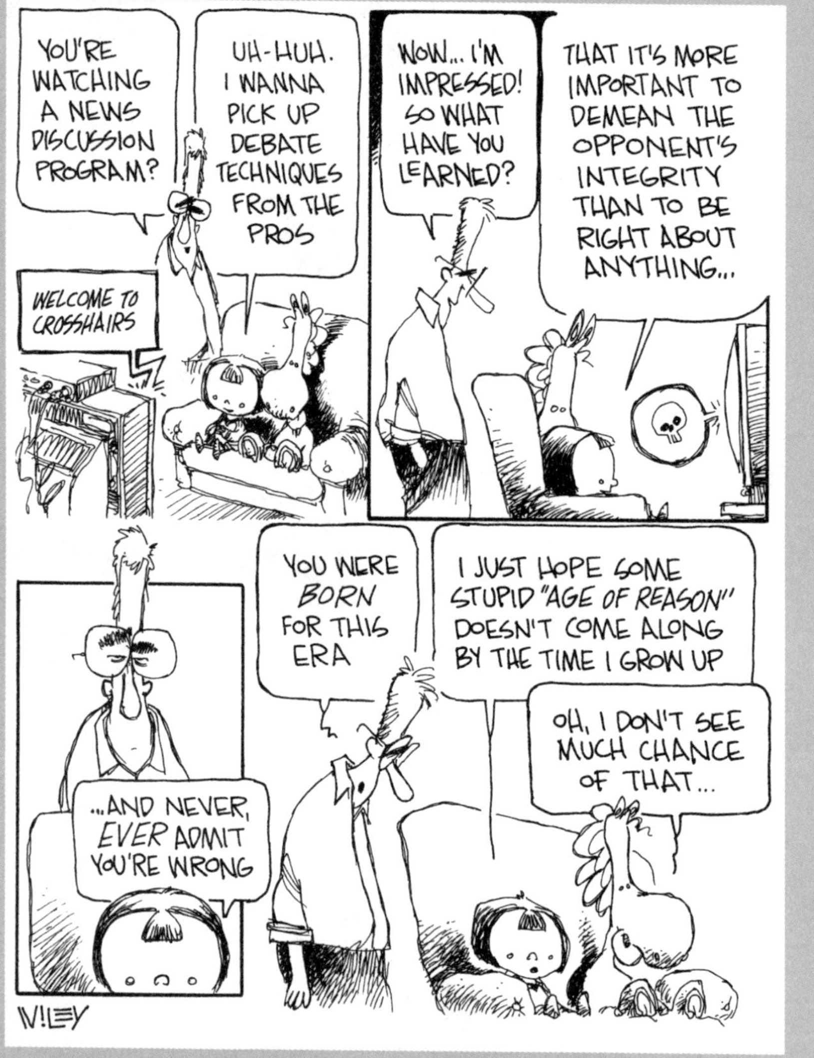
YOU'RE WATCHING A NEWS DISCUSSION PROGRAM?
WELCOME TO CROSSHAIRS
UH-HUH. I WANNA PICK UP DEBATE TECHNIQUES FROM THE PROS
WOW... I'M IMPRESSED! SO WHAT HAVE YOU LEARNED?
THAT IT'S MORE IMPORTANT TO DEMEAN THE OPPONENT'S INTEGRITY THAN TO BE RIGHT ABOUT ANYTHING...
...AND NEVER, EVER ADMIT YOU'RE WRONG
YOU WERE BORN FOR THIS ERA
I JUST HOPE SOME STUPID "AGE OF REASON" DOESN'T COME ALONG BY THE TIME I GROW UP
OH, I DON'T SEE MUCH CHANCE OF THAT...
WILEY

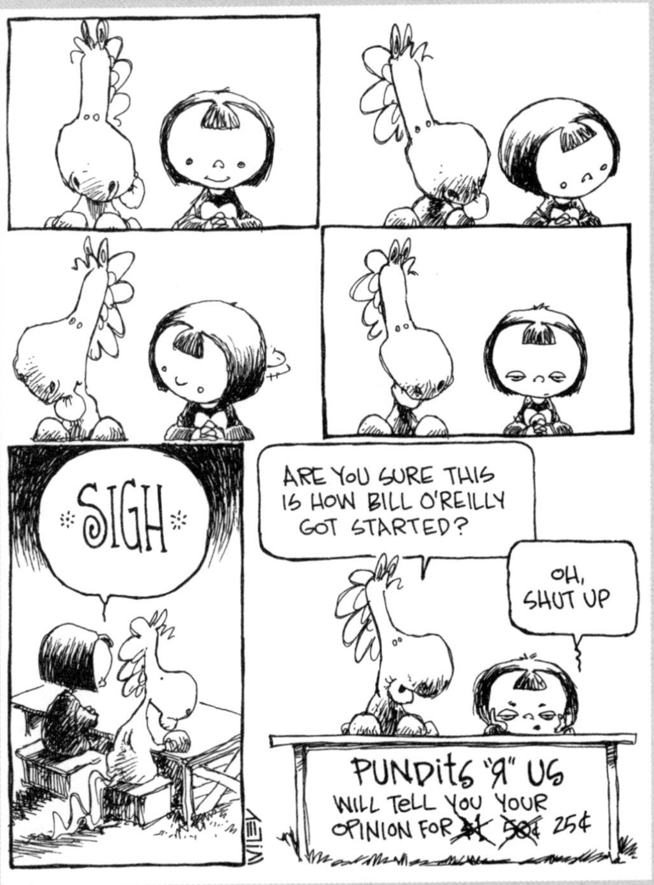
SIGH
ARE YOU SURE THIS IS HOW BILL O'REILLY GOT STARTED?
OH, SHUT UP
PUNDITS "R" US
WILL TELL YOU YOUR OPINION FOR ~~$1~~ ~~50¢~~ 25¢
WILEY

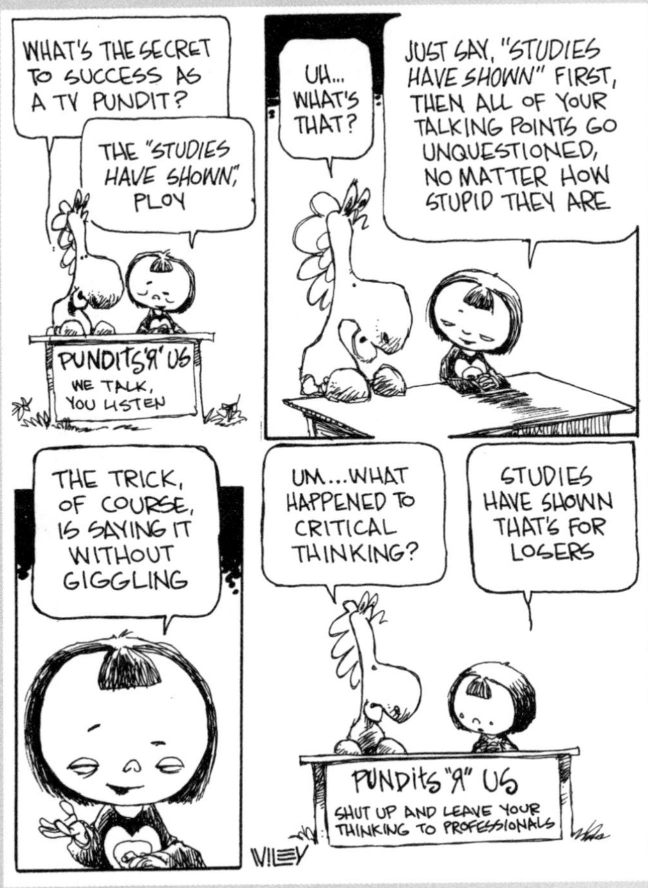
WHAT'S THE SECRET TO SUCCESS AS A TV PUNDIT?
THE "STUDIES HAVE SHOWN," PLOY
PUNDITS "R" US
WE TALK, YOU LISTEN
UH... WHAT'S THAT?
JUST SAY, "STUDIES HAVE SHOWN" FIRST, THEN ALL OF YOUR TALKING POINTS GO UNQUESTIONED, NO MATTER HOW STUPID THEY ARE
THE TRICK, OF COURSE, IS SAYING IT WITHOUT GIGGLING
UM...WHAT HAPPENED TO CRITICAL THINKING?
STUDIES HAVE SHOWN THAT'S FOR LOSERS
PUNDITS "R" US
SHUT UP AND LEAVE YOUR THINKING TO PROFESSIONALS
WILEY

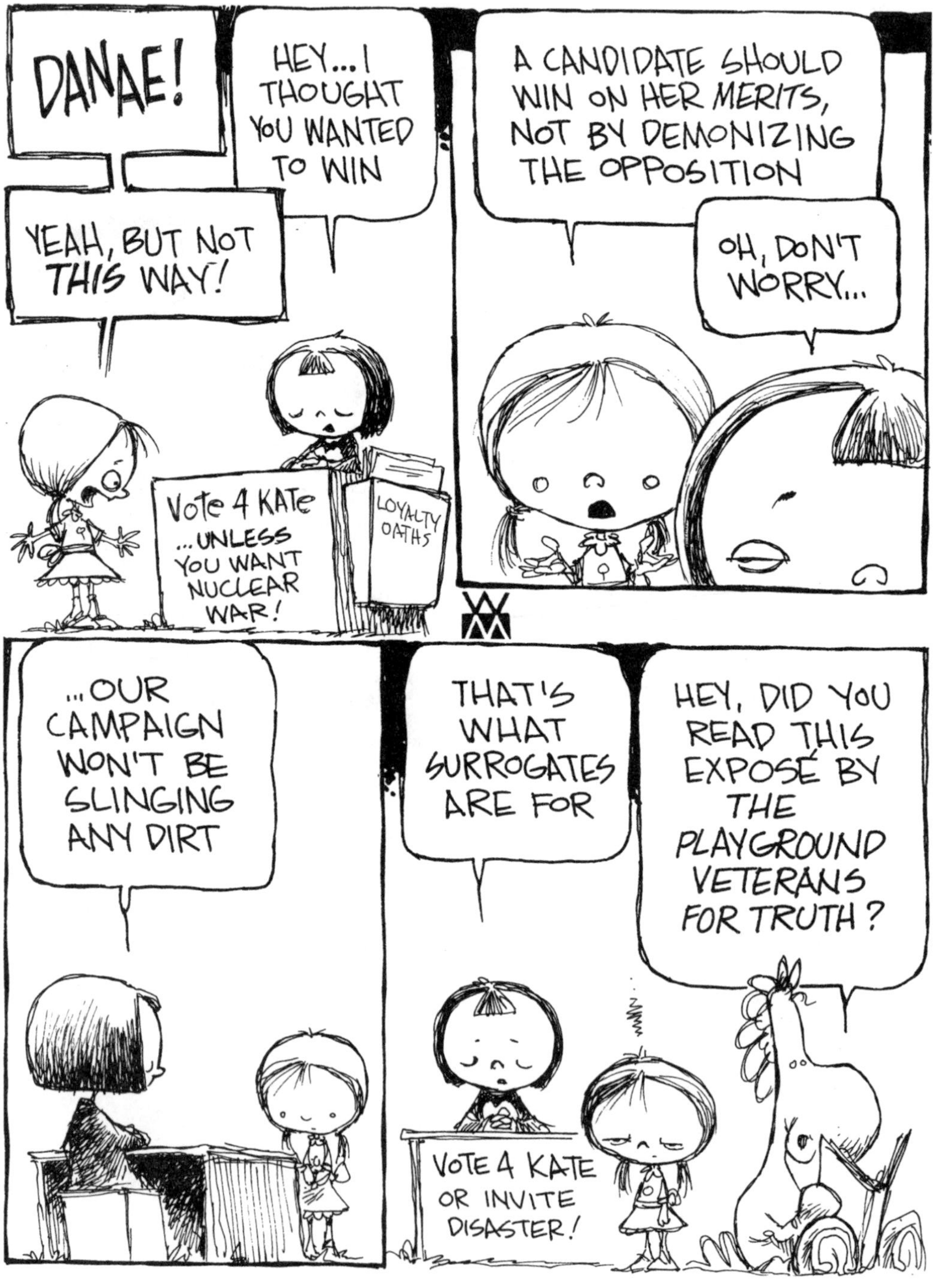
DANAE!
YEAH, BUT NOT THIS WAY!
HEY...I THOUGHT YOU WANTED TO WIN
Vote 4 KATe ...UNLESS YOU WANT NUCLEAR WAR!
LOYALTY OATHS
A CANDIDATE SHOULD WIN ON HER MERITS, NOT BY DEMONIZING THE OPPOSITION
OH, DON'T WORRY...
...OUR CAMPAIGN WON'T BE SLINGING ANY DIRT
THAT'S WHAT SURROGATES ARE FOR
HEY, DID YOU READ THIS EXPOSÉ BY THE PLAYGROUND VETERANS FOR TRUTH?
VOTE 4 KATE OR INVITE DISASTER!

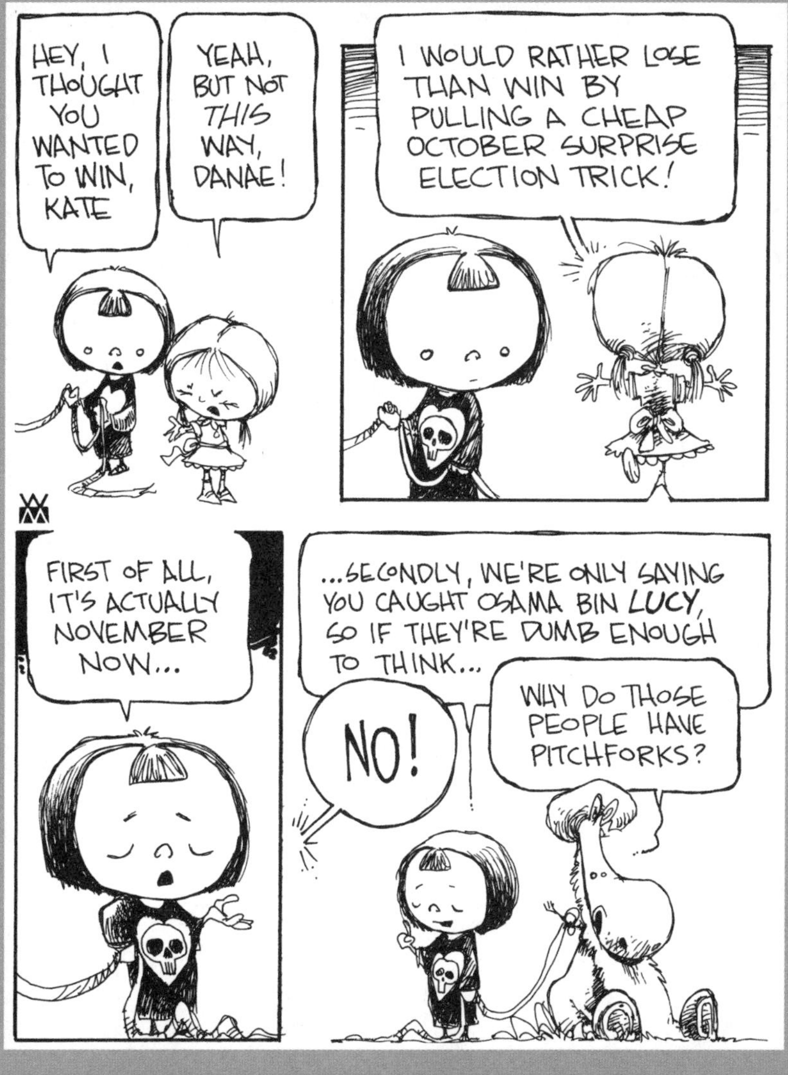
HEY, I THOUGHT YOU WANTED TO WIN, KATE
YEAH, BUT NOT *THIS* WAY, DANAE!
I WOULD RATHER LOSE THAN WIN BY PULLING A CHEAP OCTOBER SURPRISE ELECTION TRICK!
FIRST OF ALL, IT'S ACTUALLY NOVEMBER NOW...
...SECONDLY, WE'RE ONLY SAYING YOU CAUGHT OSAMA BIN *LUCY*, SO IF THEY'RE DUMB ENOUGH TO THINK...
NO!
WHY DO THOSE PEOPLE HAVE PITCHFORKS?

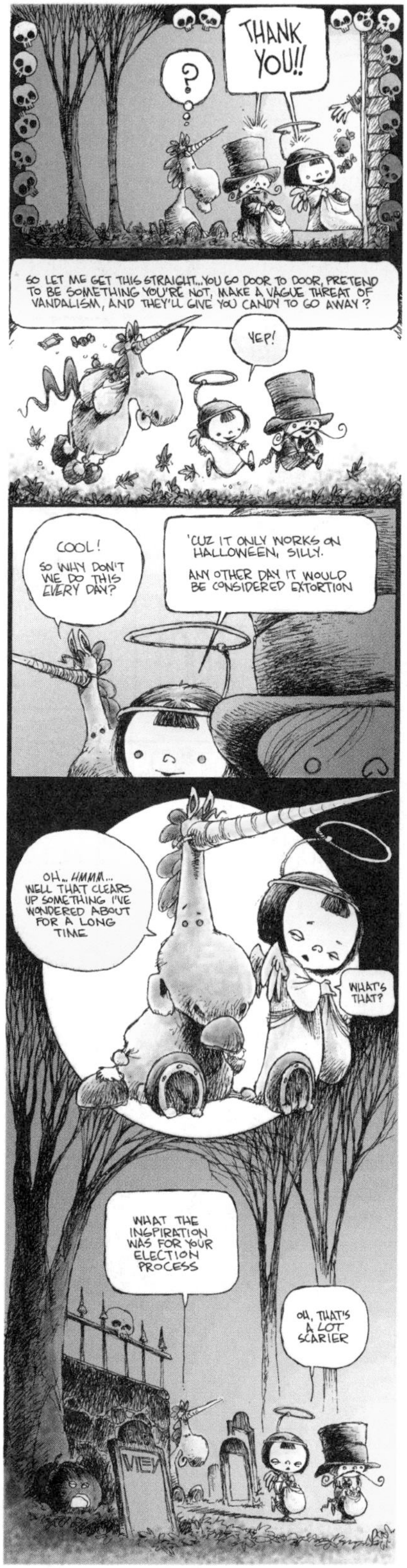
?
THANK YOU!!
SO LET ME GET THIS STRAIGHT...YOU GO DOOR TO DOOR, PRETEND TO BE SOMETHING YOU'RE NOT, MAKE A VAGUE THREAT OF VANDALISM, AND THEY'LL GIVE YOU CANDY TO GO AWAY?
YEP!
COOL! SO WHY DON'T WE DO THIS *EVERY* DAY?
'CUZ IT ONLY WORKS ON HALLOWEEN, SILLY.
ANY OTHER DAY IT WOULD BE CONSIDERED EXTORTION
OH... *HMMM*... WELL THAT CLEARS UP SOMETHING I'VE WONDERED ABOUT FOR A LONG TIME
WHAT'S THAT?
WHAT THE INSPIRATION WAS FOR YOUR ELECTION PROCESS
OH, THAT'S A LOT SCARIER

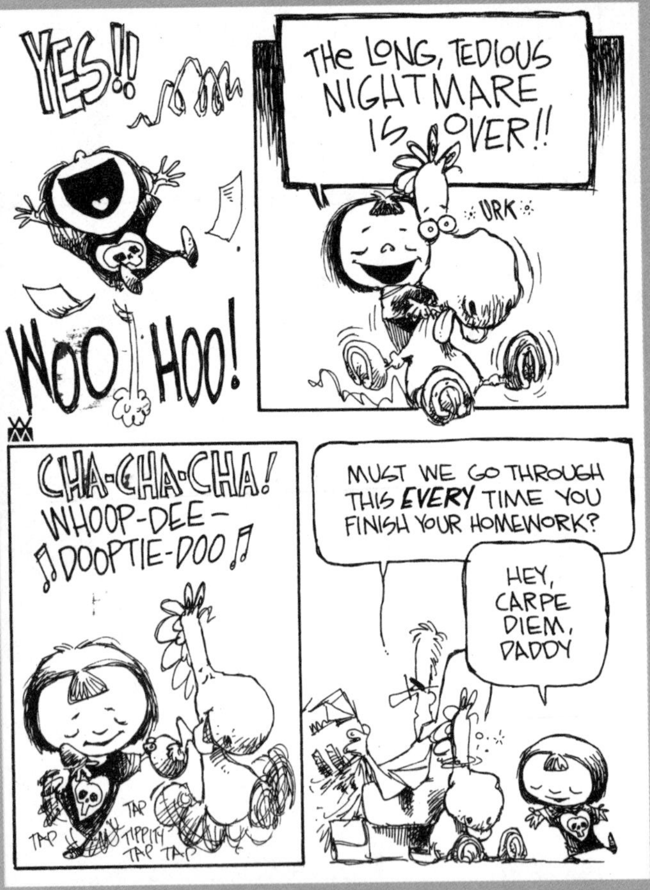
YES!!
WOO HOO!
The LONG, TEDIOUS NIGHTMARE IS OVER!!
URK
CHA-CHA-CHA! WHOOP-DEE-DOOPTIE-DOO
TAP
TAP TIPPITY TAP TAP
MUST WE GO THROUGH THIS EVERY TIME YOU FINISH YOUR HOMEWORK?
HEY, CARPE DIEM, DADDY

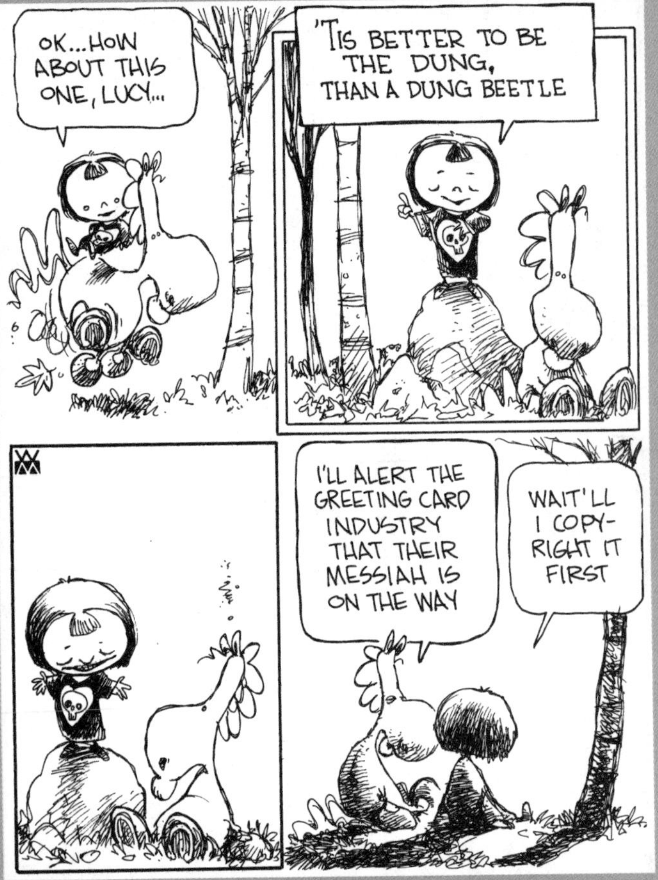
OK...HOW ABOUT THIS ONE, LUCY...
'TIS BETTER TO BE THE DUNG, THAN A DUNG BEETLE
I'LL ALERT THE GREETING CARD INDUSTRY THAT THEIR MESSIAH IS ON THE WAY
WAIT'LL I COPY-RIGHT IT FIRST

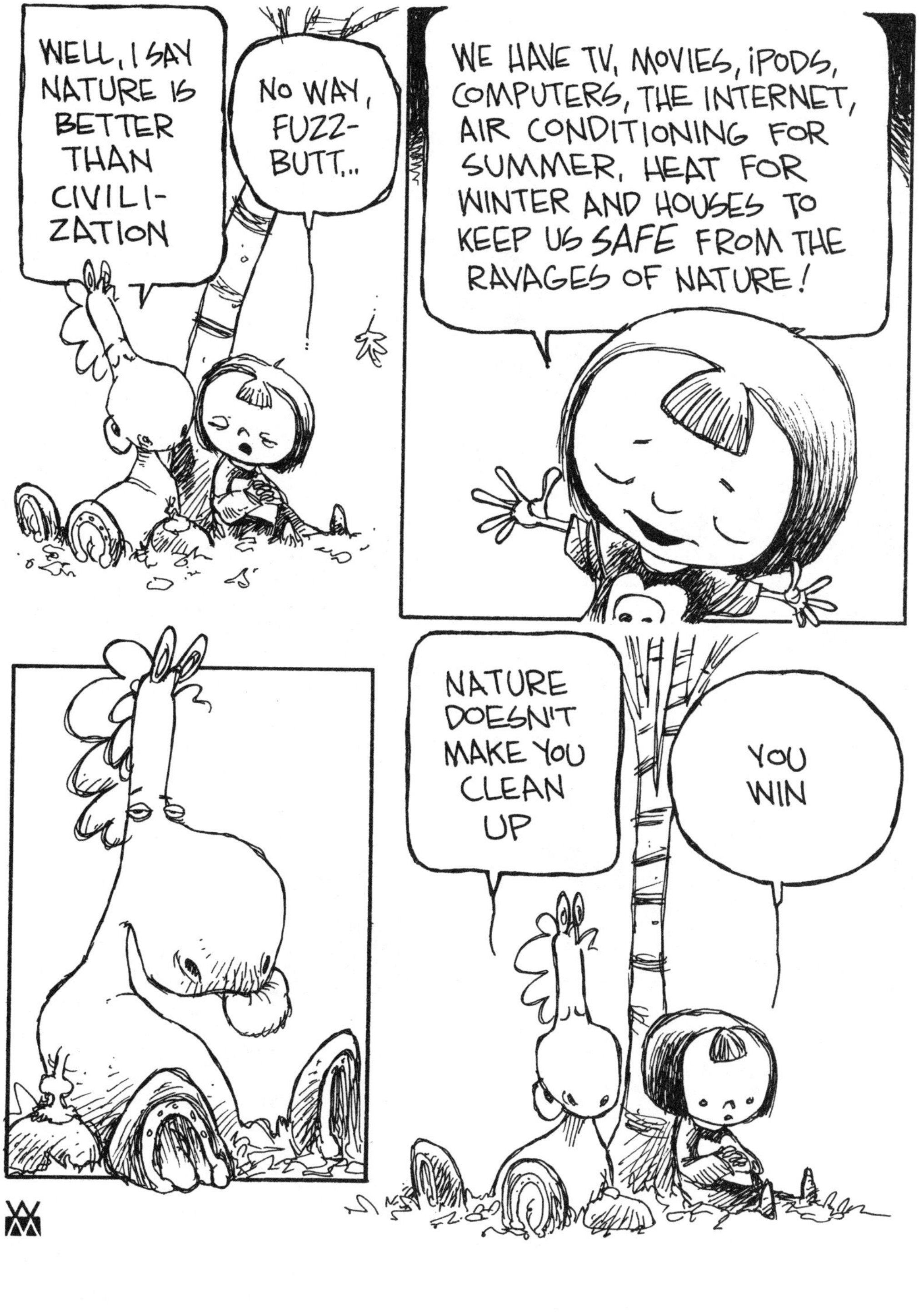
WELL, I SAY NATURE IS BETTER THAN CIVILI-ZATION
NO WAY, FUZZ-BUTT...
WE HAVE TV, MOVIES, iPODS, COMPUTERS, THE INTERNET, AIR CONDITIONING FOR SUMMER, HEAT FOR WINTER AND HOUSES TO KEEP US SAFE FROM THE RAVAGES OF NATURE!
NATURE DOESN'T MAKE YOU CLEAN UP
YOU WIN

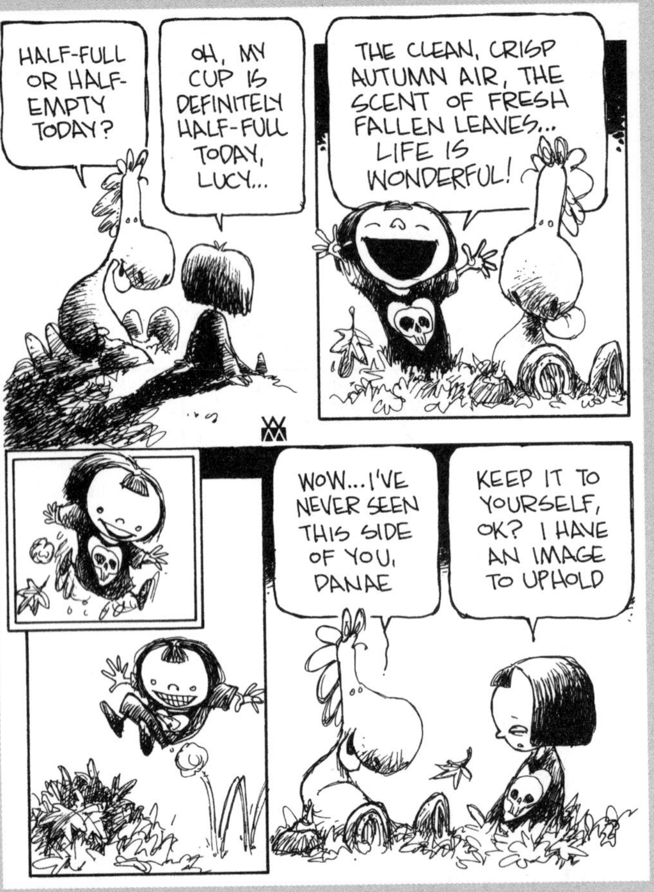
HALF-FULL OR HALF-EMPTY TODAY?
OH, MY CUP IS DEFINITELY HALF-FULL TODAY, LUCY...
THE CLEAN, CRISP AUTUMN AIR, THE SCENT OF FRESH FALLEN LEAVES... LIFE IS WONDERFUL!
WOW... I'VE NEVER SEEN THIS SIDE OF YOU, DANAE
KEEP IT TO YOURSELF, OK? I HAVE AN IMAGE TO UPHOLD

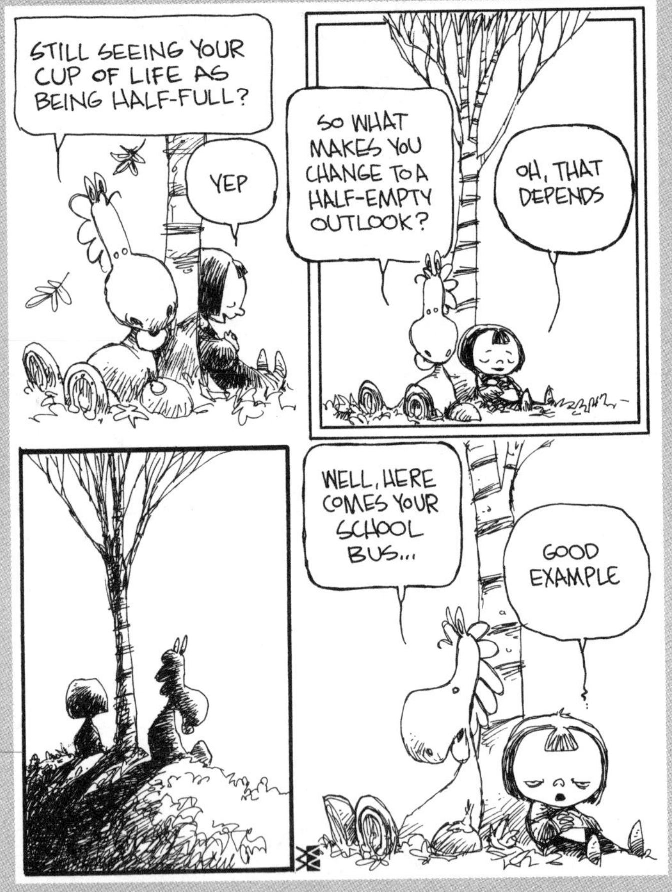
STILL SEEING YOUR CUP OF LIFE AS BEING HALF-FULL?
YEP
SO WHAT MAKES YOU CHANGE TO A HALF-EMPTY OUTLOOK?
OH, THAT DEPENDS
WELL, HERE COMES YOUR SCHOOL BUS...
GOOD EXAMPLE